# PLAYFUL DATA

## | GRAPHIC DESIGN AND ILLUSTRATION FOR INFOGRAPHICS |

Edited by Wang Shaoqiang

promopress

# PLAYFUL DATA

## GRAPHIC DESIGN AND ILLUSTRATION
## FOR INFOGRAPHICS

Editor: Wang Shaoqiang
English preface revised by: Tom Corkett

Copyright © 2018 by Sandu Publishing Co., Ltd.
Copyright © 2018 English language edition by
Promopress for sale in Europe and America.
Promopress is a brand of:
Promotora de Prensa Internacional S.A.
C/ Ausiàs March, 124
08013 Barcelona, Spain
Phone:      0034 93 245 14 64
Fax:         0034 93 265 48 83
info@promopress.es
www.promopresseditions.com
Facebook: Promopress Editions
Twitter: Promopress Editions @PromopressEd

Sponsored by Design 360°
– Concept and Design Magazine
Edited and produced by
Sandu Publishing Co., Ltd.
Book design, concepts & art direction by
Sandu Publishing Co., Ltd.
info@sandupublishing.com

Front cover project by Paul Button

ISBN 978-84-16851-34-8
D.L.: B-29318-2017

Printed in China

# CONTENTS ────────────────────────────────────

## GEOGRAPHIC DATA

## INSTRUCTION AND EXPLANATION

# PLAYING IS BEAUTIFUL

*Pablo Galeano and Francesco Furno*
*Founders of relajaelcoco*

If Peter Pan were real, he would spend a lot of his life playing as much as possible in a society that expresses itself playfully and places an emphasis on fun.

In fact, Peter Pan is real. And he is ruling a world in which many new visual products catch our attention by drawing on a deep relationship between creators and users. This relationship is a kind of game in which communicators stimulate users through devices such as infographics.

Since the 1980s, gamification—that is, the use of ideas and devices from games in nongame contexts—has become the core technique for spreading information in a new way. It is based on a light, funny idea of making serious things like data more interesting through making them light and fun.

Over the last forty years, we have witnessed a real pandemic, Peter Pan syndrome, develop and spread globally. It is "infecting" a huge part of the population and creating a more playful dynamic in which interaction between the speaker (the designer) and the receiver (the reader) is more direct and produces a rewarding dialogue. This "syndrome," which empowers composition and in many cases uses illustration as one of its most striking elements, has led playful creatives to produce infographics that let readers enjoy information in a beautiful and insightful way.

Some people may see this phenomenon as a trend that will disappear in the future. What they overlook, however, is that it represents a neoromantic point of view that keeps alive childhood to preserve positivism and the joy of life.

Our generation has started a new movement based on Rousseau's philosophical principle that the inner child never dies. Each contemporary infographer is keeping romanticism's essence alive with joyful representations of data that allow people to have fun while they are reading, whatever the type of information that they are looking at. This new idea from romanticism has mutated thanks to a deep subculture of comics and video games that filled our childhoods and kept us on a different imaginative level, and it is now what fuels creative infographic representations.

Playing helps to improve education by allowing people to grasp information on a more complex level. Education that embraces games allows people to digest a huge number of the pieces of data produced each day in our increasingly complex world. Playing with data also helps to stop data from becoming overwhelming, and it lets people pick out content with ease. In a world where we are all faced with huge volumes of targeted data, it is of vital importance to take a brief moment to relax and to enjoy the deep experience of playing with infographics.

Beautiful and fun infographics are being pioneered by people like Jing Zhang, with her microworlds based on the famous Polly Pocket toys from the 1990s, and Valerio Pellegrini, with his colorful compositions. Two common elements of their work are the beauty of never forgetting the playfulness of childhood and an awareness of how that playfulness can influence our ability to interpret lively visuals in the present.

We should give a special mention to Italy and its infographic renaissance. Italian designers and illustrators such as Francesco Franchi, Francesco Muzzi, Valerio Pellegrini, and Federica Fragapane are creating new and impactful compositions that feature audacious levels of complexity, richness, and beauty, and through doing so they have contributed to promoting a new way of conceiving infographics.

Welcoming playfulness into infographics does not mean that everything must be funny, or that gamification must be used as the essential driver of visual development. But as this volume reveals, in some cases playing is essential for communicating complex information easily by preventing feelings of frustration when it comes to reading and interpreting data. For both designers and readers, playing is a useful approach to the unknown and a profound way to experience new adventures in which creator and audience alike are involved in a fantastic and sometimes surreal storytelling.

Those who can tell stories are the chosen ones when it comes to stimulating creativity and producing a diverse and fantastic world based on real data. In this sense, it is clear that we are all kids. We are all surprised by the unknown, especially when it is a special, unique point of view that makes things different.

Remember: never stop playing.

..........................................................................................................................................

### *relajaelcoco*

Relajaelcoco is a graphic design studio founded by Pablo Galeano and Francesco Furno. It specializes in graphic design, editorial design, infographics, virtual reality, and illustration. Over the last year, the studio's main aim has been to research new ways to express and create contemporary visual systems. For relajaelcoco, good vibes and a pleasant experience are the foundation for achieving sparkling results.

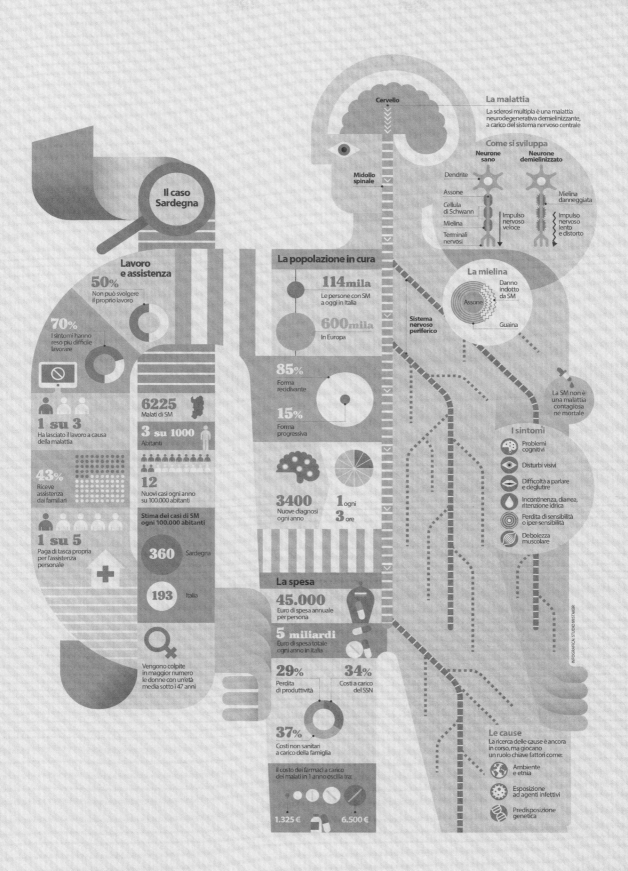

**Cervello**

**La malattia**
La sclerosi multipla è una malattia neurodegenerativa demielinizzante, a carico del sistema nervoso centrale

**Come si sviluppa**

**Neurone sano**

**Neurone demielinizzato**

Dendrite

Assone

Cellula di Schwann

Mielina

Terminali nervosi

Impulso nervoso veloce

Mielina danneggiata

Impulso nervoso lento e distorto

**Midollo spinale**

**La mielina**
Danno indotto da SM

Assone

Guaina

**Sistema nervoso periferico**

La SM non è una malattia contagiosa né mortale

**Il caso Sardegna**

**Lavoro e assistenza**

**50%**
Non può svolgere il proprio lavoro

**70%**
I sintomi hanno reso più difficile lavorare

**1 su 3**
Ha lasciato il lavoro a causa della malattia

**43%**
Riceve assistenza dai familiari

**1 su 5**
Paga di tasca propria per l'assistenza personale

Vengono colpite in maggior numero le donne con un'età media sotto i 47 anni

**6225**
Malati di SM

**3 su 1000**
Abitanti

**12**
Nuovi casi ogni anno su 100.000 abitanti

**Stima dei casi di SM ogni 100.000 abitanti**

**360** Sardegna

**193** Italia

**La popolazione in cura**

**114mila**
Le persone con SM a oggi in Italia

**600mila**
In Europa

**85%**
Forma recidivante

**15%**
Forma progressiva

**3400**
Nuove diagnosi ogni anno

**1 ogni 3 ore**

**La spesa**

**45.000**
Euro di spesa annuale per persona

**5 miliardi**
Euro di spesa totale ogni anno in Italia

**29%**
Perdita di produttività

**34%**
Costi a carico del SSN

**37%**
Costi non sanitari a carico della famiglia

il costo dei farmaci a carico dei malati in 1 anno oscilla tra:

**1.325 €** **6.500 €**

**I sintomi**

Problemi cognitivi

Disturbi visivi

Difficoltà a parlare e deglutire

Incontinenza, diarrea, ritenzione idrica

Perdita di sensibilità o iper-sensibilità

Debolezza muscolare

**Le cause**
La ricerca delle cause è ancora in corso, ma giocano un ruolo chiave fattori come:

Ambiente e etnia

Esposizione ad agenti infettivi

Predisposizione genetica

INFOGRAFICA: STUDIO MISTAKER

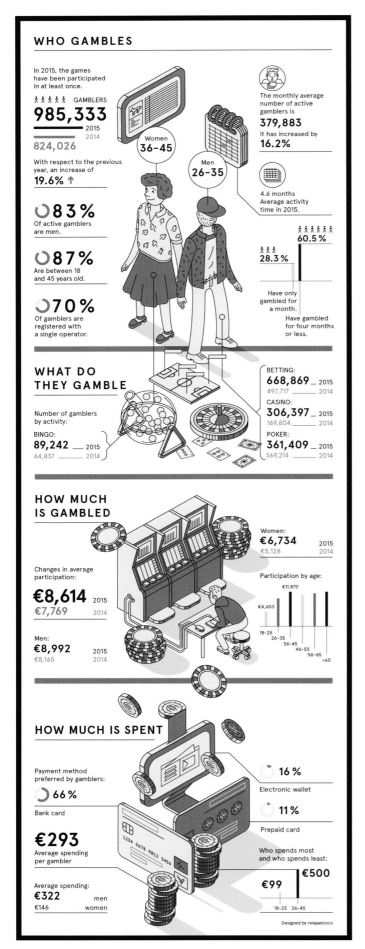

## WHO GAMBLES

In 2015, the games have been participated in at least once.

GAMBLERS
**985,333** 2015
824,026 2014

With respect to the previous year, an increase of
**19.6%** ↑

**83%**
Of active gamblers are men.

**87%**
Are between 18 and 45 years old.

**70%**
Of gamblers are registered with a single operator.

The monthly average number of active gamblers is
**379,883**
it has increased by
**16.2%**

4.6 months
Average activity time in 2015.

**60.5%**
**28.3%**

Have only gambled for a month.

Have gambled for four months or less.

Women
**36–45**

Men
**26–35**

## WHAT DO THEY GAMBLE

Number of gamblers by activity:

BINGO:
**89,242** 2015
64,837 2014

BETTING:
**668,869** 2015
497,717 2014

CASINO:
**306,397** 2015
169,804 2014

POKER:
**361,409** 2015
369,214 2014

## HOW MUCH IS GAMBLED

Changes in average participation:

**€8,614** 2015
€7,769 2014

Men:
**€8,992** 2015
€8,165 2014

Women:
**€6,734** 2015
€5,128 2014

Participation by age:
€11,870
€4,603
18–25
26–35
36–45
46–55
56–65
>65

## HOW MUCH IS SPENT

Payment method preferred by gamblers:

**66%**
Bank card

**€293**
Average spending per gambler

Average spending:
**€322** men
€146 women

**16%**
Electronic wallet

**11%**
Prepaid card

Who spends most and who spends least:

€500
**€99**
18–25  36–45

1234 5678 9012 3456

Designed by relajaelcoco

# Jugar Bien Infographic

Agency: **relajaelcoco**
Art Direction: **relajaelcoco**
Content: **Dirección General de Ordenación del Juego del Ministerio de Hacienda y Administraciones Públicas**
Client: **jugarbien.es staff**

This is an annual infographic showing the typical player profile of 2015. Relajaelcoco worked on a vertical composition (perfect for web reading) separated into four horizontal sections. Each section is divided into three columns: two sides displaying data and a central one featuring an isometric illustration to clarify the information. The project was carried out both in Spanish and English and it was published on the web page of jugarbien.es. Relajaelcoco was working with digital tools like Adobe Illustrator and Wacom Cintiq Tablet.

# WHAT DO THEY GAMBLE

Number of gamblers by activity:

BINGO:
**89,242** __ 2015
64,837 _____ 2014

BETTING:
**668,869** __ 2015
497,717 _____ 2014

CASINO:
**306,397** __ 2015
169,804 _____ 2014

POKER:
**361,409** __ 2015
369,214 _____ 2014

# HOW MUCH IS GAMBLED

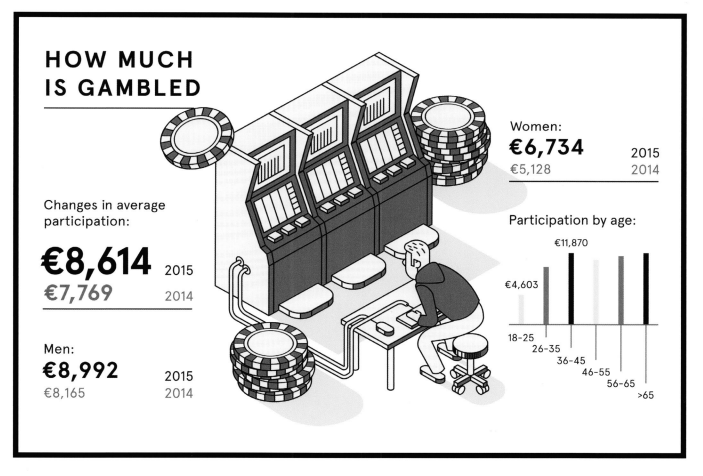

Changes in average participation:

**€8,614** 2015
**€7,769** 2014

Men:
**€8,992** 2015
€8,165 2014

Women:
**€6,734** 2015
€5,128 2014

Participation by age:

€11,870

€4,603

18–25
26–35
36–45
46–55
56–65
>65

# UIB Benefits Research

..................................................

Agency: **Estudio Pum**
Client: **UIB Benefits**

UIB Benefits Research is an annual editorial project illustrating the scenery of employee benefits offered by Brazilian insurance companies.

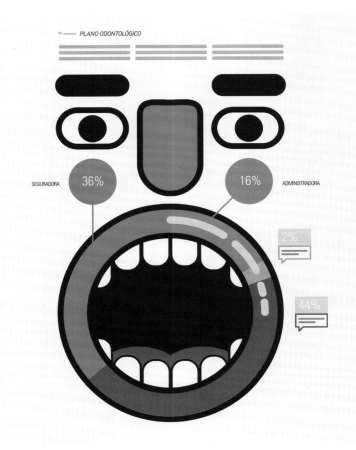

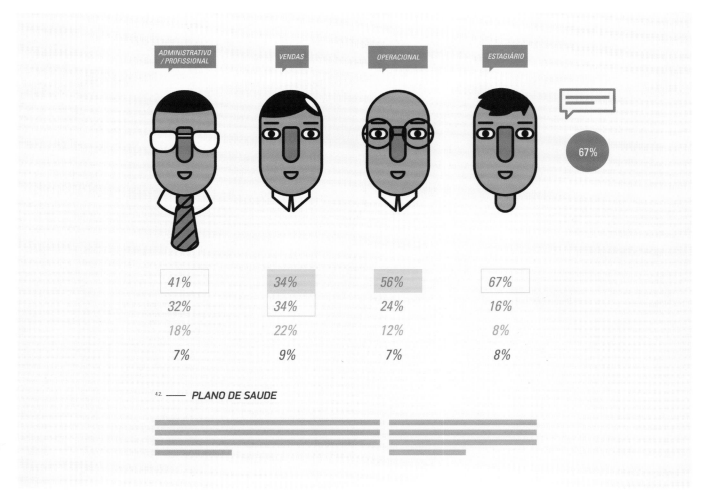

92%
INVALIDEZ
POR DOENÇA

100%
MORTE
ACIDENTAL

100%
MORTE
NATURAL

SEGURADORA

ADMINISTRADORA

36%

16%

37%

23%

56%

ASSISTÊNCIA FUNERAL

FAMILIAR 76%

INDIVIDUAL 13%

NÃO POSSUI 10%

VALORES MÉDIOS DE COBERTURA

Nº DE SALÁRIOS

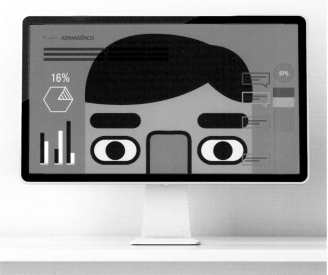

ABRANGÊNCIA

16%

87%

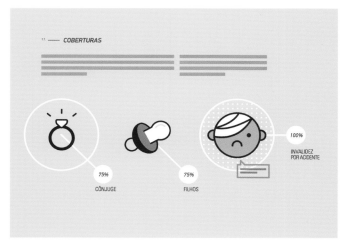

75%
CÔNJUGE

75%
FILHOS

100%
INVALIDEZ
POR ACIDENTE

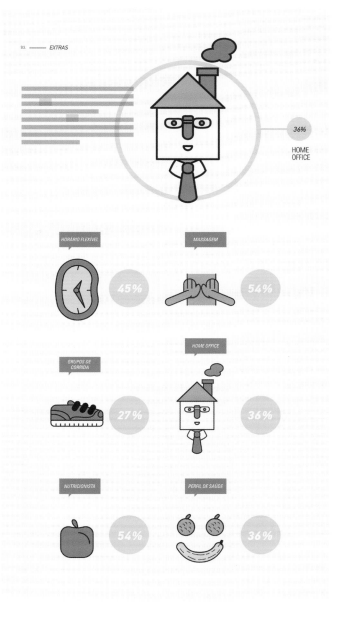

36%
HOME
OFFICE

HORÁRIO FLEXÍVEL

45%

MASSAGEM

54%

GRUPOS DE
CORRIDA

27%

HOME OFFICE

36%

NUTRICIONISTA

54%

PERFIL DE SAÚDE

36%

# Refurbishment and Energy Efficiency

Agency: **Studio Mistaker**
Art Direction: **Nino Brisindi**
Client: **La Repubblica**

Refurbishment and Energy Efficiency is an infographic project about how to refurbish one's house and use the energy efficiency subsidies to save costs.

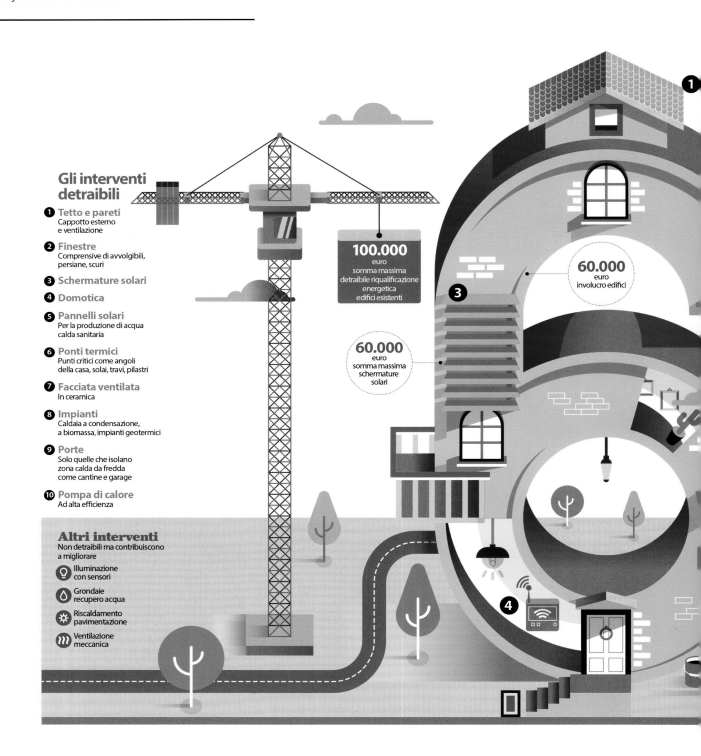

## Gli interventi detraibili

**1 Tetto e pareti**
Cappotto esterno e ventilazione

**2 Finestre**
Comprensive di avvolgibili, persiane, scuri

**3 Schermature solari**

**4 Domotica**

**5 Pannelli solari**
Per la produzione di acqua calda sanitaria

**6 Ponti termici**
Punti critici come angoli della casa, solai, travi, pilastri

**7 Facciata ventilata**
In ceramica

**8 Impianti**
Caldaia a condensazione, a biomassa, impianti geotermici

**9 Porte**
Solo quelle che isolano zona calda da fredda come cantine e garage

**10 Pompa di calore**
Ad alta efficienza

### Altri interventi
Non detraibili ma contribuiscono a migliorare

**Illuminazione** con sensori

**Grondaie** recupero acqua

**Riscaldamento** pavimentazione

**Ventilazione** meccanica

**100.000**
euro
somma massima detraibile riqualificazione energetica edifici esistenti

**60.000**
euro
involucro edifici

**60.000**
euro
somma massima schermature solari

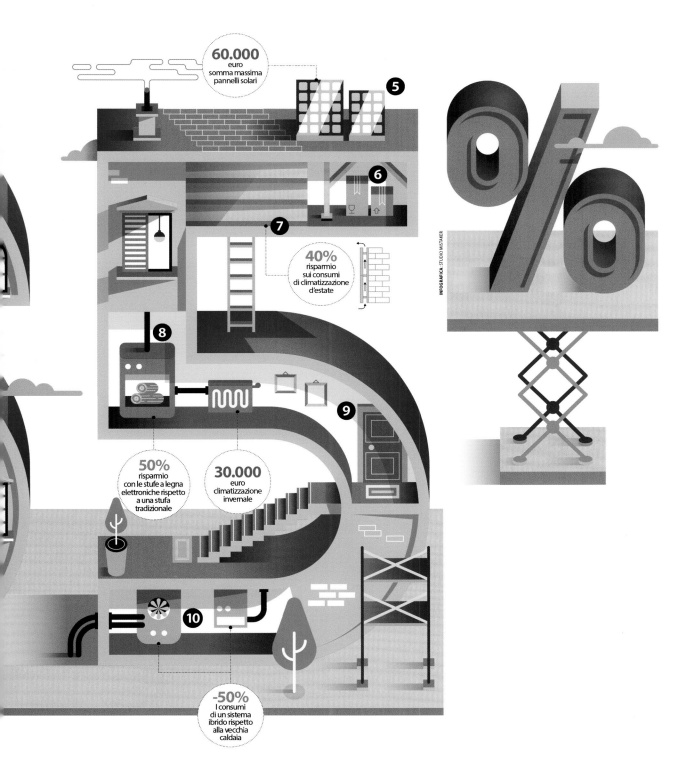

**60.000**
euro
somma massima
pannelli solari

**5**

**6**

**7**

**40%**
risparmio
sui consumi
di climatizzazione
d'estate

**8**

**9**

**50%**
risparmio
con le stufe a legna
elettroniche rispetto
a una stufa
tradizionale

**30.000**
euro
climatizzazione
invernale

**10**

**-50%**
I consumi
di un sistema
ibrido rispetto
alla vecchia
caldaia

INFOGRAFICA: STUDIO MISTAKER

# How the Consumption Changes

Agency: **Studio Mistaker**
Art Direction: **Nino Brisindi**
Client: *La Repubblica*

The infographic shows the shopping trends in Italy, which visualizes where and how much Italians spend on food, technology, and consumer goods.

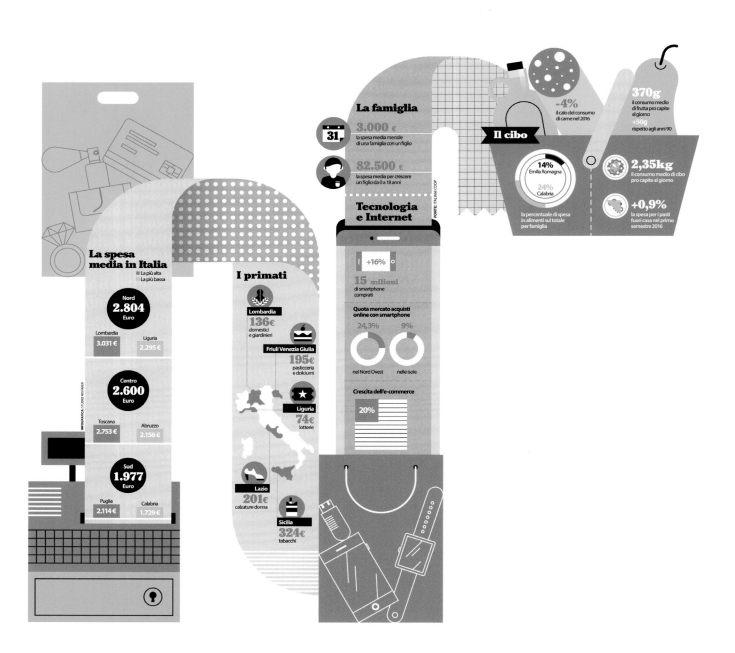

**La famiglia**

**3.000 €**
la spesa media mensile
di una famiglia con un figlio

**82.500 €**
la spesa media per crescere
un figlio da 0 a 18 anni

**Tecnologia
e Internet**

+16%

**15 milioni**
di smartphone
comprati

Quota mercato acquisti
online con smartphone

24,3%        9%

nel Nord Ovest        nelle isole

Crescita dell'e-commerce

20%

**Il cibo**

-4%
il calo del consumo
di carne nel 2016

**370g**
il consumo medio
di frutta pro capite
al giorno
+50g
rispetto agli anni 90

14%
Emilia Romagna
24%
Calabria

la percentuale di spesa
in alimenti sul totale
per famiglia

**2,35kg**
il consumo medio di cibo
pro capite al giorno

**+0,9%**
la spesa per i pasti
fuori casa nel primo
semestre 2016

FONTE: ITALIANI COOP

**La spesa
media in Italia**
■ La più alta
■ La più bassa

INFOGRAFICA: STUDIO MISTAKER

Nord
**2.804**
Euro

Lombardia
**3.031 €**

Liguria
**2.295 €**

Centro
**2.600**
Euro

Toscana
**2.753 €**

Abruzzo
**2.156 €**

Sud
**1.977**
Euro

Puglia
**2.114 €**

Calabria
**1.729 €**

**I primati**

Lombardia
**136€**
domestici
e giardinieri

Friuli Venezia Giulia
**195€**
pasticceria
e dolciumi

Liguria
**74€**
lotterie

Lazio
**201€**
calzature donna

Sicilia
**324€**
tabacchi

# The Fight Against Multiple Sclerosis

Agency: **Studio Mistaker**
Art Direction: **Nino Brisindi**
Client: *La Repubblica*

The infographic indicates the fight against multiple sclerosis in Italy. Many researches are carried out with a medical focus on the disease and on people who are affected by it.

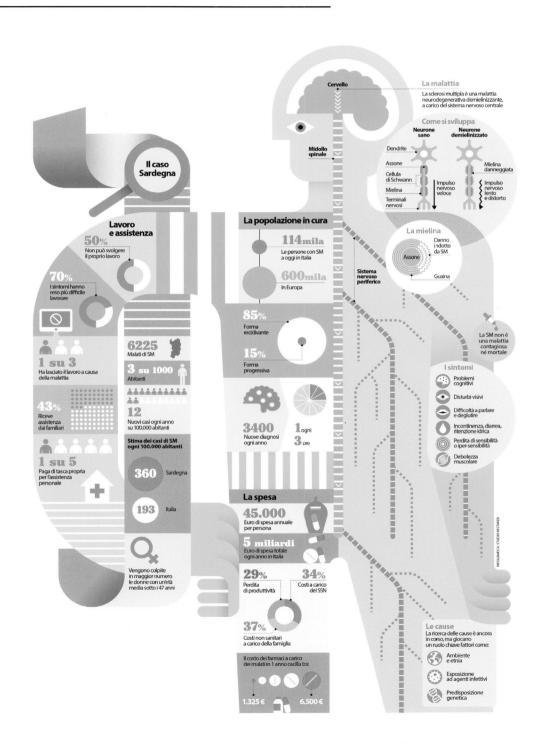

**SIN CITY** PRESENTS

# CRIMES OF **VIOLENCE**

As the Federal Police Convention gets underway next week in Sin City, we ask how effective are the systems we have in place to counter crimes of violence and crimes of alcohol? How safe are our cities?

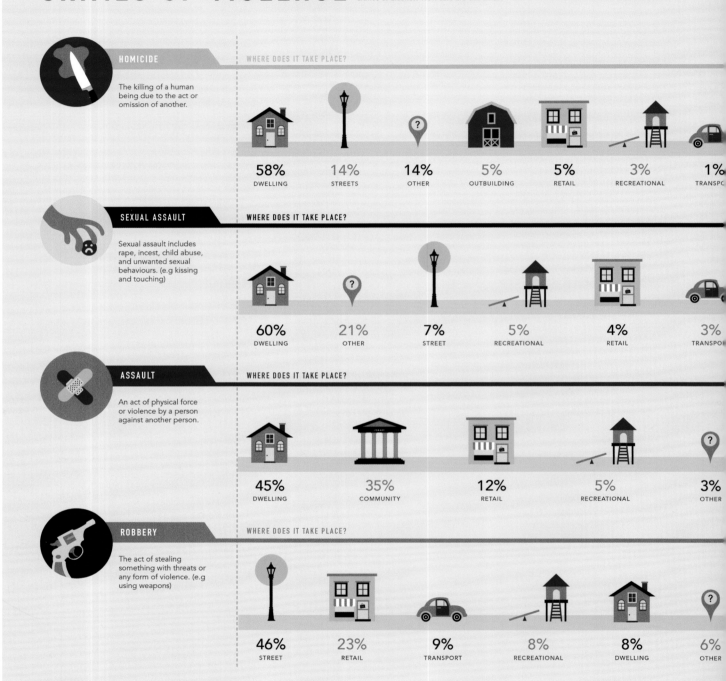

## HOMICIDE

The killing of a human being due to the act or omission of another.

WHERE DOES IT TAKE PLACE?

| 58% | 14% | 14% | 5% | 5% | 3% | 1% |
|---|---|---|---|---|---|---|
| DWELLING | STREETS | OTHER | OUTBUILDING | RETAIL | RECREATIONAL | TRANSPO |

## SEXUAL ASSAULT

Sexual assault includes rape, incest, child abuse, and unwanted sexual behaviours. (e.g kissing and touching)

WHERE DOES IT TAKE PLACE?

| 60% | 21% | 7% | 5% | 4% | 3% |
|---|---|---|---|---|---|
| DWELLING | OTHER | STREET | RECREATIONAL | RETAIL | TRANSPO |

## ASSAULT

An act of physical force or violence by a person against another person.

WHERE DOES IT TAKE PLACE?

| 45% | 35% | 12% | 5% | 3% |
|---|---|---|---|---|
| DWELLING | COMMUNITY | RETAIL | RECREATIONAL | OTHER |

## ROBBERY

The act of stealing something with threats or any form of violence. (e.g using weapons)

WHERE DOES IT TAKE PLACE?

| 46% | 23% | 9% | 8% | 8% | 6% |
|---|---|---|---|---|---|
| STREET | RETAIL | TRANSPORT | RECREATIONAL | DWELLING | OTHER |

**REFERENCES (AS OF 2010–11)**
http://www.aic.gov.au/statistics/violent%20crime.html
http://www.aic.gov.au/publications/previous%20series/vt/1-9/vt01.html
http://www.legalaid.vic.gov.au/find-legal-answers/sex-and-law/sexual-assault
http://www.police.nsw.gov.au/__data/assets/pdf_file/0010/331777/easy-english-fact-sheets_booklets.pdf
http://vocal.org.au/support-for-victims-of-crime/compensation/

*Some values are rounded off and approximated to 2-3 significant figures.

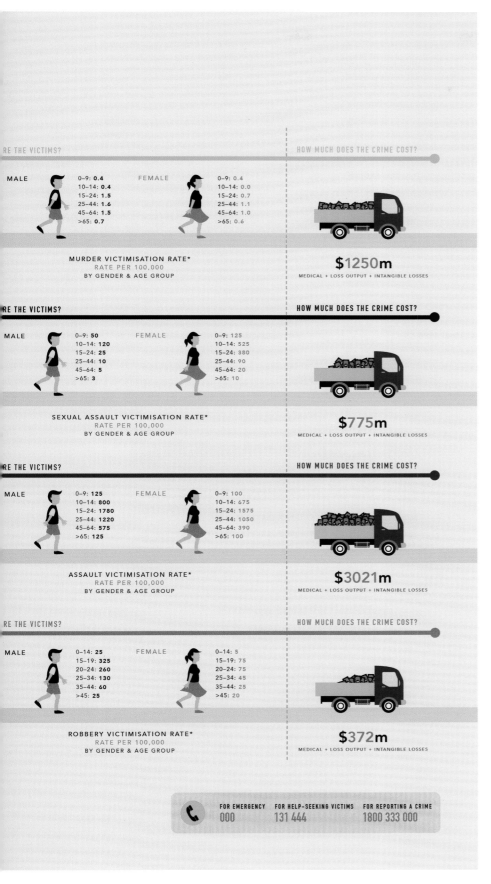

RE THE VICTIMS?

MALE    0–9: **0.4**     FEMALE    0–9: 0.4
            10–14: **0.4**                   10–14: 0.0
            15–24: **1.5**                   15–24: 0.7
            25–44: **1.6**                   25–44: 1.1
            45–64: **1.5**                   45–64: 1.0
            >65: **0.7**                    >65: 0.6

HOW MUCH DOES THE CRIME COST?

**MURDER VICTIMISATION RATE\***
RATE PER 100,000
BY GENDER & AGE GROUP

**$1250m**
MEDICAL + LOSS OUTPUT + INTANGIBLE LOSSES

RE THE VICTIMS?

MALE    0–9: **50**     FEMALE    0–9: 125
            10–14: **120**                   10–14: 525
            15–24: **25**                   15–24: 380
            25–44: **10**                   25–44: 90
            45–64: **5**                   45–64: 20
            >65: **3**                    >65: 10

HOW MUCH DOES THE CRIME COST?

**SEXUAL ASSAULT VICTIMISATION RATE\***
RATE PER 100,000
BY GENDER & AGE GROUP

**$775m**
MEDICAL + LOSS OUTPUT + INTANGIBLE LOSSES

RE THE VICTIMS?

MALE    0–9: **125**     FEMALE    0–9: 100
            10–14: **800**                   10–14: 675
            15–24: **1780**                  15–24: 1575
            25–44: **1220**                  25–44: 1050
            45–64: **575**                   45–64: 390
            >65: **125**                   >65: 100

HOW MUCH DOES THE CRIME COST?

**ASSAULT VICTIMISATION RATE\***
RATE PER 100,000
BY GENDER & AGE GROUP

**$3021m**
MEDICAL + LOSS OUTPUT + INTANGIBLE LOSSES

RE THE VICTIMS?

MALE    0–14: **25**     FEMALE    0–14: 5
            15–19: **325**                  15–19: 75
            20–24: **260**                  20–24: 75
            25–34: **130**                  25–34: 45
            35–44: **60**                   35–44: 25
            >45: **25**                   >45: 20

HOW MUCH DOES THE CRIME COST?

**ROBBERY VICTIMISATION RATE\***
RATE PER 100,000
BY GENDER & AGE GROUP

**$372m**
MEDICAL + LOSS OUTPUT + INTANGIBLE LOSSES

FOR EMERGENCY    FOR HELP-SEEKING VICTIMS    FOR REPORTING A CRIME
000               131 444                    1800 333 000

# Crimes of Violence

Design: **Kevin Teh**

This A3-sized infographic was an assessment task offered by the Billy Blue College of Design. It was designed to educate the younger audience about the crimes of violence by using illustrations in bright colors and straightforward data. Statistics of four types of crimes—homicide, sexual assault, assault, and robbery—are presented, each with details of the location, victims, and cost.

# Infographic Series: Getty Images

Agency: **Surgery & Redcow**
Client: **Getty Images**

Surgery & Redcow has developed an illustrative style for a series of infographics that would compliment the history of the company, while at the same time being perceived as contemporary, forward-thinking, and cutting-edge.

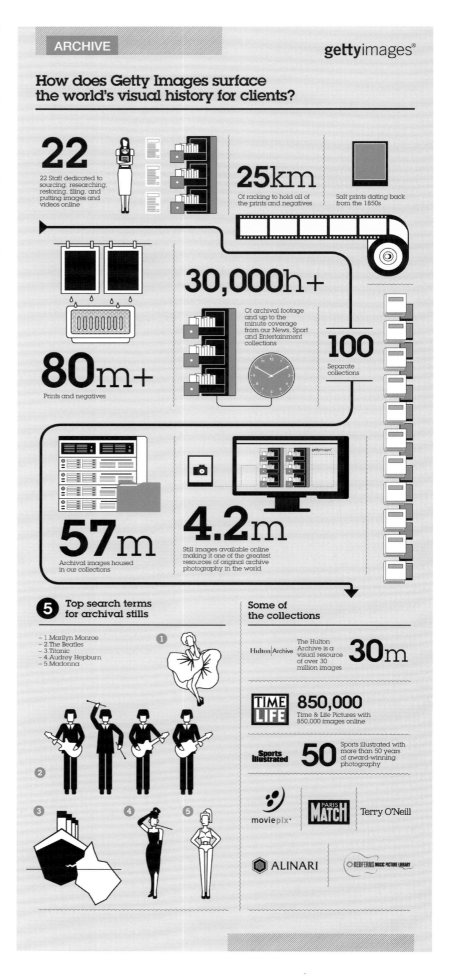

ARCHIVE

**gettyimages®**

## How does Getty Images surface the world's visual history for clients?

**22**
22 Staff dedicated to sourcing, researching, restoring, filing, and putting images and videos online

**25km**
Of racking to hold all of the prints and negatives

Salt prints dating back from the 1850s

**30,000h+**
Of archival footage and up to the minute coverage from our News, Sport and Entertainment collections

**100**
Separate collections

**80m+**
Prints and negatives

**57m**
Archival images housed in our collections

**4.2m**
Still images available online making it one of the greatest resources of original archive photography in the world

**5** Top search terms for archival stills

– 1.Marilyn Monroe
– 2.The Beatles
– 3.Titanic
– 4.Audrey Hepburn
– 5.Madonna

**Some of the collections**

Hulton|Archive — The Hulton Archive is a visual resource of over 30 million images **30m**

TIME LIFE — **850,000** Time & Life Pictures with 850,000 images online

Sports Illustrated — **50** Sports illustrated with more than 50 years of award-winning photography

moviepix®

PARIS MATCH

Terry O'Neill

ALINARI

REDFERNS MUSIC PICTURE LIBRARY

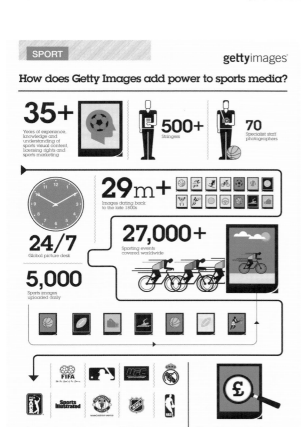

## How does Getty Images add power to sports media?

**35+** Years of experience, knowledge and understanding of sports visual content, licensing rights and sports marketing

**500+** Stringers

**70** Specialist staff photographers

**29m+** Images dating back to the late 1800s

**24/7** Global picture desk

**5,000** Sports images uploaded daily

**27,000+** Sporting events covered worldwide

Getty Images represent the unique content of some of the biggest names in sport, covering activity on the field and behind the scenes complimented by a wide range of commercial services for our partners and their licensees.

Get everything you need – 3rd party services, price negotiation, rights and clearance, image guarantee, project management, planning and research

FIFA · Sports Illustrated · UFC

---

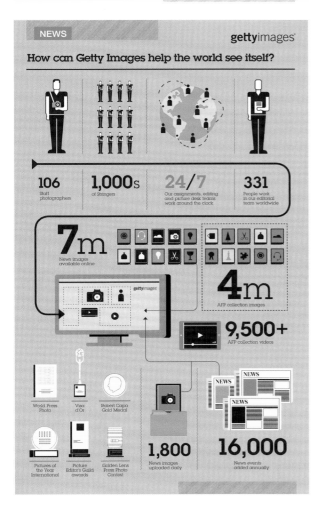

NEWS — gettyimages

## How can Getty Images help the world see itself?

**106** Staff photographers

**1,000s** of Stringers

**24/7** Our assignments, editing and picture desk teams work around the clock

**331** People work in our editorial team worldwide

**7m** News images available online

**4m** AFP collection images

**9,500+** AFP collection videos

World Press Photo · Visa d'Or · Robert Capa Gold Medal

Pictures of the Year International · Picture Editor's Guild awards · Golden Lens Press Photo Contest

**1,800** News images uploaded daily

**16,000** News events added annually

---

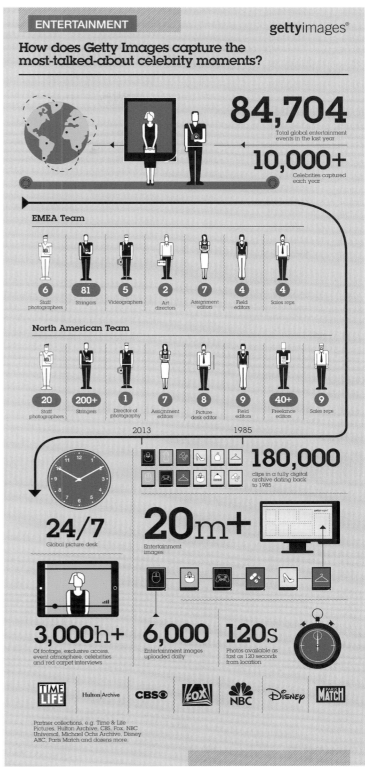

ENTERTAINMENT — gettyimages

## How does Getty Images capture the most-talked-about celebrity moments?

**84,704** Total global entertainment events in the last year

**10,000+** Celebrities captured each year

### EMEA Team

| | | | | | | |
|---|---|---|---|---|---|---|
| 6 Staff photographers | 81 Stringers | 5 Videographers | 2 Art directors | 7 Assignment editors | 4 Field editors | 4 Sales reps |

### North American Team

| | | | | | | | |
|---|---|---|---|---|---|---|---|
| 20 Staff photographers | 200+ Stringers | 1 Director of photography | 7 Assignment editors | 8 Picture desk editor | 9 Field editors | 40+ Freelance editors | 9 Sales reps |

2013  1985

**180,000** clips in a fully digital archive dating back to 1985

**24/7** Global picture desk

**20m+** Entertainment images

**3,000h+** Of footage, exclusive access, event atmosphere, celebrities and red carpet interviews

**6,000** Entertainment images uploaded daily

**120s** Photos available as fast as 120 seconds from location

TIME LIFE · Hulton Archive · CBS · FOX · NBC · Disney · PARIS MATCH

Partner collections, e.g. Time & Life Pictures, Hulton Archive, CBS, Fox, NBC Universal, Michael Ochs Archive, Disney ABC, Paris Match and dozens more.

# Raconteur Dashboard: Swiss Watch Sales

.....................................................................................................................

Agency: **Surgery & Redcow**
Client: *Raconteur*

Swiss Watch Sales was among a series of infographics dashboards that Surgery & Redcow produced for *Raconteur*. Each dashboard highlights interesting aspects of the data and combines it with engaging visuals from the topic. A minimalist approach makes the dashboard easy to read and understand.

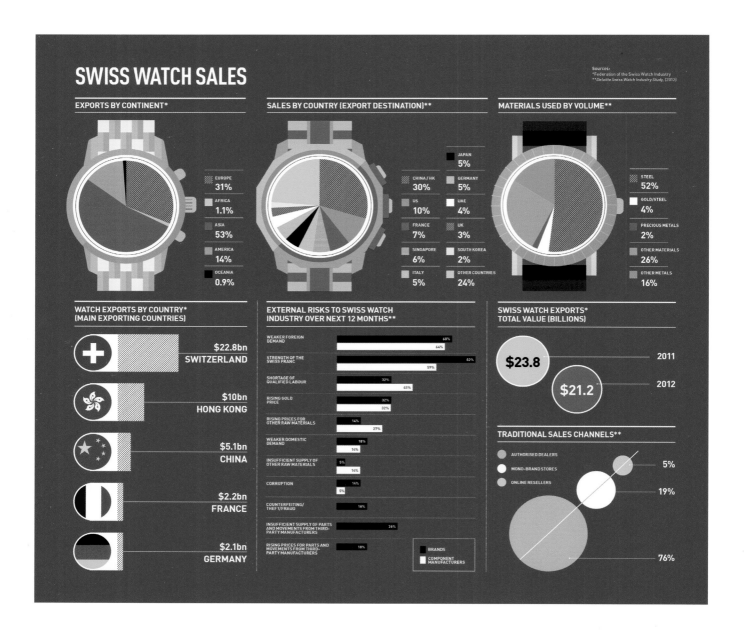

## Cycling's Dark Years

........................................

Design: **Paul Button**

Client: *Corriere della Sera*

This project for *Corriere della Sera: La Lettura* was inspired by the designer's own curiosity. Before Lance Armstrong gained public attention for his success in the Tour de France, he had received a lot of criticisms because the public questioned how he could be clean when his rivals were accused of implicating in doping. Paul decided to create a visualization that would depict the top 10 finishers from every Tour de France whom Armstrong had defeated and how far they fell behind him.

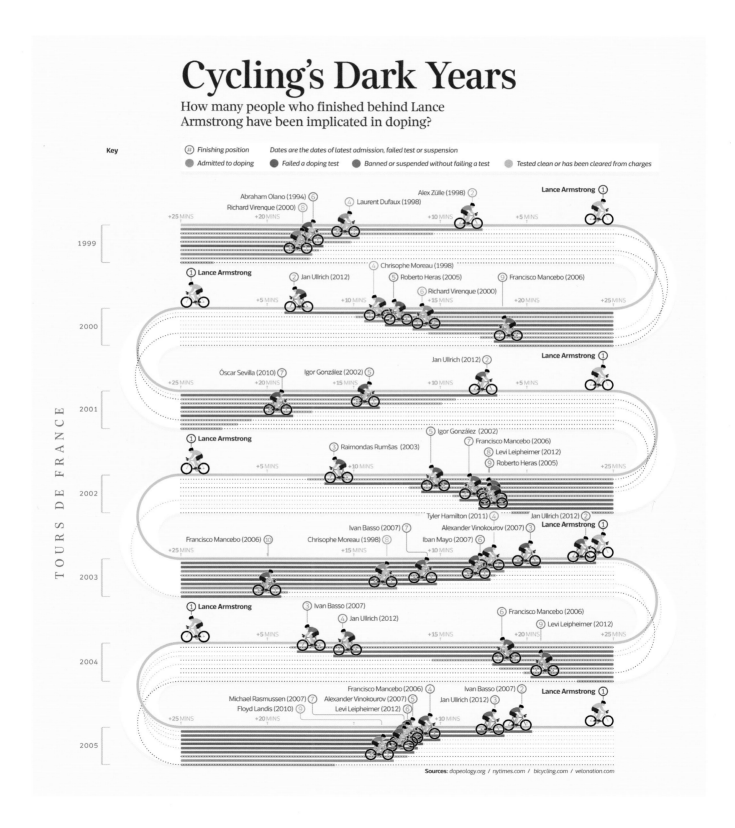

# Cycling's Dark Years

How many people who finished behind Lance Armstrong have been implicated in doping?

**Sources:** *dopeology.org / nytimes.com / bicycling.com / velonation.com*

# Toyota Editorial Illustration Infographic

Agency: **Surgery & Redcow**
Client: **Toyota**

Commissioned by Sunday Publishing, Surgery & Redcow has created an editorial infographic project for Toyota's internal magazine.

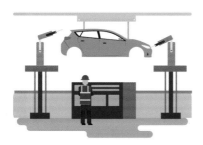

## MUS SEN OF CONS EQUEE POR SI SAE FACE REPAM RATIAS

*Atur? Lore dest lit alibus minciis abore cor sunt et ipsam dus nonsequo mo vellupi endent esed quo qui doluptur autet alicipsa pro blatem. Em abo. Nam quiam num dolum asped utem quae volupta*

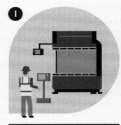

**①**

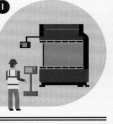

**②**

# 25

BLUE WHALES STACKED ON TOP OF EACH OTHER WOULD EXERT THE SAME PRESSURE AS THE MACHINES THAT TURN STEEL SHEETS INTO THE PANELS OF THE NEW AURIS

# 1

THE AMOUNT C
CAR VARIATION
IN **1992**

# 12(

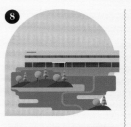

**⑧**

**⑨**

# 00

AMOUNT OF WASTE PUT INTO INCINERATION IN **2008** THE BURNASTON SITE

# 99%

OF THE WASTE
MAKING THE NE
RECYCLED OR F

| 250 km/h | 250 km/h | 250 km/ |
|----------|----------|---------|
| **1992** | **1993** | **1995** |

## TOYOTA CAR MODELS TIMELINE

| CARINA E SEDAN | CARINA E HATCHBACK | CARINA E ESTA |
|----------------|--------------------|---------------|

**06** www.facebook.com/toyotauk

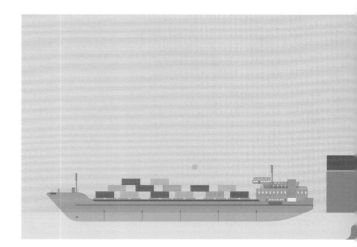

**3**

**1,077**
EMPLOYEES WORKED IN THE BURNASTON IN **1992**

**3,877** EMPLOYEES WORKED IN THE BURNASTON IN **2013**

**4**

**17**
THE NUMBER OF COUNTRIES EXPORTED TO IN **1992**

**52** NUMBER OF COUNTRIES EXPORTED TO IN **2013**

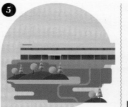

**5**

**00**
AMOUNT OF WASTE PUT INTO LANDFILL IN **2002** THE BURNASTON SITE

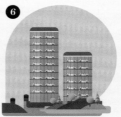

**6**

**40,000**
OF THE VEHICLES CREATED IN FIRST FULL YEAR OF PRODUCTION

**280,000**
OF THE VEHICLES CREATED IN **2006**

**7**

**16/12/ 1992**
THE DAY PRODUCTION STARTED

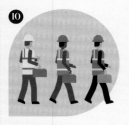

**10**

**300+**
TOYOTA MEMBERS WORKING AT BURNASTON TODAY WERE PART OF THE MANUFACTURING TEAM WHEN PRODUCTION BEGAN IN **1992**

**11**

**66s**
A NEW AURIS OR AVENSIS IS DRIVEN OFF THE PRODUCTION LINE

**12**

**322**
THE NUMBER OF SEPARATE PROCESSES INVOLVED IN THE ASSEMBLY OF EACH AURIS

**13**

**1,200**
THE NUMBER OF STATIC CHECKS THE NEW AURIS UNDERGOES AS PART OF QUALITY ASSURANCE TESTING

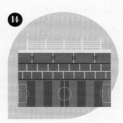

**14**

**329x**
THE BURNASTON SITE IS THE SIZE OF TH PITCH AT OLD TRAFFORD

| 1997 | 1998 | 2001 | 2003 | 2007 | 2008 | 2010 | 2012 |
|---|---|---|---|---|---|---|---|
| 0 km/h | 250 km/h | 250 km/h | 250 km/h | 250 km/h | 250 km/h | 250 km/h | 250 km/h |
| AVENSIS | CAROLLA HATCHBACK | CAROLLA HATCHBACK MODEL CHANGE | AVENSIS 2ND GEN | AURIS | AVENSIS 3RD GEN | AURIS HYBRID SYNERGY DRIVE | AURIS 2ND GEN |

www.facebook.com/toyotauk **07**

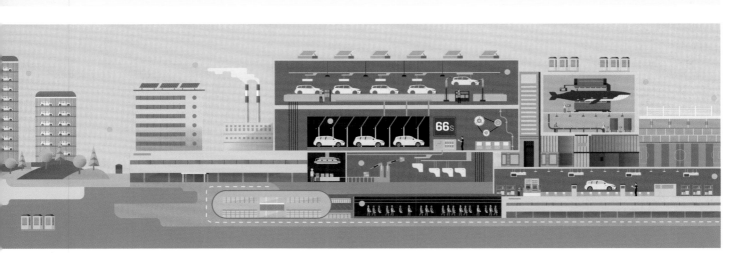

# What People Are Afraid of in Russia

Agency: **Design-Bureau Shuka**
Design: **Rodion Kitaev**

Rodion Kitaev created a series of infographics showing the various fears experienced by Russian citizens for *Bolshoy Gorod* magazine, using pencil and Photoshop.

Автокатастрофы
**68,4%**

Бедствий
**35,8%**

Нападения на улице
**64,2%**

Сойти с ума
**42%**

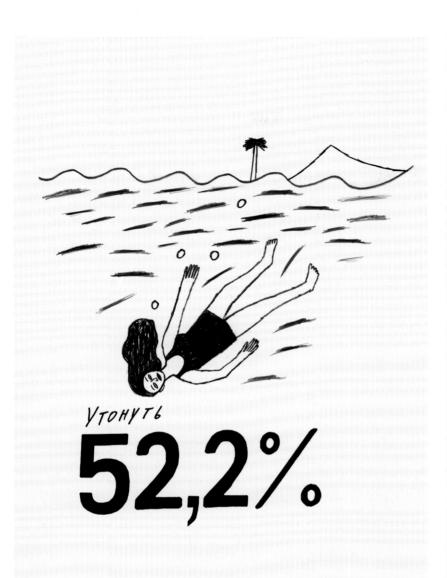

Утонуть

# 52,2%

Болезней (инфекции, рака)

# 60,2%

Собак

# 8,1%

Экономического кризиса

# 6%

Стоматологов

# 2,8%

# The Wrinklebabes:
# Six Months on Instagram

........................................

Agency: **Studio Inform**
Design: **Lysanne de Water**

This is a self-initiated project to record the designer's cat and to practice her data visualization skills. The circles represent a period of six months, with each dot representing a day. Up to three posts are visualized in the outer three circles. The inner circle shows the date on which a photo was featured by another account.

The size of the circles indicates the number of likes (or views) that a post has received. Mint green signifies a photo post, purple a video post; pink denotes the video views and green the featured posts. The data is derived from the posts from December 10th, 2015 to June 10th, 2016.

## top 5 most liked posts

2.202 likes     1.795 likes     1.753 likes     1.630 likes     1.534 likes

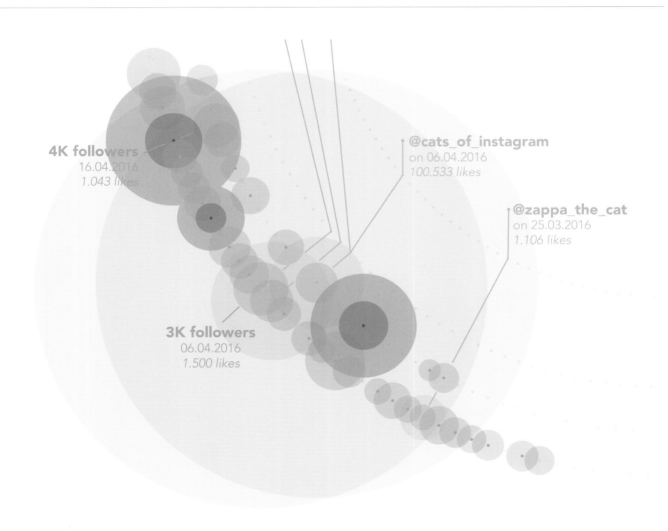

4K followers
16.04.2016
1.043 likes

@cats_of_instagram
on 06.04.2016
100.533 likes

@zappa_the_cat
on 25.03.2016
1.106 likes

3K followers
06.04.2016
1.500 likes

# @thewrinklebabes

## six months on instagram

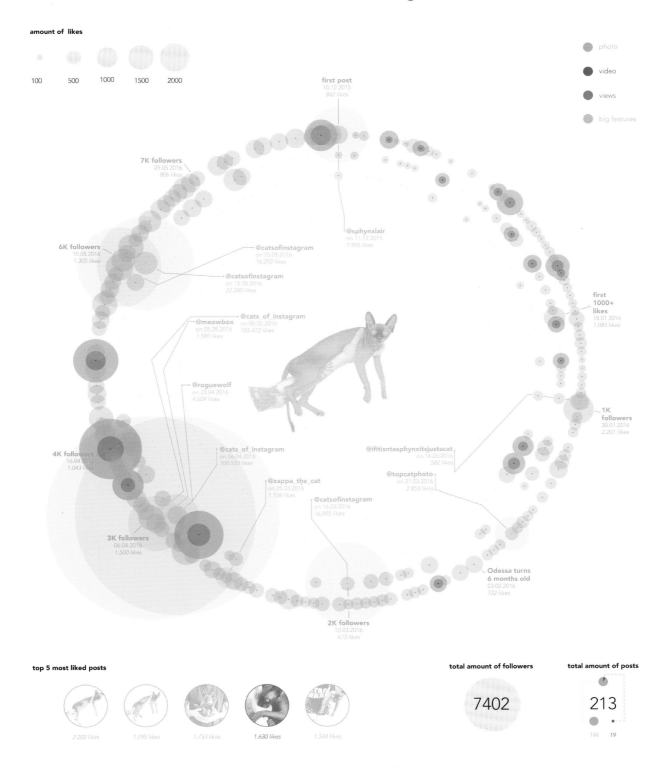

amount of likes

100  500  1000  1500  2000

photo
video
views
big features

**first post**
10.12.2015
842 likes

**7K followers**
29.05.2016
806 likes

**6K followers**
10.05.2016
1.305 likes

**@catsofinstagram**
on 23.05.2016
16.292 likes

**@catsofinstagram**
on 15.05.2016
22.240 likes

**@sphynxlair**
on 11.12.2015
7.995 likes

**@meowbox**
on 05.05.2016
7.590 likes

**@cats_of_instagram**
on 06.05.2016
105.472 likes

**first 1000+ likes**
18.01.2016
1.085 likes

**@roguewolf**
on 23.04.2016
4.609 likes

**1K followers**
30.01.2016
2.201 likes

**4K followers**
16.04.2016
1.043 likes

**@cats_of_instagram**
on 06.04.2016
100.533 likes

**@ifitisntasphynxitsjustacat**
on 16.03.2016
582 likes

**@topcatphoto**
on 21.03.2016
2.853 likes

**@zappa_the_cat**
on 25.03.2016
1.106 likes

**@catsofinstagram**
on 16.03.2016
16.895 likes

**3K followers**
06.04.2016
1.500 likes

**Odessa turns 6 months old**
23.02.2016
722 likes

**2K followers**
10.03.2016
473 likes

---

**top 5 most liked posts**

2.202 likes  1.795 likes  1.753 likes  1.630 likes  1.534 likes

**total amount of followers**

7402

**total amount of posts**

213

194    19

# Fume Leads to Death

....................................................

Design: **Liow Heng Chun**

Fume Leads to Death aims to break the stereotyped and conventional presentation of an awareness poster—often with gross imageries of damaged body parts and somber colors—concerning the detrimental effects of smoking by implementing whimsical illustrations and eye-catching color schemes (while retaining a certain degree of clinical appearance) to encourage a more pleasant viewing experience and to enable the audience to understand the content. The website link on top of the infographic directs viewers to the official website of Blackmores (fictional client) and help them to find out how they can benefit from Blackmores supplements in the endeavor of quitting smoking.

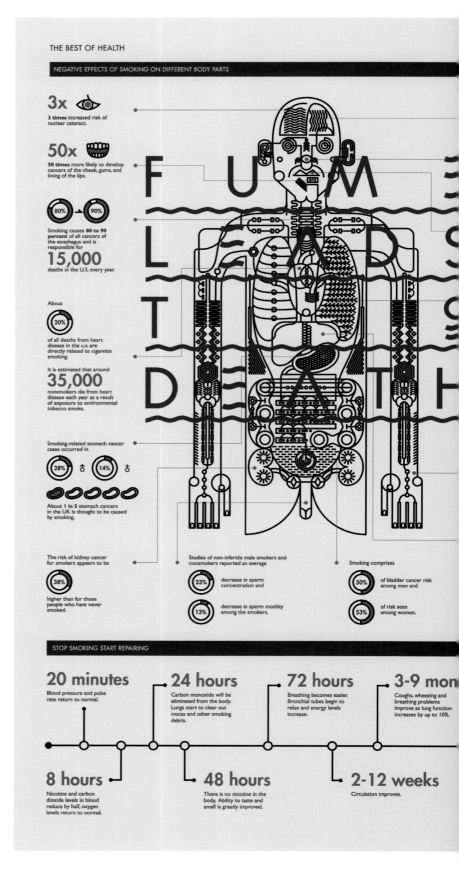

THE BEST OF HEALTH

NEGATIVE EFFECTS OF SMOKING ON DIFFERENT BODY PARTS

**3x**
3 **times** increased risk of nuclear cataract.

**50x**
**50 times** more likely to develop cancers of the cheek, gums, and lining of the lips.

**80%** → **90%**
Smoking causes **80 to 90 percent** of all cancers of the esophagus and is responsible for
**15,000**
deaths in the U.S. every year.

About
**20%**
of all deaths from heart disease in the u.s. are directly related to cigarette smoking.

It is estimated that around
**35,000**
nonsmokers die from heart disease each year as a result of exposure to environmental tobacco smoke.

Smoking-related stomach cancer cases occurred in
**28%** ♂ **14%** ♀
About 1 in 5 stomach cancers in the UK is thought to be caused by smoking.

The risk of kidney cancer for smokers appears to be
**38%**
higher than for those people who have never smoked.

Studies of non-infertile male smokers and nonsmokers reported an average
**23%** decrease in sperm concentration and
**13%** decrease in sperm motility among the smokers.

Smoking comprises
**50%** of bladder cancer risk among men and
**53%** of risk seen among women.

STOP SMOKING START REPAIRING

**20 minutes**
Blood pressure and pulse rate return to normal.

**24 hours**
Carbon monoxide will be eliminated from the body. Lungs start to clear out mucas and other smoking debris.

**72 hours**
Breathing becomes easier. Bronchial tubes begin to relax and energy levels increase.

**3-9 mon**
Coughs, wheezing and breathing problems improve as lung function increases by up to 10%.

**8 hours**
Nicotine and carbon dioxide levels in blood reduce by half, oxygen levels return to normal.

**48 hours**
There is no nicotine in the body. Ability to taste and smell is greatly improved.

**2-12 weeks**
Circulation improves.

...f stroke is **nearly doubled**
...erson who smokes.

...rs are **twice** as likely to have a
...d sense of smell than their
...oking counterparts.

...imately **90 percent** of the
...ed oral cancer are
...o-caused.

**23x**

...ho smoke are **23 times** more
...o develop lung cancer than
...ho do not smoke, and female
...rs are **13 times** more likely to
...o the disease.

**13x**

...ng cancer deaths in men and

...ng cancer deaths in women
...ed by smoking.

...rs have a

...e in their risk of squamous cell
... one of the most common
...ancers today.

...rs have

... of excess risk of death
... from liver cancer.

## 10 years

Risk of lung cancer falls to
half that of a smoker. Risk
of heart attack falls to the
same as someone who has
never smoked.

## 5 years

Risk of heart attack falls to
about half compared to a
person who is still smoking.

---

## FACTS ABOUT SECONDHAND SMOKES

There are more than

**4,000**
chemicals in tobacco
smoke.

**250**
are known to
be harmful.

**50**
are known to
cause cancer.

**TOBACCO SMOKE INCLUDES**

Acetone
Ammonia
Arsenic
Butane
Cadmium
Carbon monoxide
DDT
Methanol
Vinyl Chloride

**AS FOUND IN**

Paint stripper
Floor cleaner
Ant poison
Lighter fuel
Car batteries
Car exhaust fumes
Insecticide
Rocket fuel
Plastics

**NON-SMOKING AREAS DO NOT WORK.** it takes less than

## 10 minutes
for the smoke particles to fill the air, making the level
of the cancer-causing pollutants in the smoking
area and non-smoking area the same

## 2 minutes
after cigarettes have been extingusihed.

Particles pollution level in
**SMOKING AREA**

Particles pollution level in
**NON-SMOKING AREA**

## 30 minutes
Exposure to second hand smokes.

= **2-4**
Smoking
cigarettes

One recent study in the british
medical journal found that
exposure to second hand smoke
increases the risk of heart
disease among non-smokers by

 60%

 40%
of all children are
regularly exposed to
second hand smoke at
home.

31%
of the death attributable to
second hand smoke occur in
children.

(x100,000) children

It is estimated that

**1,000,000**
asthmatic children have their condition worsened by
exposure to environmental tobacco smoke.

(x100,000) infections

Secondhand smoke is responsible
for about

**300,000**
lower respiratory tract infections in
children under 18 months of age,
and lung infections resulting in

**7,500-
15,000**
hospitalizations each year.

Secondhand smoke
cause almost

**75,000**
death in the United
States each year.

(x1,000) deaths

(x1,000) death from
lung cancer

(x10,000) death from
heart disease

Including approximately

**3,000**
from lung cancer.

and

**60,000**
from heart disease.

---

## FACTS ABOUT NATURE AND TOBACCO

Each year nearly

## 600 million
trees are destroyed to provide fuel
to dry tobacco.

Smokers toss at least

## 4.5 trillion
cigarettes butts each year.

---

## FACTS ABOUT GLOBAL USE OF TOBACCO

# 1,350,000,000

PEOPLE SMOKE WORLDWIDE

1 out of every **5** people
smoke worldwide.

**One third** of the male
population in the world
smokes tobacco.

**1,000**/24h

1000 persons younger than 18 years
of age become regular smokers everyday.

**Percentage of Adults Who Were Current Smokers in 2010**

By Gender

| | |
|---|---|
| 21.5% | adult men |
| 17.3% | adult women |

By Age

| | |
|---|---|
| 20.1% | 18-24 years old |
| 22.0% | 25-44 years old |
| 21.1% | 45-64 years old |
| 9.5% | 65 years old and older |

If current trends continue, the number of
smoker is expected to increase to

**1,600,000,000**
by the year 2025.

Approximately

**10,000,000**
cigarettes are purchased a minute.

**15,000,000,000**
cigarettes are sold every day.

**5,000,000,000,000**
cigarettes are sold annually.

One survey found that

60%
of Chinese adults did not
know that smoking can
cause lung cancer while

96%
were unaware it can
cause heart disease.

---

## FACTS ABOUT DEATH AND TOBACCO

75%
of smokers say they want
to quit smoking.

Only **5 of every 100** people
who attempt to quit smoking
succeed.

Every
## 8 sec
someone dies from
tobacco use.

Every
## 5,000,000
deaths per year in the world
caused by cigarette smoking.

or about **one in five deaths** annually.

More than alcohol, car accidents,
suicides, AIDS, homicide and illegal
drugs **COMBINED.**

(x100,000) people

If current trends continue, by the year 2020,
tobacco is projected to kill about

**7,000,000**
people a year worldwide.

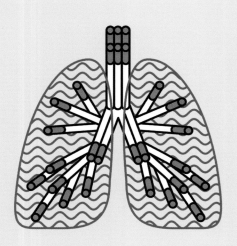

**MAKE YOUR CHOICES.
IT IS YOUR LIFE.**

Smoking causes
**5,000,000**
death every year. If the current trend
continues, by the year 2020, tobacco
is projected to kill about
**7,000,000**
people a year worldwide.

Put it out before it puts you out.

BLACKMORES                                      www.blackmore.com.au

**MAKE YOUR CHOICES.
IT IS YOUR LIFE.**

Smoking causes
**5,000,000**
death every year. If the current trend
continues, by the year 2020, tobacco
is projected to kill about
**7,000,000**
people a year worldwide.

Put it out before it puts you out.

BLACKMORES                                      www.blackmore.com.au

**(x100,000) children**

It is estimated that
# 1,000,000
asthmatic children have their condition worsened by
exposure to environmental tobacco smoke.

**(x100,000) infections**

Secondhand smoke is responsible
for about
# 300,000
lower respiratory tract infections in
children under 18 months of age,
and lung infections resulting in
# 7,500-
# 15,000
hospitalizations each year.

Secondhand smoke
cause almost
# 75,000
death in the United
States each year.

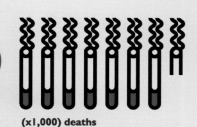

**(x1,000) deaths**

**MAKE YOUR CHOICES.
IT IS YOUR LIFE.**

Smoking causes
**5,000,000**
death every year. If the current trend
continues, by the year 2020, tobacco
is projected to kill about
**7,000,000**
people a year worldwide.

Put it out before it puts you out.

BLACKMORES

www.blackmore.com.au

# Alle paarden verzamelen

In de RAI begint morgen de 57ste editie van Jumping Amsterdam. Wat is er nou zo leuk aan, dat al die paarden naar de stad komen?

tekst VINCENT SMITS graphic CHANTAL VAN WESSEL

'B riljant, maar volledig nutteloos." Zo omschrijft de Britse komiek Eddie Izzard in een van zijn sketches de dressuursport. "Tenzij je je paard in een kast wil parkeren."

Het is een soort onbegrip waar paardensportliefhebbers vaker tegen aanlopen. Dressuur? Onbegrijpelijk getrippel van paarden, wel of niet op muziek. Springen? Dat is toch zielig voor die dieren. Paardensport in het algemeen, wat is daar nou leuk aan?

Die vraag wordt vanaf morgen beantwoord in de RAI, waar de 57ste Jumping Amsterdam is. Vier dagen zal daar de top van de spring- en dressuursport acte de présence geven. Het is een van de oudste indoorconcoursen van Europa en geniet binnen de paardensport een bijzondere reputatie. "Jumping leeft enorm onder de ruiters," zegt Rob Ehrens, bondscoach van de Nederlandse springruiters. "Er is tegelijkertijd een wereldbekerwedstrijd in Zürich waar ik twee plekken voor mag weggeven, maar alleen Harrie Smolders gaat. Die andere plek kan ik niet eens vullen. Iedereen wil naar Amsterdam. Vorig jaar ging er zelfs helemaal niemand naar Zürich."

Het concours is dan ook een topevenement, aldus Ehrens. "Het publiek leeft ongelofelijk mee. Het blijft zitten voor de prijsuitreiking en juicht en joelt voor onze mensen. Dat mis ik vaak bij andere evenementen. Het maakt wel verschil of je bij een Grand Prix een barrage moet rijden in een entourage met vijftig mensen op de tribune die hooguit een applausje geven of dat je in een volle bak moet rijden waar iedereen meedoet."

Het bijzondere van Jumping is dat het een volksevenement is, zegt Hans Bakker, voorzitter van Jumping Amsterdam en directeur van de RAI. "Dat krijgen we ook te horen van mensen van de Internationale Hippische Sport Federatie. Veel concoursen zijn toch vaak een beetje stijf. Daar gaat het om de chique tafels. Jumping is een drie-eenheid van wereldtopsport, entertainment –

binnen en buiten de ring – en e Als er bij de prijsuitreiking *Gee* wordt gedraaid, zingt iedereer

Directeur Annemarie van trots op dat veel ruiters en ama ping komen, hoewel bijvoorbe Grote Prijs van Aken sportief g niet. Een goede organisatie is "We willen dat ruiters een goe dat ze zijn voorzien van een na fortabel en snel van het hotel r vervoerd. Daarnaast moeten d verdienen in bepaalde rubriek ranking en proberen we te zorg trainingstijden hebben. Dat he zijn vruchten afgeworpen. We nen op een heel mooi deelnem

Goed, voor de ruiters is het bezoekers? Annette van Trigt, *dio Sport*, komt al jaren op Jum een snelkookpan. Het evenem gen. Daarom zit je er als toesch dernissen staan bijna tegen de ze van spreken het zweet van d vliegt je om de oren. Als je je houdt, zoals ik, kom je in een w

Zij adviseert bezoekers om kijken bij de ring in de andere I inrijden. "Dan kun je de paard als je geen verstand hebt van d sant en ingewikkeld het is."

**Imposant dier**
Van Trigt maakt documentaire wereld. "De basis voor mijn do is op Jumping gelegd. Ik heb h in levenden lijve gezien." Ruite Totilas de ene na de andere gr suursport, totdat een Duitser d voor meer dan tien miljoen eu zie je wat zo'n imposant dier lo is met zijn proef, strekt hij zijn

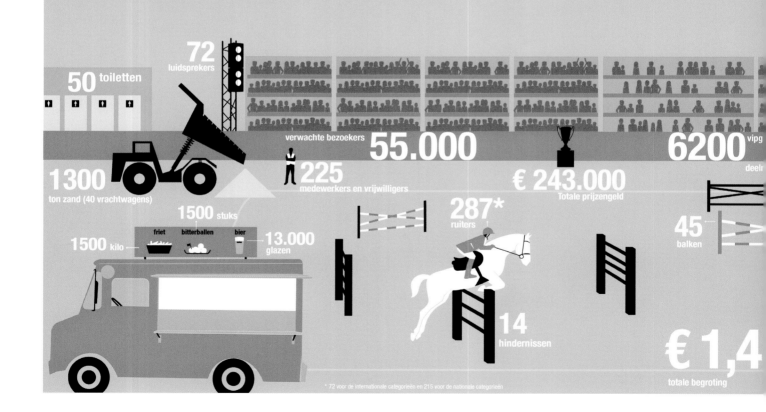

wijl het publiek op de banken staat."

"Topsport is het hart van het evenement maar dat gaat op Jumping samen met entertainment en een Amsterdamse tintje," zegt Van Putten-Bunschoten. Zo zijn er ook acts in de piste. Dit jaar onder anderen van een Catalaanse paardentrainer die met zijn twee arabieren en twee honden een bijzondere show geeft. Er zijn allerlei stands en er is 's avonds op het 'Leidseplein' – alle plekken hebben Amsterdamse straatnamen – een show met Amsterdamse artiesten. "Het is ook een leuk evenement voor mensen die gewoon een avondje uit willen."

Jumping is belangrijk voor de stad, aldus voorzitter Hans Bakker. "Afgezien dat de hotels en horeca goede zaken doen, is het ook een van de weinige jaarlijkse grote sportevenementen van Amsterdam. Je hebt de Wielerzesdaagse, de Marathon van Amsterdam en Jumping. Dat is toch een beetje karig voor een hoofdstad met ambities. Als je een metropool wilt zijn, moet je zorgen dat je ook op sportgebied meekomt. De NOS schiet de beelden van Jumping, maar je ziet ze wereldwijd terug. Dat doet ook wat voor de uitstraling van Amsterdam in de rest van de wereld. Ik was een keer in een hotel in Madrid. Zag ik op televisie anderhalf uur beelden van Jumping. En dat was een half jaar na het evenement."

Vorig jaar kende de Grote Prijs van Amsterdam op de laatste dag een bijzonder spannende finale, waarin Nederlander Willem Greve in de barrage de eerste plaats wist binnen te slepen. "De tribunes waren tot de nok toe gevuld, de viptribunes barstten uit hun voegen en er was topsport van de bovenste plank te zien," zegt Van Putten-Bunschoten. "Als mensen me dan vragen waarom ik het hele jaar werk voor vier dagen, wijs ik naar zo'n moment. Daar krijg je echt kippenvel van."

## Tapijt op stal

De organisatie van Jumping Amsterdam vergt een jaar, maar de fysieke opbouw begint pas op de zondag voor het concours. "In totaal hebben we daar 3,5 dag voor," zegt directeur Annemarike van Putten-Bunschoten.

Jumping beslaat drie hallen – het hele Hollandcomplex: een hal waar de piste en tribunes zijn met daar omheen wat stands, dan is er de hal voor standhouders en het promodorp. Daar is ook het Leidseplein (het cateringplein), waar in het weekeinde 's avonds het feestje is. Daar is ook de openbare inrijring waar de deelnemers van dichtbij zijn te zien. En dan is er nog een afgesloten hal met een kleine 190 stallen. Daar is ook een losrijpiste die niet toegankelijk is voor het publiek en waar ruiters kunnen trainen.

"Op zondag wordt het tapijt gelegd in de entreehal en wordt het licht en geluid opgehangen in de hal waar de piste komt. Dan komt ook de standhouder met vrachtwagens voor paardenvervoer de trucks parkeren, want die kan er daarna niet meer bij," aldus Van Putten-Bunschoten. "Op maandagochtend vijf uur klopt tribunebouwer Kuijf op de deur."

Dan wordt de bodem gelegd. Maandagochtend komen veertig vrachtwagens met zand naar de RAI. "Je mag het eigenlijk geen zand noemen. Het is een bodem met een gelmix die een bepaalde vering heeft. Daar zit heel veel onderhoud in, ook tijdens het evenement. De bodem moet een bepaalde vochtigheidsgraad bezitten. Vergelijk het met de ijsmeester in Thialf. Als het ijs niet goed is, wordt er ook niet goed geschaatst."

In de hal waar de stallen komen, wordt de vloer eerst geïmpregneerd, daarna komt er een laag plastic overheen gevolgd door een laag tapijt. "Dat is om te voorkomen dat ze drie weken later op een beurs nog steeds de ammoniak en de paarden ruiken. De paarden staan dus op tapijt met daarop stro, zaagsel of vlas." Donderdag komen de meeste paarden aan, vóór de controle van de veearts.

Op het drukste moment heeft Jumping Amsterdam 225 mensen rondlopen, het merendeel vrijwilliger. "Sommigen doen het al meer dan dertig jaar. We proberen ze door het jaar heen leuke dingen aan te bieden, zoals kaartjes voor een concours. Zonder al die vrijwilligers zou Jumping geen haalbare kaart zijn."

Het hele evenement vergt sowieso veel planning, zegt Van Putten-Bunschoten: "We hebben een draaiboek van minuut tot minuut. Het luistert zó nauw. Het is eigenlijk een show van half negen 's ochtends tot kwart voor twaalf 's avonds."

# Jumping Amsterdam

Agency: **Vizualism**
Design: **Chantal van Wessel, Het Parool**

Jumping Amsterdam is a Dutch international horse show. Instead of showing the usual pictures of horses, Vizualism interpreted this show by numbers and data.

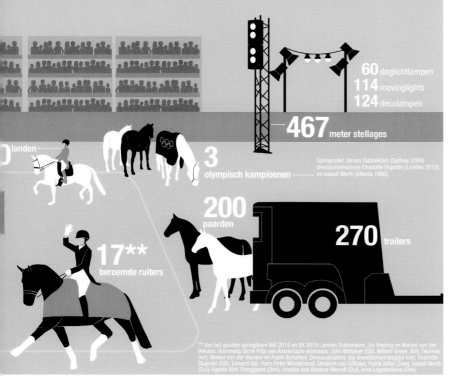

60 daglichtlampen
114 movinglights
124 decolampen

467 meter stellages

Springruiter Jeroen Dubbeldam (Sydney 2000) dressuuramazones Charlotte Dujardin (Londen 2012) en Isabell Werth (Atlanta 1996).

3 olympisch kampioenen

200 paarden

270 trailers

17** beroemde ruiters

** Van het gouden springteam WK 2014 en EK 2015: Jeroen Dubbeldam, Jur Vrieling en Maikel van der Vleuten. Voormalig Grote Prijs van Amsterdam-winnaars: John Whitaker (GB), Willem Greve, Billy Twomey (Ier), Maikel van der Vleuten en Frank Schuttert. Dressuurruiters, top wereldbekerranglijst met: Charlotte Dujardin (GB), Edward Gal, Hans Peter Minderhoud, Diederik van Silfhout, Patrik Kittel (Zwe), Isabell Werth (Dui), Agnete Kirk Thinggaard (Den), Jessica von Bredow-Werndl (Dui), Inna Logutenkova (Oek).

# The Hobbit: The Desolation of Smaug

..................................................................................

Design: **TukiToku**
Content: **Zaki Jufri**
Client: **inSing**

Having worked with numerous clients including inSing, *Forbes* Indonesia, and UPS, TukiToku has not stopped himself from creating his own personal projects—a move derived from his inventive passion and provocative perspectives in the arts. Taking a special interest in whatever comes to his attention, TukiToku is not limited by any visual style or medium. Commissioned by inSing.com, this is an infographics project showing *The Hobbit: The Desolation of Smaug* by the numbers.

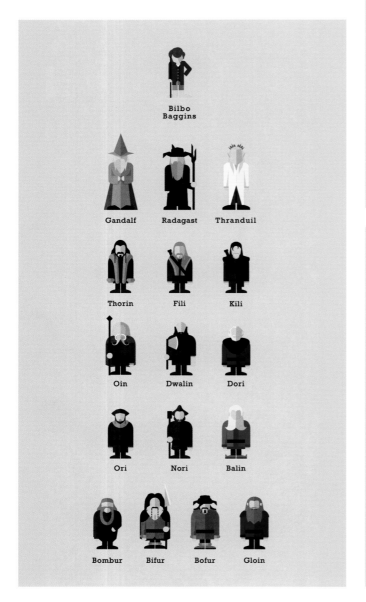

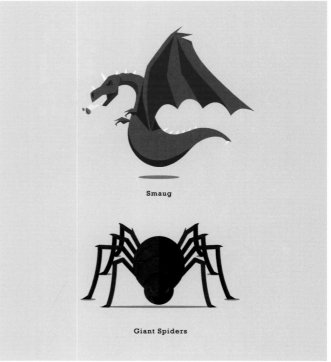

# THE HOBBIT

## THE DESOLATION OF SMAUG

### BY THE NUMBERS

**01**
Dragon–Smaug

**03**
Films in the Trilogy

**02**
Wizards–Gandalf
& Radagast

**01**
Hobbit–Bilbo Baggins

Bilbo
Baggins

Gandalf  Radagast

**13**
Empty wine
barrels in which
the Dwarves escape
Thranduil's Realm

**100+**
Hobbit feet
for Bilbo

**01**
Elvenking–
Thranduil

Thranduil

Bombur

**05**
Hours to complete
hair, make-up,
prosthetics,
and wardrobe for
each of the
13 Dwarves

Kili

**08**
Legs on the giant
Spiders infesting
Mirkwood Forest

Thorin   Fili

Bofur

Dori

Dwalin

Oin

Balin

**10 kg**
Human hair
for wigmaking

Gloin

Nori

**48 fps**
Higher frame rate
used for the Trilogy

**547**
Travelling weapons
for the 13 Dwarves

**80**
The age of the
oldest vintage
microphone
used to record
the score for
"The Hobbit:
The Desolation
of Smaug

Bifur

**752**
Wigs. Nearly everyone
in the film is wigged

**1,200**
'Extras' that needed
to be cast for the
Trilogy

Ori

**5,000+**
Approximate
population of
Lake-Town

**13**
Dwarves– Thorin, Balin,
Dwalin, Fili, Kili
Bofur, Bombur, Bifur, Oin,
Gloin, Dori, Nori and Ori

**170,000**
Punched aluminium gold plated
coins trickled over Smaug's Lair

**140,000**
Cups of coffee made
by craft services
throughout production

inSing.com movies

# Internet para Toda la Humanidad Infographic

Design: **Samu Coronado**
Client: *Yorokobu*

This two-page infographic for the mensual magazine *Yorokobu* shows the different satellites and drones that distinct technologic powers are launching in order to bring the Internet to the whole globe.

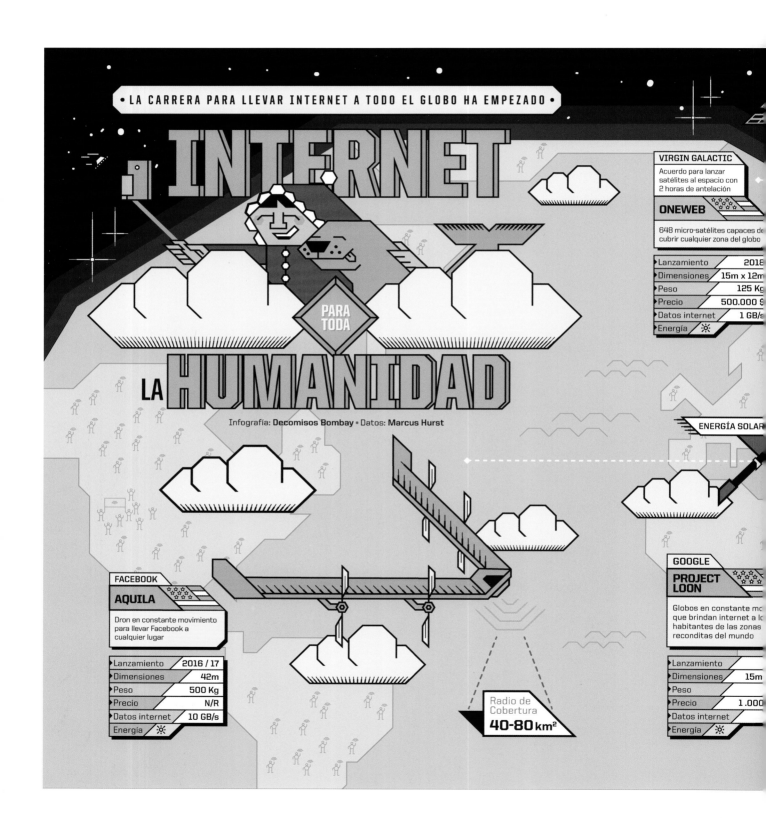

• LA CARRERA PARA LLEVAR INTERNET A TODO EL GLOBO HA EMPEZADO •

INTERNET
PARA TODA
LA HUMANIDAD

Infografía: **Decomisos Bombay** • Datos: **Marcus Hurst**

**VIRGIN GALACTIC**
Acuerdo para lanzar
satélites al espacio con
2 horas de antelación

**ONEWEB**
648 micro-satélites capaces de
cubrir cualquier zona del globo

| | |
|---|---|
| ▶Lanzamiento | 2018 |
| ▶Dimensiones | 15m x 12m |
| ▶Peso | 125 Kg |
| ▶Precio | 500.000 $ |
| ▶Datos internet | 1 GB/s |
| ▶Energía | ☼ |

**ENERGÍA SOLAR**

**FACEBOOK**
**AQUILA**
Dron en constante movimiento
para llevar Facebook a
cualquier lugar

| | |
|---|---|
| ▶Lanzamiento | 2016 / 17 |
| ▶Dimensiones | 42m |
| ▶Peso | 500 Kg |
| ▶Precio | N/R |
| ▶Datos internet | 10 GB/s |
| ▶Energía | ☼ |

**GOOGLE**
**PROJECT LOON**
Globos en constante mo
que brindan internet a lo
habitantes de las zonas
reconditas del mundo

| | |
|---|---|
| ▶Lanzamiento | |
| ▶Dimensiones | 15m |
| ▶Peso | |
| ▶Precio | 1.000 |
| ▶Datos internet | |
| ▶Energía | ☼ |

Radio de
Cobertura
**40-80 km²**

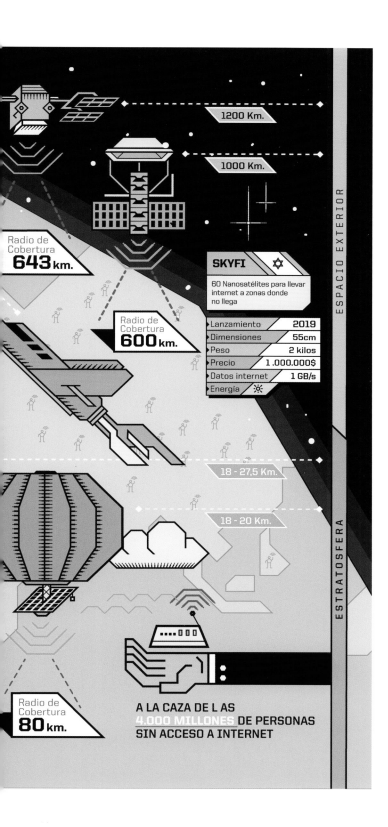

Radio de Cobertura
**643** km.

Radio de Cobertura
**600** km.

1200 Km.

1000 Km.

18 - 27,5 Km.

18 - 20 Km.

ESPACIO EXTERIOR

ESTRATOSFERA

**SKYFI** ✡

60 Nanosatélites para llevar internet a zonas donde no llega

| Lanzamiento | 2019 |
|---|---|
| Dimensiones | 55cm |
| Peso | 2 kilos |
| Precio | 1.000.000$ |
| Datos internet | 1 GB/s |
| Energía | ☼ |

Radio de Cobertura
**80** km.

A LA CAZA DE L AS
**4.000 MILLONES** DE PERSONAS
SIN ACCESO A INTERNET

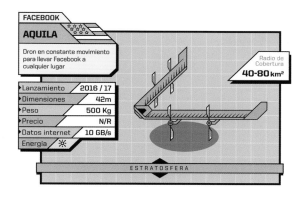

**FACEBOOK**

**AQUILA** ★★★

Dron en constante movimiento para llevar Facebook a cualquier lugar

| Lanzamiento | 2016 / 17 |
|---|---|
| Dimensiones | 42m |
| Peso | 500 Kg |
| Precio | N/R |
| Datos internet | 10 GB/s |
| Energía | ☼ |

Radio de Cobertura
**40-80 km²**

ESTRATOSFERA

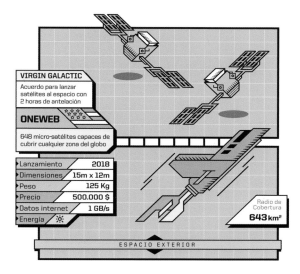

**VIRGIN GALACTIC** ★★★

Acuerdo para lanzar satélites al espacio con 2 horas de antelación

**ONEWEB**

648 micro-satélites capaces de cubrir cualquier zona del globo

| Lanzamiento | 2018 |
|---|---|
| Dimensiones | 15m x 12m |
| Peso | 125 Kg |
| Precio | 500.000 $ |
| Datos internet | 1 GB/s |
| Energía | ☼ |

Radio de Cobertura
**643 km²**

ESPACIO EXTERIOR

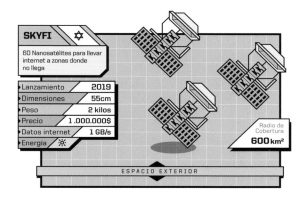

**SKYFI** ✡

60 Nanosatélites para llevar internet a zonas donde no llega

| Lanzamiento | 2019 |
|---|---|
| Dimensiones | 55cm |
| Peso | 2 kilos |
| Precio | 1.000.000$ |
| Datos internet | 1 GB/s |
| Energía | ☼ |

Radio de Cobertura
**600 km²**

ESPACIO EXTERIOR

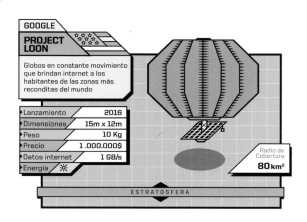

**GOOGLE** ★★★

**PROJECT LOON**

Globos en constante movimiento que brindan internet a los habitantes de las zonas más reconditas del mundo

| Lanzamiento | 2016 |
|---|---|
| Dimensiones | 15m x 12m |
| Peso | 10 Kg |
| Precio | 1.000.000$ |
| Datos internet | 1 GB/s |
| Energía | ☼ |

Radio de Cobertura
**80 km²**

ESTRATOSFERA

# Porcolipsis

...........................

Design: **Angel Sanz Correa**
Art Direction: **Angel Sanz Correa**
Data: **Mar Romero**
Client: **BCN Més**

*BCN Més* reached out to Angel Sanz Correa to design an infographic poster about the Catalan pork industry and its excesses. Angel decided to go with the illustrative style of traditional stationary from local butchers and meat shops, which uses a strange combination of naïve, positive, yet creepy and gory depictions of pigs being slaughtered. It fits the context considering the contradiction of such industry: local people are very proud of the industry because it powers the nation's economy, yet it also pollutes the land and damages small businesses.

# PORCOLIPSIS!

## L'EIX DELS PORCS CATALANS

14 MILIONS DE PORCS NEIXEN I CREIXEN A CATALUNYA CADA ANY. UNS 50.000 AL DIA ARRIBEN ALS ESCORXADORS DE LA NOSTRA COMARCA. EL SECTOR REPRESENTA MÉS DEL 3% DEL PIB CATALÀ I UNES POQUES EMPRESES ESTAN A CÀRREC. UNA HISTÒRIA *AGRIDUCE* SOBRE L'EXCÉS DE LA CARN. EL SEU FINAL FELIÇ DEPÈN DE TU, CONSUMIDOR OMNÍVOR.

UN PROJECTE DE BCN MÉS. ABRIL DE 2016.
DADES: MAR ROMERO.
DISSENY: ANGEL SANZ CORREA.

**BCNMES**

## EXPORTACIONS

CATALUNYA ÉS LA COMUNITAT QUE MÉS EXPORTA – 76% – I IMPORTA – 37% – DE TOT EL TERRITORI NACIONAL

CARN FRESCA - 37,4% -
CONGELADA - 20,4% -
I EMBOTITS - 17,9% -

## PROCÉS DE PRODUCCIÓ DEL PORC:

### 1. ALIMENTACIÓ

1.1 Importació de soja transgènica des de Brasil

1.2 Processat: al Port de Bcn, la soja es transforma en pinso

DESPESA ACUMULADA: 0€/KG
T. +0% | PREU VENDA: 0€/KG

### 2. PRODUCCIÓ

2.1 Venda de semen de porc a granges de truges

2.2 Fase d'inseminació i de gestació (3 mesos)

2.3 Fase inicial de lactància del porc (23 dies) *el porc pesa 18-20kg*

2.4 Fase d'engreixament a la granja "integrada" (5 mesos) *el porc pesa 110kg*

DESPESA ACUMULADA: 1,49€/KG
T. +12% | PREU VENDA: 1,67€/KG

### 3. "PORCOCIDI"

3.1 Sacrifici (de 50.000 porcs / dia)

3.2 Procés a les sales d'especejaments i sales de filetejat

DESPESA ACUMULADA: 2,15€/KG
T. +23% | PREU VENDA: 2,65€/KG

### 4. DISTRIBUCIÓ

4.1 Transport a majoristes de tot el territori català, nacional i internacional

DESPESA ACUMULADA: 2,93€/KG
T. +13% | PREU VENDA: 3,32€/KG

### 5. VENDA

5.1 Transport a minoristes i venda final al client al mercat o supermercat

DESPESA ACUMULADA: 4,00€/KG
T. +12% | PREU VENDA: 4,56€/KG

CADA ANY ES MATEN APROXIMADAMENT **19 milions!** DE PORCS - ÉS A DIR, UNS 50.000 AL DIA...

LA *PETXADA D'AIGUA* D'UN PORC DE PRODUCCIÓ INDUSTRIAL ÉS DE:
**3.428** L/KG

I TANT VOLUM D'AIGUA EQUIVAL A:
**330** H MIN DE DUTXA!

LES EMISSIONS PER PRODUÏR CADA KG DE PORC SÓN EQUIVALENTS A CONDUIR 40KMS EN COTXE DE GASOLINA: 6,72KG[3]

6,7 GR/M2 $CO_2$

### LLEIDA
*LA PROVÍNCIA AMB MÉS CAPS DE BESTIAR*
CAPS DE BESTIAR: ★ 4.256.070 #1 DE 4 EN CAPS
SACRIFICIS: 2.151.964 porcs/any #3 DE 4 EN SACRIFICIS
A LLEIDA HI HA APROXIMADAMENT 10 PORCS X PERSONA

### NOGUERA
CAPS: 919.000 #2 EN CAPS DE BESTIAR

### SEGRIÀ
CAPS: 943.000 #1 EN CAPS DE BESTIAR

### GIRONA
CAPS DE BESTIAR: 873.376 #3 DE 4 EN CAPS
SACRIFICIS: 6.660.673 porcs/any #2 DE 4 EN SACRIFICIS

OSONA ÉS LA COMARCA AMB MÉS DENSITAT DE PORCS

### OSONA
CAPS: 794.000 #3 EN CAPS DE BESTIAR
SACRIFICIS: +5 milions/any #1 EN SACRIF.

### SEGARRA
SACRIFICIS: 1,3 milions/any #4 EN SACRIF.

### BAGES
SACRIFICIS: 1,7 milions/any #3 EN SACRIF.

### LA SELVA
SACRIFICIS: 3,7 milions/any #2 EN SACRIF.

LES 4 COMARQUES JUNTES SUPOSEN EL: 70,4% DE TOTS ELS SACRIFICIS

*LA PROVÍNCIA AMB MÉS SACRIFICIS*

### BARCELONA
CAPS DE BESTIAR: 1.838.437 #2 DE 4 EN CAPS
SACRIFICIS: ★ 7.902.229 porcs/any #1 DE 4 EN SACRIF.

### BARCELONÈS
CAPS: 0 L'ÚNICA SENSE CAPS DE BESTIAR

### TARRAGONA
CAPS DE BESTIAR: 489.332 #4 DE 4 EN CAPS
SACRIFICIS: 14.572 porcs/any #4 DE 4 EN SACRIFICIS

*Distribució*
**CATALUNYA**
DELS CAPS DE BESTIAR
I SACRIFICIS
·EL 2014·

**3'5** % DEL PIB CATALÀ ÉS COBERT PEL SECTOR PORCÍ. TURISME COBREIX EL 12%

**29000** EMPLEATS PEL SECTOR PORCÍ

**70** % DE LES DESPESES TOTALS DE LA PRODUCCIÓ SÓN L'ALIMENTACIÓ

20%FIXES, 4%MEDICINES, 3%EXTRA

NOMÉS **25** % ...DE LES GRANJES CATALANES NO ESTAN INTEGRADES

*el* **Pes** D'UN PORC ADULT TÍPIC

SÓN: **110** KG

QUE EQUIVAL A:

**63'5** KG DE CARN QUE COMPARTIRAN 5 CATALANS

**CONSUM, A** (DE CARN DE PORC / PES I DESPESES)

·EL· **12'4** KG **76'2** € CÀPITA X ANY ·14·

**CATALUNYA**

**Volum** DE PORCS SACRIFICATS

A BARCELONA

**100** EL 1998 %
**+78** % EL 2008 ‰

### A CATALUNYA:
**33** % DE LES AIGÜES ESTAN CONTAMINADES PER NITRATS

### A OSONA:
**50** % DE LES FONTS DE LA COMARCA TAMBÉ ESTAN CONTAMINADES PER NITRATS

ECOLOGIA

### TAMBÉ A OSONA:
**58** % ...ÉS EL TOTAL DE L'EXCEDENT DE PURINS DE LA COMARCA AMB MÉS DENSITAT DE PORCS

### A MÉS, A OSONA:
**52** % DEL PIB DE LA REGIÓ ESTÀ RELACIONAT AMB EL SECTOR PORCÍ

- RESIDUS -

>200
100-200
<100

SEGRIÀ | PLÀ D'URGELL | NOGUERA | OSONA

C-25 CARRETERA DE L'EIX TRANSVERSAL

CONCENTRACIÓ DE NITRATS (KG NITRATS / HECTÀREA) A CATALUNYA. LES DUES ZONES MÉS CRÍTIQUES ESTAN CONNECTADES PER LA CARRETERA DE L'EIX TRANSVERSAL: OSONA I LES COMARQUES CENTRALS DE LLEIDA

- REFERÈNCIES -
1: DADES DEL DEPARTAMENT D'AGRICULTURA, ALIMENTACIÓ I ACCIÓ RURAL, 2008.
2: DADES DE LLOTJA DE LLEIDA I GOVERN.CAT DEL 2015.
3: DADES DE GRUP DE DEFENSA DEL TER, HOEKSTRA, A., GARCIA-CALVO, E., 2014, *SUSTAINABILITY OF THE WATER FOOTPRINT OF THE SPANISH PORK INDUSTRY*.
4: DADES EXTRETES DE L'ESTUDI DE MCLEOD ET. AL. (2013) MACLEOD, M., GERBER, P., MOTTET, A., TEMPIO, G., FALCUCCI, A., OPIO, C., VELINGA, T., HENDERSON, B. & STEINFELD, H. 2013. *GREEN-HOUSE GAS EMISSIONS FROM PIG AND CHICKEN SUPPLY CHAINS - A GLOBAL LIFE CYCLE ASSESSMENT DE LA FOOD AND AGRICULTURE ORGANIZATION OF THE UNITED NATIONS.*

Design: **Samu Coronado**
Client: *Yorokobu*

This two-page infographic for the mensual magazine *Yorokobu* studies the rivalry that has been established in the last few years between different elevators manufacturers, which has forced them to build bigger test towers as taller buildings have been built, especially in emerging countries. The data is collected from different publications like *Financial Times*, *Scientific American*, *The New Yorker*, *PBS*, *Economist*, *Buzzfeed*, etc.

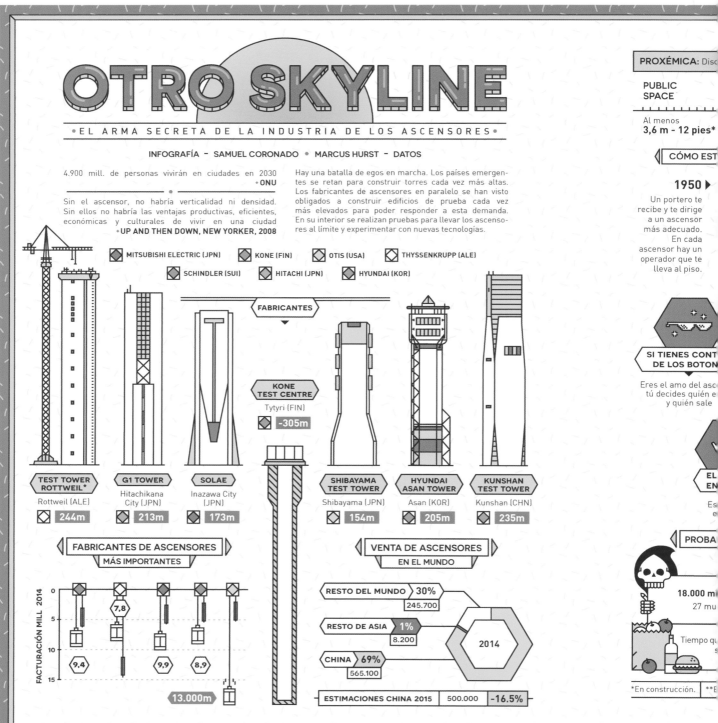

# OTRO SKYLINE

• EL ARMA SECRETA DE LA INDUSTRIA DE LOS ASCENSORES •

INFOGRAFÍA - SAMUEL CORONADO • MARCUS HURST - DATOS

4.900 mill. de personas vivirán en ciudades en 2030
• ONU

Sin el ascensor, no habría verticalidad ni densidad. Sin ellos no habría las ventajas productivas, eficientes, económicas y culturales de vivir en una ciudad
• UP AND THEN DOWN, NEW YORKER, 2008

Hay una batalla de egos en marcha. Los países emergentes se retan para construir torres cada vez más altas. Los fabricantes de ascensores en paralelo se han visto obligados a construir edificios de prueba cada vez más elevados para poder responder a esta demanda. En su interior se realizan pruebas para llevar los ascensores al límite y experimentar con nuevas tecnologías.

MITSUBISHI ELECTRIC (JPN)　　KONE (FIN)　　OTIS (USA)　　THYSSENKRUPP (ALE)
SCHINDLER (SUI)　　HITACHI (JPN)　　HYUNDAI (KOR)

FABRICANTES

KONE TEST CENTRE
Tytyri (FIN)
-305m

**TEST TOWER ROTTWEIL\***
Rottweil (ALE)
244m

**G1 TOWER**
Hitachikana City (JPN)
213m

**SOLAE**
Inazawa City (JPN)
173m

**SHIBAYAMA TEST TOWER**
Shibayama (JPN)
154m

**HYUNDAI ASAN TOWER**
Asan (KOR)
205m

**KUNSHAN TEST TOWER**
Kunshan (CHN)
235m

**FABRICANTES DE ASCENSORES**
**MÁS IMPORTANTES**

FACTURACIÓN MILL 2014
0
5
10
15

7,8
9,4　　9,9　8,9
13.000m

**VENTA DE ASCENSORES**
**EN EL MUNDO**

RESTO DEL MUNDO 30%
245.700
RESTO DE ASIA 1%
8.200
CHINA 69%
565.100

2014

ESTIMACIONES CHINA 2015　500.000　-16.5%

\*En construcción.

PROXÉMICA: Dis...

PUBLIC SPACE
Al menos
**3,6 m - 12 pies\***

CÓMO EST...

**1950 ▶**
Un portero te recibe y te dirige a un ascensor más adecuado. En cada ascensor hay un operador que te lleva al piso.

SI TIENES CONT...
DE LOS BOTON...
Eres el amo del asc... tú decides quién e... y quién sale

EL
EN...
Es...

PROBA...
18.000 mi...
27 mu...
Tiempo q...

\*\*E...

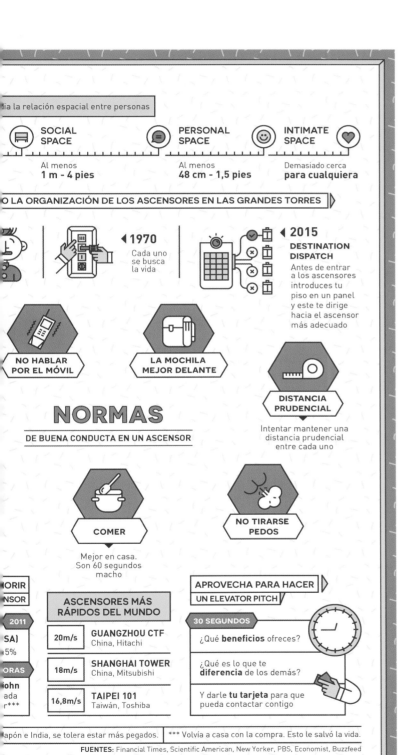

...dia la relación espacial entre personas

| SOCIAL SPACE | PERSONAL SPACE | INTIMATE SPACE |
|---|---|---|
| Al menos **1 m - 4 pies** | Al menos **48 cm - 1,5 pies** | Demasiado cerca **para cualquiera** |

...O LA ORGANIZACIÓN DE LOS ASCENSORES EN LAS GRANDES TORRES

◀ **1970**
Cada uno se busca la vida

◀ **2015**
**DESTINATION DISPATCH**
Antes de entrar a los ascensores introduces tu piso en un panel y este te dirige hacia el ascensor más adecuado

**NO HABLAR POR EL MÓVIL**

**LA MOCHILA MEJOR DELANTE**

**DISTANCIA PRUDENCIAL**
Intentar mantener una distancia prudencial entre cada uno

# NORMAS
## DE BUENA CONDUCTA EN UN ASCENSOR

**COMER**
Mejor en casa. Son 60 segundos macho

**NO TIRARSE PEDOS**

...ORIR
...NSOR

...2011

...SA)
...5%

...ORAS

...ohn
...ada
...r***

| ASCENSORES MÁS RÁPIDOS DEL MUNDO | |
|---|---|
| 20m/s | **GUANGZHOU CTF** China, Hitachi |
| 18m/s | **SHANGHAI TOWER** China, Mitsubishi |
| 16,8m/s | **TAIPEI 101** Taiwán, Toshiba |

**APROVECHA PARA HACER UN ELEVATOR PITCH**

**30 SEGUNDOS**
¿Qué **beneficios** ofreces?
¿Qué es lo que te **diferencia** de los demás?
Y darle **tu tarjeta** para que pueda contactar contigo

...apón e India, se tolera estar más pegados. | *** Volvía a casa con la compra. Esto le salvó la vida.

**FUENTES:** Financial Times, Scientific American, New Yorker, PBS, Economist, Buzzfeed

**KONE TEST CENTRE**
-305m

**TEST TOWER ROTTWEIL**
244m

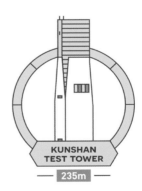
**KUNSHAN TEST TOWER**
235m

**G1 TOWER**
213m

**SHIBAYAMA TEST TOWER**
154m

**HYUNDAI ASAN TOWER**
205m

# Bob Dylan's Words:
## Analysis of Bob Dylan's Vocabulary

.........................................................

Design: **Federica Fragapane**
Art Direction: **Federica Fragapane**
Data: **ItaliaNLP Lab**
Client: *Corriere della Sera*

The visualization shows an analysis of the lyrics written by Bob Dylan (years 1962-2015). For each year were analyzed the albums whose songs are available on Dylan's official website. For each song, the terms used more than once have been extracted. The terms were then grouped into thematic areas. For each year are shown: the thematic area of the words, the frequency for each area, the predominance within a subject of a certain grammatical category, and the average number of words for each song.

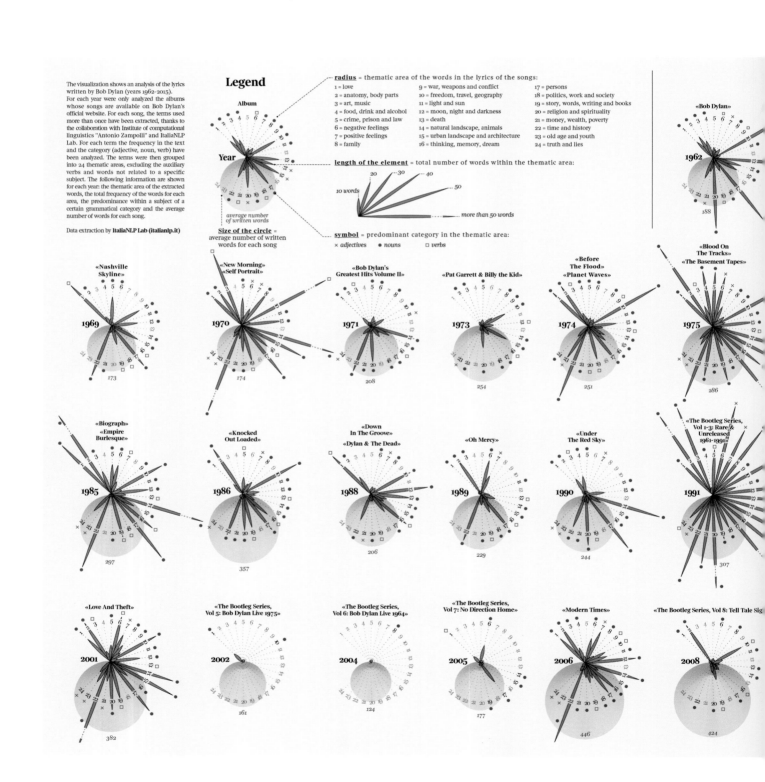

The visualization shows an analysis of the lyrics written by Bob Dylan (years 1962-2015). For each year were only analyzed the albums whose songs are available on Bob Dylan's official website. For each song, the terms used more than once have been extracted, thanks to the collaboration with Institute of computational linguistics "Antonio Zampolli" and ItaliaNLP Lab. For each term the frequency in the text and the category (adjective, noun, verb) have been analyzed. The terms were then grouped into 24 thematic areas, excluding the auxiliary verbs and words not related to a specific subject. The following information are shown for each year: the thematic area of the extracted words, the total frequency of the words for each area, the predominance within a subject of a certain grammatical category and the average number of words for each song.

Data extraction by ItaliaNLP Lab (italianlp.it)

**Legend**

**Album**

**Year**

*average number of written words*

**Size of the circle** = average number of written words for each song

**radius** = thematic area of the words in the lyrics of the songs:

1 = love
2 = anatomy, body parts
3 = art, music
4 = food, drink and alcohol
5 = crime, prison and law
6 = negative feelings
7 = positive feelings
8 = family

9 = war, weapons and conflict
10 = freedom, travel, geography
11 = light and sun
12 = moon, night and darkness
13 = death
14 = natural landscape, animals
15 = urban landscape and architecture
16 = thinking, memory, dream

17 = persons
18 = politics, work and society
19 = story, words, writing and books
20 = religion and spirituality
21 = money, wealth, poverty
22 = time and history
23 = old age and youth
24 = truth and lies

**length of the element** = total number of words within the thematic area:

10 words   20   30   40   50   more than 50 words

**symbol** = predominant category in the thematic area:
× *adjectives*   ● *nouns*   □ *verbs*

«Nashville Skyline» **1969** 173

«New Morning» «Self Portrait» **1970** 174

«Bob Dylan's Greatest Hits Volume II» **1971** 208

«Pat Garrett & Billy the Kid» **1973** 254

«Before The Flood» «Planet Waves» **1974** 251

«Blood On The Tracks» «The Basement Tapes» **1975** 286

«Bob Dylan» **1962** 188

«Biograph» «Empire Burlesque» **1985** 297

«Knocked Out Loaded» **1986** 357

«Down In The Groove» «Dylan & The Dead» **1988** 206

«Oh Mercy» **1989** 229

«Under The Red Sky» **1990** 244

«The Bootleg Series, Vol 1-3: Rare & Unreleased 1961-1991» **1991** 307

«Love And Theft» **2001** 382

«The Bootleg Series, Vol 5: Bob Dylan Live 1975» **2002** 161

«The Bootleg Series, Vol 6: Bob Dylan Live 1964» **2004** 124

«The Bootleg Series, Vol 7: No Direction Home» **2005** 177

«Modern Times» **2006** 446

«The Bootleg Series, Vol 8: Tell Tale Sig» **2008** 424

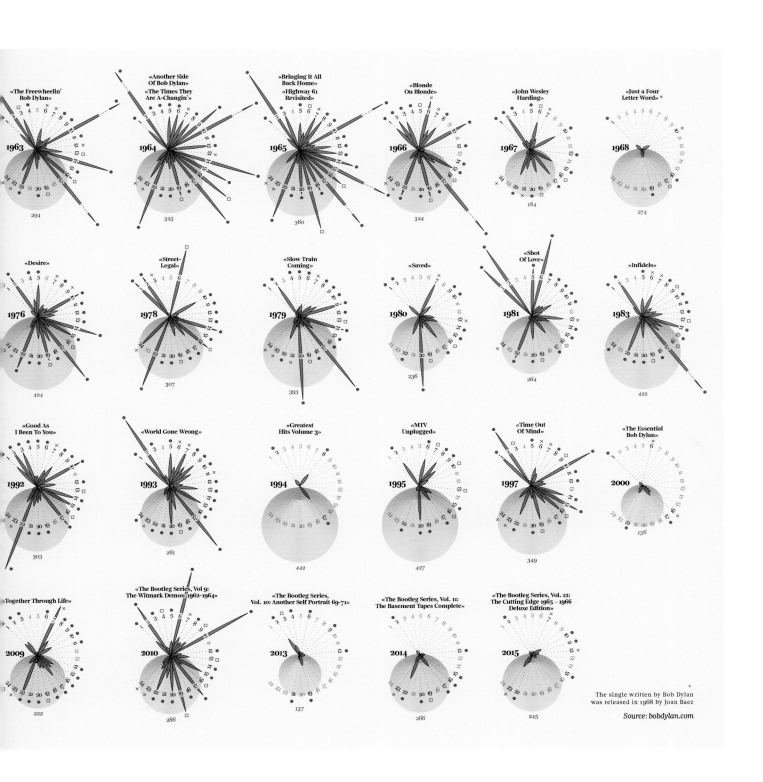

«The Freewheelin' Bob Dylan»
1963
294

«Another Side Of Bob Dylan»
«The Times They Are A-Changin'»
1964
325

«Bringing It All Back Home»
«Highway 61 Revisited»
1965
360

«Blonde On Blonde»
1966
324

«John Wesley Harding»
1967
184

«Just a Four Letter Word» *
1968
274

«Desire»
1976
424

«Street-Legal»
1978
307

«Slow Train Coming»
1979
393

«Saved»
1980
236

«Shot Of Love»
1981
264

«Infidels»
1983
422

«Good As I Been To You»
1992
303

«World Gone Wrong»
1993
261

«Greatest Hits Volume 3»
1994
442

«MTV Unplugged»
1995
427

«Time Out Of Mind»
1997
349

«The Essential Bob Dylan»
2000
136

«Together Through Life»
2009
222

«The Bootleg Series, Vol 9: The Witmark Demos: 1962-1964»
2010
286

«The Bootleg Series, Vol. 10: Another Self Portrait 69-71»
2013
137

«The Bootleg Series, Vol. 11: The Basement Tapes Complete»
2014
266

«The Bootleg Series, Vol. 12: The Cutting Edge 1965 – 1966 Deluxe Edition»
2015
245

*
The single written by Bob Dylan was released in 1968 by Joan Baez

*Source: bobdylan.com*

# Literary Meals

**Design: Federica Fragapane**
Art Direction: **Federica Fragapane**
Client: *Corriere della Sera*

The visualization shows the meals described in 49 novels. The descriptions and the novels have been selected by Dinah Fried, who has collected them in the book *Fictitious Dishes: An Album of Literature's Most Memorable Meals*. For each novel are indicated: author, title, year of publication, and meals mentioned in the description. For each meal are indicated: type of food, predominant compound (carbohydrates, fats, proteins, vitamins or others), and calories. For each novel is shown the total glycemic load.

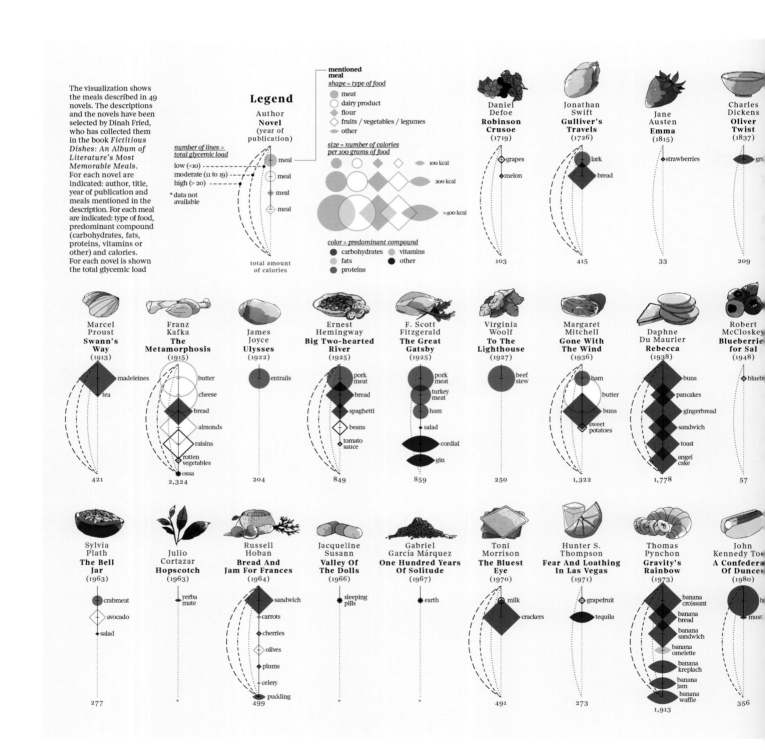

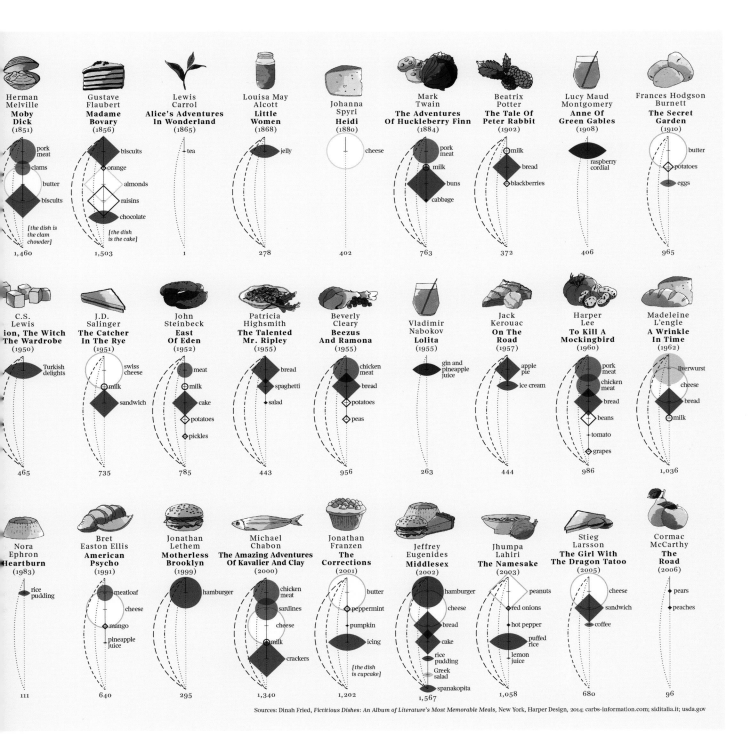

Herman Melville
**Moby Dick**
(1851)

pork meat
clams
butter
biscuits

*[the dish is the clam chowder]*

1,460

Gustave Flaubert
**Madame Bovary**
(1856)

biscuits
orange
almonds
raisins
chocolate

*[the dish is the cake]*

1,503

Lewis Carrol
**Alice's Adventures In Wonderland**
(1865)

tea

1

Louisa May Alcott
**Little Women**
(1868)

jelly

278

Johanna Spyri
**Heidi**
(1880)

cheese

402

Mark Twain
**The Adventures Of Huckleberry Finn**
(1884)

pork meat
milk
buns
cabbage

763

Beatrix Potter
**The Tale Of Peter Rabbit**
(1902)

milk
bread
blackberries

372

Lucy Maud Montgomery
**Anne Of Green Gables**
(1908)

raspberry cordial

406

Frances Hodgson Burnett
**The Secret Garden**
(1910)

butter
potatoes
eggs

965

C.S. Lewis
**ion, The Witch The Wardrobe**
(1950)

Turkish delights

465

J.D. Salinger
**The Catcher In The Rye**
(1951)

swiss cheese
milk
sandwich

735

John Steinbeck
**East Of Eden**
(1952)

meat
milk
cake
potatoes
pickles

785

Patricia Highsmith
**The Talented Mr. Ripley**
(1955)

bread
spaghetti
salad

443

Beverly Cleary
**Beezus And Ramona**
(1955)

chicken meat
bread
potatoes
peas

956

Vladimir Nabokov
**Lolita**
(1955)

gin and pineapple juice

263

Jack Kerouac
**On The Road**
(1957)

apple pie
ice cream

444

Harper Lee
**To Kill A Mockingbird**
(1960)

pork meat
chicken meat
bread
beans
tomato
grapes

986

Madeleine L'engle
**A Wrinkle In Time**
(1962)

liverwurst
cheese
bread
milk

1,036

Nora Ephron
**Heartburn**
(1983)

rice pudding

111

Bret Easton Ellis
**American Psycho**
(1991)

meatloaf
cheese
mango
pineapple juice

640

Jonathan Lethem
**Motherless Brooklyn**
(1999)

hamburger

295

Michael Chabon
**The Amazing Adventures Of Kavalier And Clay**
(2000)

chicken meat
sardines
cheese
milk
crackers

1,340

Jonathan Franzen
**The Corrections**
(2001)

butter
peppermint
pumpkin
icing

*[the dish is cupcake]*

1,202

Jeffrey Eugenides
**Middlesex**
(2002)

hamburger
cheese
bread
cake
rice pudding
Greek salad
spanakopita

1,567

Jhumpa Lahiri
**The Namesake**
(2003)

peanuts
red onions
hot pepper
puffed rice
lemon juice

1,058

Stieg Larsson
**The Girl With The Dragon Tatoo**
(2005)

cheese
sandwich
coffee

680

Cormac McCarthy
**The Road**
(2006)

pears
peaches

96

Sources: Dinah Fried, *Fictitious Dishes: An Album of Literature's Most Memorable Meals*, New York, Harper Design, 2014; carbs-information.com; siditalia.it; usda.gov

# Sonnet Signatures

Design: **Nicholas Rougeux**

Sonnet Signatures visualizes each of Shakespeare's 154 sonnets by charting the letters used within each one. This requires some extra thought when looking at the sonnets but it is of secondary importance. What is more interesting to consider is the hidden shapes revealed by looking at the centuries-old poetry through a different lens. This lens gives each sonnet its own identity like a person's signature. No two are the same—or even similar. Connections between the shape and the meaning of a sonnet is coincidental but a welcome interpretation. The signatures are not meant to assign meaning but to inspire others to think about them differently than before.

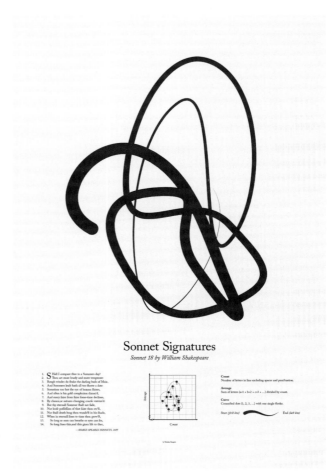

## Sonnet Signatures
*Sonnet 18 by William Shakespeare*

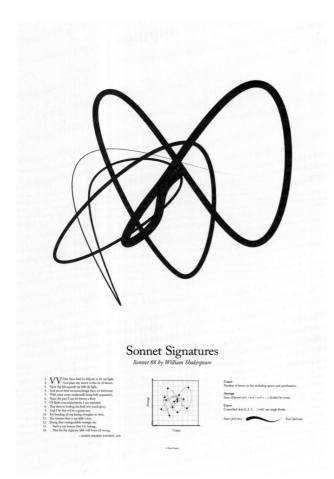

## Sonnet Signatures
*Sonnet 88 by William Shakespeare*

## Sonnet Signatures
*Sonnet 58 by William Shakespeare*

# Sonnet Signatures

*Sonnets by William Shakespeare*

1. S Hall I compare thee to a Summers day?
2. Thou art more louely and more temperate:
3. Rough windes do fhake the darling buds of Maie,
4. And Sommers leafe hath all too fhorte a date:
5. Sometime too hot the eye of heauen fhines,
6. And often is his gold complexion dimm'd,
7. And euery faire from faire fome-time declines,
8. By chance,or natures changing courfe vntrim'd:
9. But thy eternall Sommer fhall not fade,
10. Nor loofe poffeffion of that faire thou ow'ft,
11. Nor fhall death brag thou wandr'ft in his fhade,
12. When in eternall lines to time thou grow'ft,
13. So long as men can breathe or eyes can fee,
14. So long liues this,and this giues life to thee,

—*Sonnet 18, SHAKE-SPEARES SONNETS, 1609*

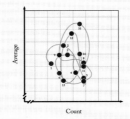

**Count**
Number of letters in line excluding spaces and punctuation.

**Average**
Sum of letters (a=1 + b=2 + c=3 + ...) divided by count.

**Curve**
Connected dots (1, 2, 3, ...) with one single stroke.

Start *(firſt line)* ⟶ End *(laſt line)*

by Nicholas Rougeux

# The Art in π

. . . . . . . . . . . . . . . . . . . . .

Design: **Nadieh Bremer**

Each digit of the number "π" is converted into a step direction, with 360 degrees split into 10 different directions (for 0,...,9). The viewers then follow the path that the digits of "π" make. By comparing 1000 to 10,000 to 100,000 digit paths, it becomes apparent that the number "π" is quite random; the viewer can never predict how the next path will "walk" based on what came before.

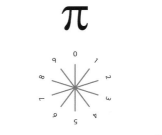

start                              end

1000
digits of π

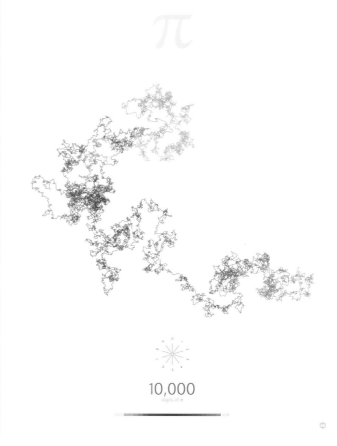

10,000
digits of π

start                    end

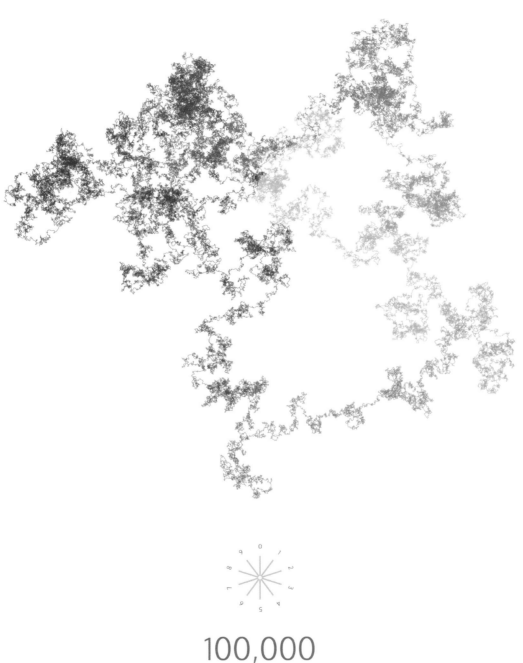

100,000
digits of π

start ▬▬▬▬▬▬▬▬▬▬▬▬▬▬▬ end

# Olympic Feathers

...................................................

Design: **Nadieh Bremer**

This visualization shows all the 5000 gold medal winners of the Summer Olympics since the very first games in 1896 down to the 2016's event. Each circle represents a group of similar sports and each slice/feather within is a type of sport. The years radiate outward. The reddish backgrounds are female events and the blue backgrounds the male events. Finally, each medal is colored according to the continent that won the game. Users can hover the medals to see the winning athlete or the team to find their own interesting stories. Nadieh did the data preparation using Microsoft Excel and R, sketched ideas on paper, and built the visualization with D3.js. The whole project can be viewed on the web.

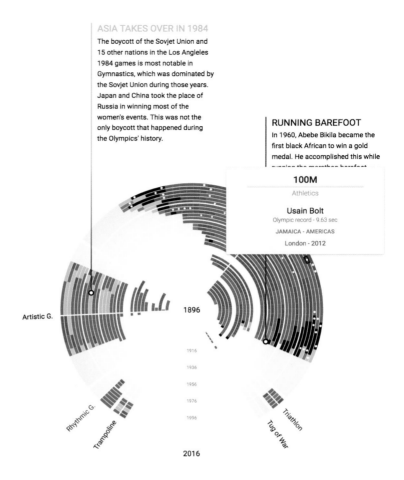

### RUNNING BAREFOOT

In 1960, Abebe Bikila became the first black African to win a gold medal. He accomplished this while

**100M**

Athletics

**Usain Bolt**

Olympic record - 9.63 sec

JAMAICA - AMERICAS

London - 2012

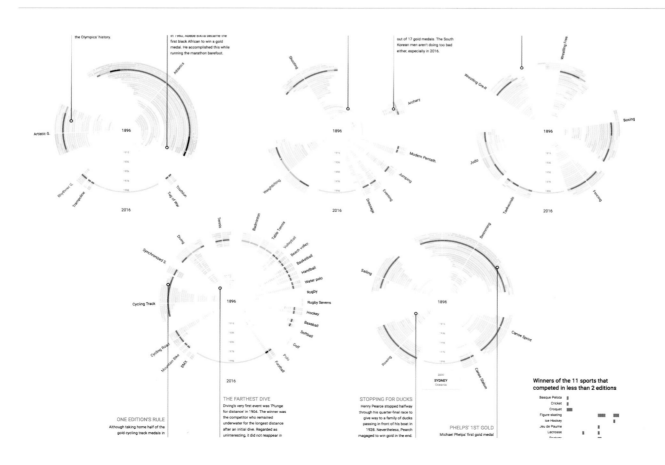

ONE EDITION'S RULE

Although taking home half of the gold cycling track medals in

THE FARTHEST DIVE

Diving's very first event was 'Plunge for distance' in 1904. The winner was the competitor who remained underwater for the longest distance after an initial dive. Regarded as uninteresting, it did not reappear in

STOPPING FOR DUCKS

Henry Pearce stopped halfway through his quarter-final race to give way to a family of ducks passing in front of his boat in 1928. Nevertheless, Pearch magaged to win gold in the end.

PHELPS' 1ST GOLD

Michael Phelps' first gold medal

Winners of the 11 sports that competed in less than 2 editions

# ALL OLYMPIC GOLD MEDAL WINNERS
## summer editions since 1896

More than 5000 Olympic events have had a winner, rewarded with a gold medal from 1904 onwards, in the Summer Olympics since the first games of 1896. Investigate the visuals below to see how each of these medals has been won in the 56 different sporting disciplines that have competed at the games, of which 41 are still held at Rio 2016.

Most of the Olympic sports started out being a men only event. Thankfully this started to change during the 2nd half of the last century. Even the number of medals that can be won for one discipline is slowly becoming the same for both genders. Today at Rio there are 3 disciplines left in which only one gender can compete; the Greco-Roman wrestling, already at the games since the very first edition, is done solely by men. Rhythmic gymnastics & synchronized swimming on the other hand, both at the Olympics since 1984, are only performed by women.

Although Rio could have been celebrating the 31st Olympic Games, 3 editions have been canceled, due to WW I in 1916 and WW II in 1940 & 1944. And yes, Tug of war has truly been part of 5 Olympic Games, from 1900 to 1920. Hover over the medals to see the winning athlete or team or hover over the time-line in the bottom of each circle to find your own interesting stories.

*Instead of a medal being represented by a specific width, in these visuals 1 medal always has the same arc length. This makes sure that the more recent the edition of the games, the more emphasis it gets due to the increasing size of the ring.*

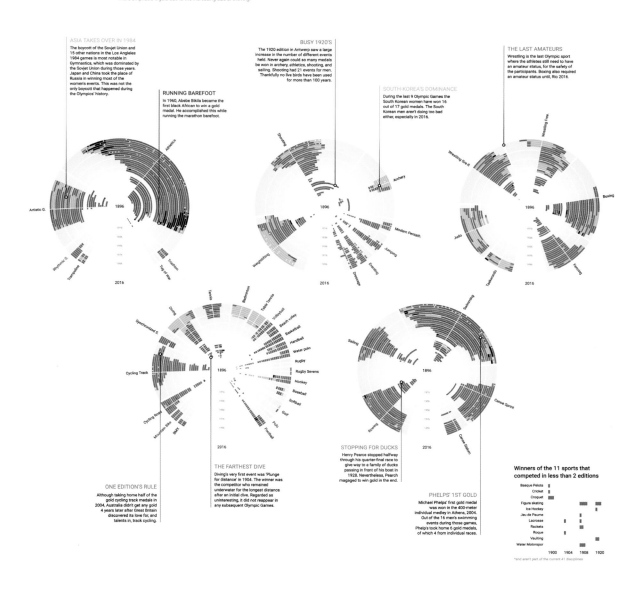

### ASIA TAKES OVER IN 1984
The boycott of the Sovjet Union and 15 other nations in the Los Angeles 1984 games is most notable in Gymnastics, which was dominated by the Sovjet Union during those years. Japan and China took the place of Russia in winning most of the women's events. This was not the only boycott that happened during the Olympics' history.

### RUNNING BAREFOOT
In 1960, Abebe Bikila became the first black African to win a gold medal. He accomplished this while running the marathon barefoot.

### BUSY 1920'S
The 1920 edition in Antwerp saw a large increase in the number of different events held. Never again could so many medals be won in archery, athletics, shooting, and sailing. Shooting had 21 events for men. Thankfully no live birds have been used for more than 100 years.

### SOUTH-KOREA'S DOMINANCE
During the last 9 Olympic Games the South Korean women have won 16 out of 17 gold medals. The South Korean men aren't doing too bad either, especially in 2016.

### THE LAST AMATEURS
Wrestling is the last Olympic sport where the athletes still need to have an amateur status, for the safety of the participants. Boxing also required an amateur status until, Rio 2016.

### ONE EDITION'S RULE
Although taking home half of the gold cycling track medals in 2004, Australia didn't get any gold 4 years later after Great Britain discovered its love for, and talents in, track cycling.

### THE FARTHEST DIVE
Diving's very first event was 'Plunge for distance' in 1904. The winner was the competitor who remained underwater for the longest distance after an initial dive. Regarded as uninteresting, it did not reappear in any subsequent Olympic Games.

### STOPPING FOR DUCKS
Henry Pearce stopped halfway through his quarter-final race to give way to a family of ducks passing in front of his boat in 1928. Nevertheless, Pearch managed to win gold in the end.

### PHELPS' 1ST GOLD
Michael Phelps' first gold medal was won in the 400-meter individual medley in Athens, 2004. Out of the 16 men's swimming events during those games, Phelp's took home 6 gold medals, of which 4 from individual races.

### Winners of the 11 sports that competed in less than 2 editions

Basque Pelota
Cricket
Croquet
Figure skating
Ice Hockey
Jeu de Paume
Lacrosse
Rackets
Roque
Vaulting
Water Motorspor

1900   1904   1908   1920

*end aren't part of the current 41 disciplines

## HOW TO READ A FEATHER

Each circle represents a grouping of several different (but approximately) similar themed sports, such as water or ball sports. Within a circle we find slices. Let's call each slice a feather to make it easier to distinguish as a whole. Each feather represents one discipline.

A feather is split up into 31 sections, radiating outward. Starting from the first Olympic Games in 1896 at the center to the current Olympic Games in Rio in 2016 at the other end. Each discipline is twice as wide as the maximum number of medals that could ever be won during one edition for a gender (men and women get the same width).

The next split is by gender. For the example feather to the right, the small bars going upward on the light red background are gold medals won by women. The bars going towards the bottom, with the light blue background are gold medals won by men.

All the medals have the same arc length and you can see in the bottom (men) section of the example feather to the right how wide 1 medal is for each edition of the Olympics. For medals won by a men & woman team or two gold medals in the same event each person gets 0.5 medal assigned. The medal bars are colored according to the continent in which the country of the winning athlete or team lies. Furthermore, for each edition and gender, the bars are stacked from the continent that won the most medals to the least.

Finally, some sport disciplines have Olympic records, such as athletics and swimming. As an extra level of detail, the events in which the gold medalist reached a currently standing Olympic record (after Rio 2016) are marked with a white dot. You can see the record when you hover over the medal.

### A FEATHER = ONE DISCIPLINE

Olympic / World record
Women
Discipline
Men
1896    2016

Europe    Africa    Americas
Asia    Oceania

Design concept with pen & (digital) paper, data wrangling in R, & coding with d3.v4.js by Nadieh Bremer  |  VisualCinnamon.com
With valuable design advice from Jeroen de Lange  |  Read all about the raw data, data preparation and preprocessing for the visualization here

# The Rhythm of Food

........................................

Creative Direction, Data Visualization & Design:
**Moritz Stefaner**
Collaboration: **Google News Lab, Simon Rogers, Alberto Cairo**
Design and Development: **Yuri Vishnevsky**
Illustration: **Stefanie Weigele**
Content: **Destry Sibley**
Development Support: **Dominikus Baur**

What can we learn about food culture by looking at Google search data? When do people search for smoothies, soup, or fruit salad? Which foods are trending, and which ones have seen their best days?

To find out, Google News Lab partnered with Truth & Beauty, Moritz Stefaner's consultancy, to focus on the cutting-edge data visualizations. Together, they launched the Rhythm of Food, a visualization project that sheds light on the many facets of food seasonality, based on twelve years of Google search data.

In the course of this project, they analyzed hundreds of ingredients, recipes, and other food-related search terms. A good starting point was FooDB. All Google search data are sourced from Google Trends. The web application was built using ES2015, Webpack, React, Material UI, and D3 (version 4).

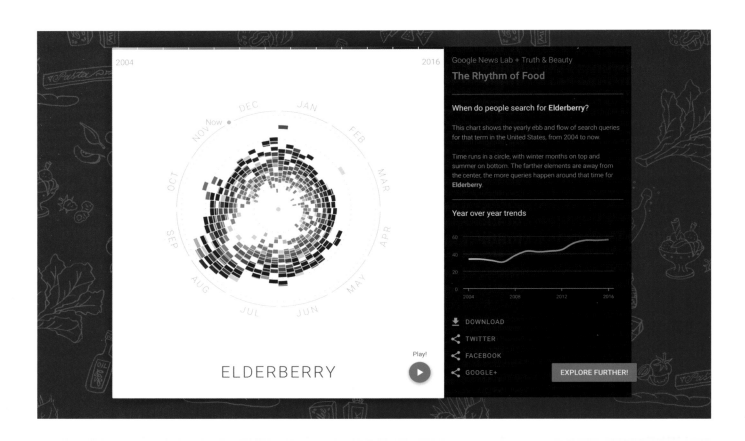

How do we search for food? Google search interest can reveal key food trends over the years.

From the rise and fall of recipes over diets and drinks to cooking trends and regional cuisines.

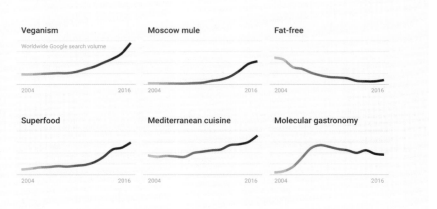

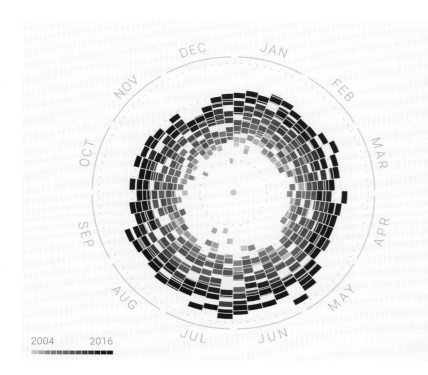

2004      2016

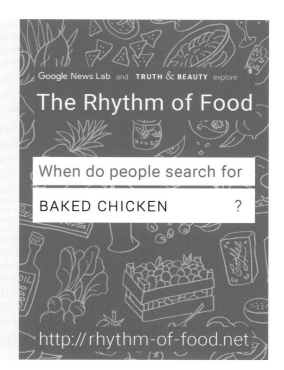

Google News Lab and **TRUTH & BEAUTY** explore

# The Rhythm of Food

When do people search for

BAKED CHICKEN          ?

http://rhythm-of-food.net

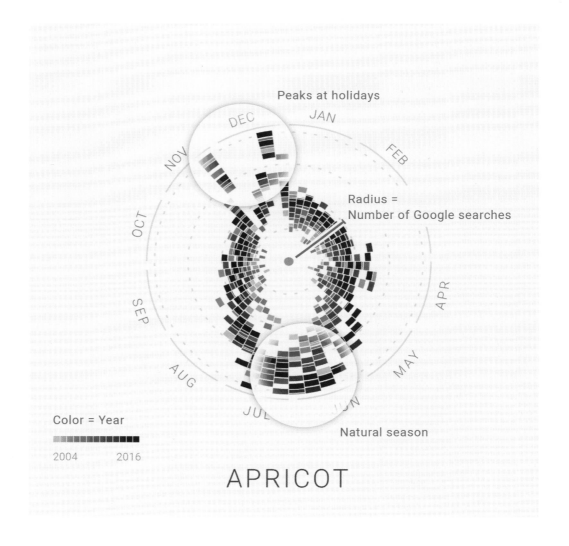

Peaks at holidays

Radius =
Number of Google searches

Color = Year

2004      2016

Natural season

APRICOT

GOOSEBERRY

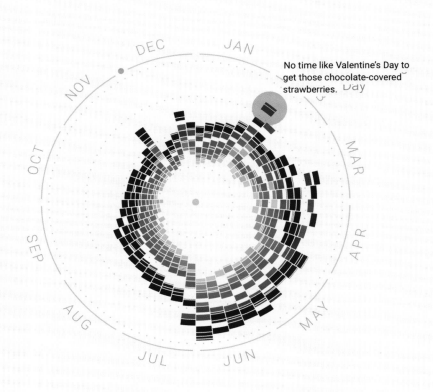

No time like Valentine's Day to get those chocolate-covered strawberries.

STRAWBERRY

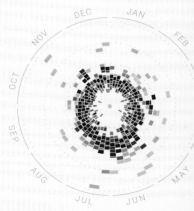

BOYSENBERRY

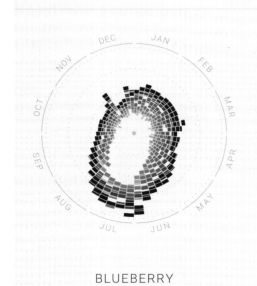

BLUEBERRY

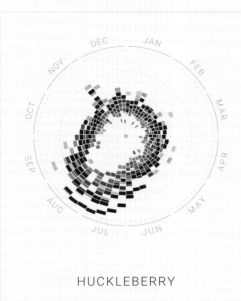

HUCKLEBERRY

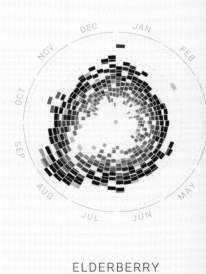

ELDERBERRY

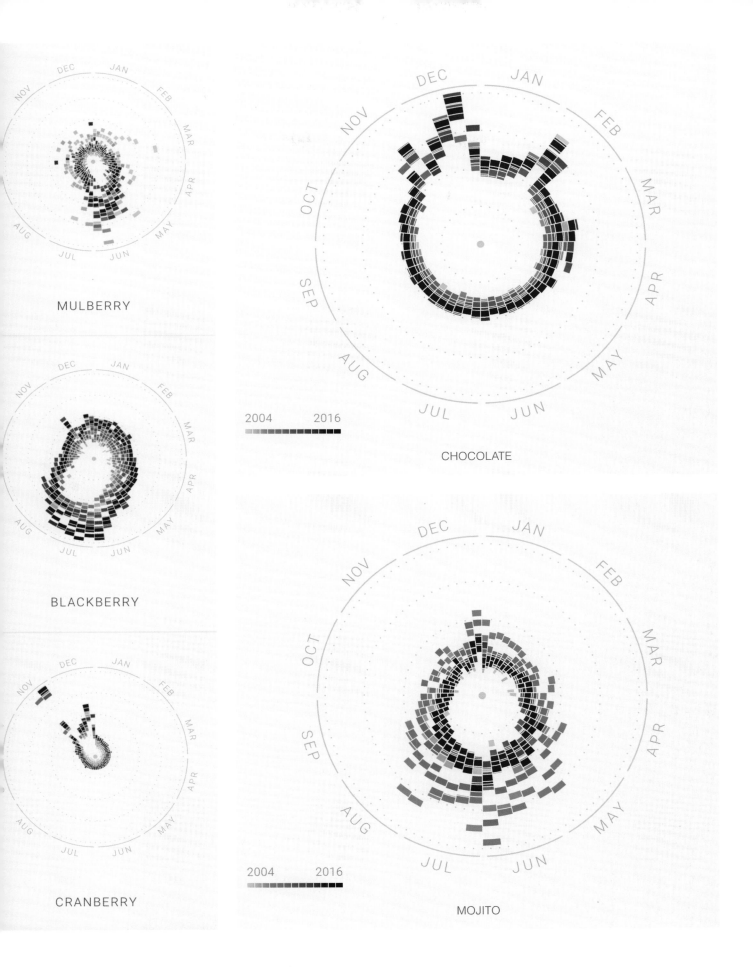

MULBERRY

BLACKBERRY

CRANBERRY

2004     2016

CHOCOLATE

2004     2016

MOJITO

# Red Bull:
# The Sixth Sense

..............................

Agency: **CLEVER°FRANKE**
Client: **Red Bull**

At Red Bull Playrooms, one of the most popular events during Amsterdam Dance Event (ADE), music, art, and technology come together to stimulate all senses. For the 2016 edition of ADE, Red Bull and fashion label BYBORRE invited CLEVER°FRANKE to create a unique live data visualization for this exclusive event.

By combining hardware with data-analysis, they developed "The Sixth Sense," a platform that created personalized and real-time data visualizations. This platform responded to the actions, movements, and temperature of each individual visitor. All guests wore a personal bracelet designed by BYBORRE, equipped with technology from the Dutch Center for Mathematics (Centrum Wiskunde & Informatica; CWI). Through these hybrid bracelets, the designers collected activity, movement, and temperature data.

Afterwards, all guests received their "Flight of the Night"—a unique, personalized souvenir, summarizing their data visualization of the night. Each personal visualization consisted of a colored spiral: the colors indicated how much time the guest had spent in every room; the thickness of the line indicated the activity of the guest in every room. The more movement, the thicker the line.

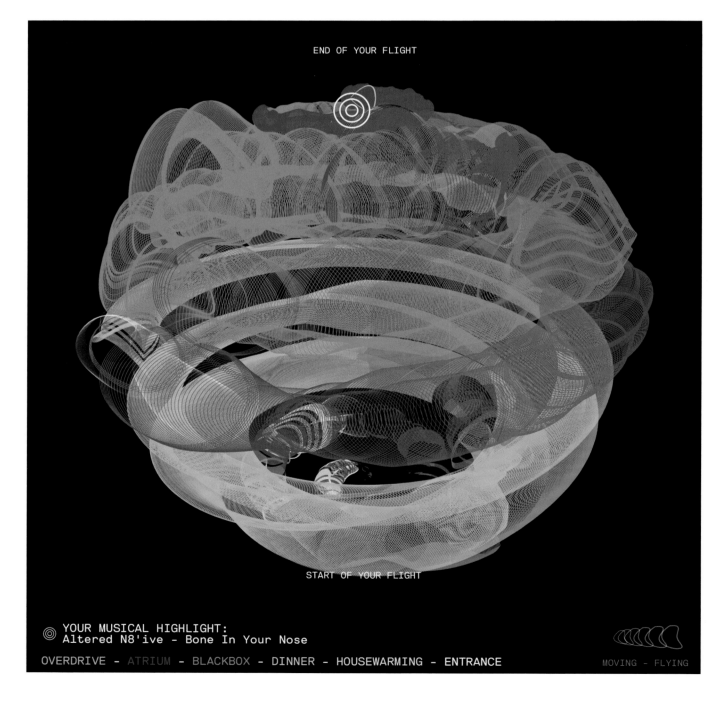

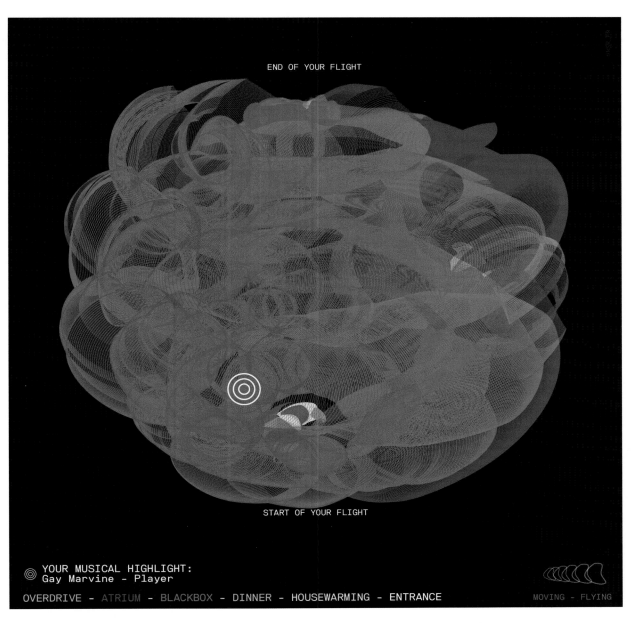

END OF YOUR FLIGHT

START OF YOUR FLIGHT

◎ YOUR MUSICAL HIGHLIGHT:
Gay Marvine - Player

OVERDRIVE - ATRIUM - BLACKBOX - DINNER - HOUSEWARMING - ENTRANCE          MOVING - FLYING

NOW SHOWING:
ATRIUM

TEMPERATURE 23.49C          PEOPLE 133          ENERGY CHILLING

LIVE DATA FEED: 20:25

BASSIE

TEMP 41.4          ENERGY MOVIN'          TIME HERE 0

# Europe Is Gay-friendly

..............................................

Design: **Massimiliano Mauro**
Art Direction: **Corrado Garcia**
Journalist: **Marco Boscolo**
Client: *Wired*

This visualization is to show the tolerance to homosexuality in each country. The data is separated into two sections. For the first section, the data set is visualized as a rainbow where each country occupies a ray. From left to right the countries are arranged according to a gay-friendly index that represents the country itself. At first glace, it is possible to understand what gay-right is missing, partially recognized or forbidden.

For the second section, LGBT unions measure with a survey what Italian people think about marriage, adoption, and attitude according to the gender. The interviewed can answer with four grade of agreement: complete disagreement, slightly disagreement, slightly agreement, and complete agreement.

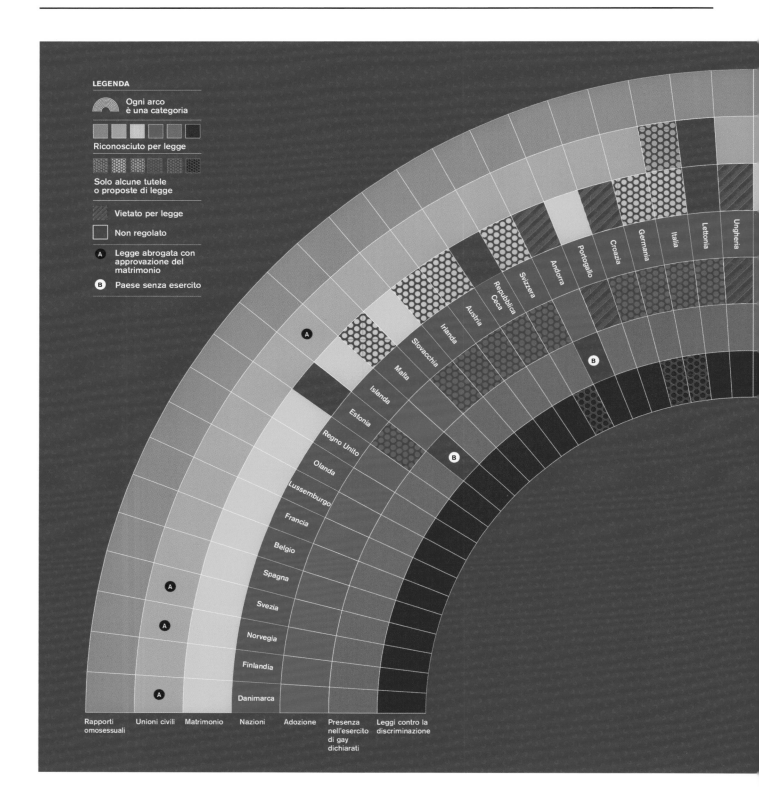

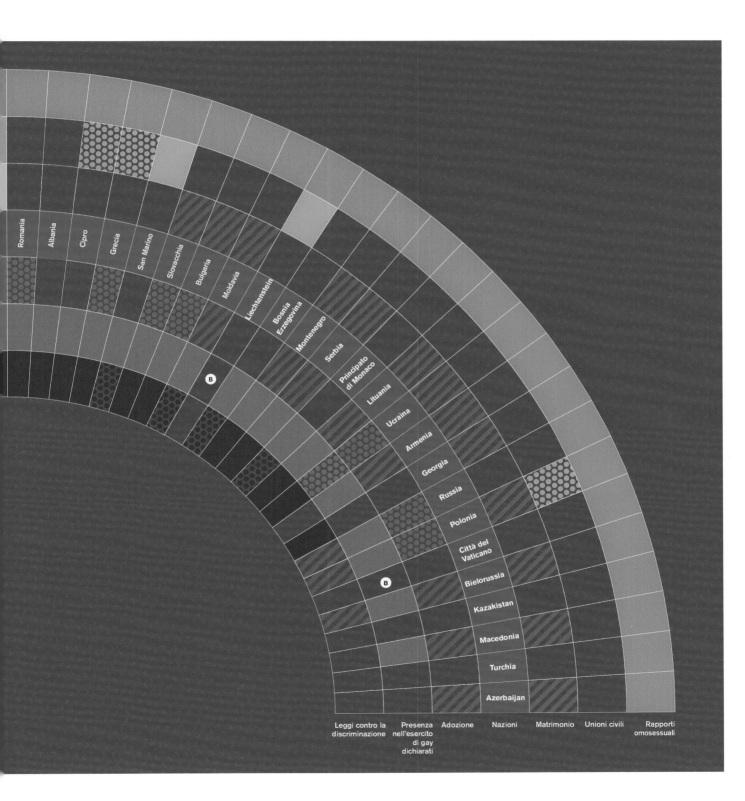

Romania
Albania
Cipro
Grecia
San Marino
Slovacchia
Bulgaria
Moldavia
Liechtenstein
Bosnia Erzegovina
Montenegro
Serbia
Principato di Monaco
Lituania
Ucraina
Armenia
Georgia
Russia
Polonia
Città del Vaticano
Bielorussia
Kazakistan
Macedonia
Turchia
Azerbaijan

Leggi contro la discriminazione
Presenza nell'esercito di gay dichiarati
Adozione
Nazioni
Matrimonio
Unioni civili
Rapporti omosessuali

**La cronistoria**
**I diritti conquistati in Europa passo dopo passo.**

**Unione Europea**
8 febbraio 1994
Risoluzione per la parità dei diritti degli omosessuali e delle lesbiche.

**Olanda**
1 gennaio 1998
Il Parlamento vota a favore di alcuni diritti paritari fra cui le unioni civili.

**Francia**
15 novembre 1999
Approvazione dei Pacs, i Patti civili di solidarietà anche per le coppie gay.

**Germania**
16 febbraio 2001
Legge sulle convivenze registrate, riservate agli omosessuali.

**Portogallo**
11 maggio 2001
Due leggi sulle unioni di fatto per coppie legate da più di due anni.

**Svizzera 22**
settembre 2002
Il cantone di Zurigo apre alle unioni domestiche registrate.

**Belgio**
30 gennaio 2003
Le coppie dello stesso sesso si possono sposare.

**Svezia**
30 gennaio 2003
Il Parlamento svedese vota la legge sulle sambolag (convivenze).

**Lussemburgo**
12 maggio 2004
Sono approvate le partnership registrate per coppie etero e gay.

# E se il tuo vicino di casa fosse gay?

L'adozione per le coppie omosessuali è ancora un tabù per quasi l'80% della popolazione italiana, ma sul matrimonio gay siamo molto più avanti dei nostri politici: una persona su due lo trova accettabile. È quello che emerge dall'indagine Istat dedicata alla percezione dell'omosessualità nel nostro paese. Dai baci in pubblico al coming out, ecco gli altri dati.

LEGENDA
NON D'ACCORDO  POCO D'ACCORDO  ABBASTANZA D'ACCORDO  MOLTO D'ACCORDO

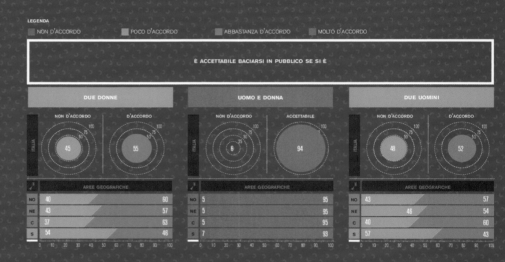

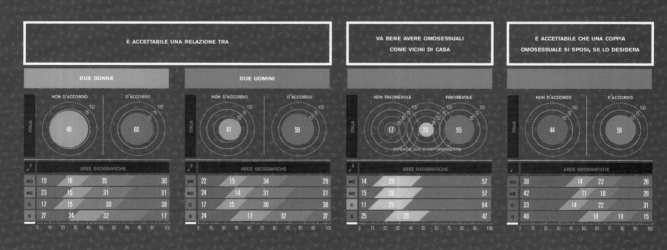

| Regno Unito 18 novembre 2004 | Spagna 30 giugno 2005 | Rep. Ceca 15 marzo 2006 | Svezia - Norvegia maggio - giugno 2009 | Portogallo 17 maggio 2010 | Islanda 27 giugno 2010 | Irlanda 19 luglio 2010 | Danimarca 15 giugno 2012 | Regno Unito 12 marzo 2014 | Lussemburgo 1 gennaio 2015 |
|---|---|---|---|---|---|---|---|---|---|
| Grazie al Civil Partnership Act le coppie gay possono unirsi legalmente. | Il matrimonio civile è esteso anche alle coppie dello stesso sesso. | Passa la legge Registrované Partnership sulle unioni registrate. | Il matrimonio viene esteso alle coppie omosessuali. | Il Parlamento apre al matrimonio omosessuale, senza adozioni. | Passa il matrimonio, abrogata la legge del 2006 sulle unioni. | Il Civil Partnership Bill riconosce le coppie omosessuali. | Abrogata la legge sulle unioni registrate del 1989. Sì al matrimonio. | Matrimonio tra persone dello stesso sesso (tranne l'Irlanda del Nord). | Entra in vigore il matrimonio per le coppie dello stesso sesso. |

## È GIUSTO CHE UNA COPPIA ADOTTI UN BAMBINO

DUE DONNE

ITALIA — NON D'ACCORDO 77 / D'ACCORDO 23

AREE GEOGRAFICHE

| | NO | | | |
|---|---|---|---|---|
| NO | 54 | 20 | 14 | 12 |
| NE | 60 | 16 | 13 | 11 |
| C | 56 | 16 | 15 | 13 |
| S | 65 | 16 | 11 | 8 |

DUE UOMINI

ITALIA — NON D'ACCORDO 81 / D'ACCORDO 19

AREE GEOGRAFICHE

| | | | | |
|---|---|---|---|---|
| NO | 59 | 20 | 11 | 10 |
| NE | 64 | 16 | 10 | 10 |
| C | 60 | 16 | 13 | 11 |
| S | 70 | 15 | 9 | 6 |

## SE GLI OMOSESSUALI FOSSERO PIÙ DISCRETI SAREBBERO ACCETTATI PIÙ FACILMENTE

ITALIA — NON D'ACCORDO 44 / D'ACCORDO 56

AREE GEOGRAFICHE

| | | | | |
|---|---|---|---|---|
| NO | 27 | 18 | 34 | 21 |
| NE | 27 | 16 | 30 | 27 |
| C | 26 | 20 | 32 | 22 |
| S | 21 | 22 | 34 | 23 |

## LA COSA MIGLIORE PER UN OMOSESSUALE È NON DIRE AGLI ALTRI DI ESSERLO

ITALIA — NON D'ACCORDO 70 / D'ACCORDO 30

AREE GEOGRAFICHE

| | | | | |
|---|---|---|---|---|
| NO | 48 | 23 | 19 | 10 |
| NE | 45 | 22 | 20 | 13 |
| C | 51 | 24 | 16 | 9 |
| S | 42 | 27 | 21 | 10 |

## È GIUSTO CHE UNA COPPIA DI OMOSESSUALI CHE CONVIVE POSSA AVERE PER LEGGE GLI STESSI DIRITTI DI UNA COPPIA SPOSATA

ITALIA — NON D'ACCORDO 37 / D'ACCORDO 63

AREE GEOGRAFICHE

| | | | | |
|---|---|---|---|---|
| NO | 21 | 11 | 26 | 42 |
| NE | 25 | 9 | 21 | 45 |
| C | 19 | 9 | 26 | 46 |
| S | 31 | 18 | 25 | 26 |

## L'OMOSESSUALITÀ È UNA MINACCIA PER LA FAMIGLIA

ITALIA — NON D'ACCORDO 75 / D'ACCORDO 25

AREE GEOGRAFICHE

| | | | | |
|---|---|---|---|---|
| NO | 55 | 22 | 14 | 9 |
| NE | 55 | 19 | 15 | 11 |
| C | 60 | 20 | 12 | 8 |
| S | 43 | 27 | 20 | 10 |

## IN GENERALE, LE LESBICHE SONO DONNE MASCOLINE

ITALIA — NON D'ACCORDO 62 / D'ACCORDO 38

AREE GEOGRAFICHE

| | | | | |
|---|---|---|---|---|
| NO | 32 | 34 | 26 | 8 |
| NE | 33 | 30 | 25 | 12 |
| C | 35 | 31 | 25 | 9 |
| S | 22 | 34 | 30 | 14 |

## IN GENERALE, I GAY SONO UOMINI EFFEMINATI

ITALIA — NON D'ACCORDO 57 / D'ACCORDO 43

AREE GEOGRAFICHE

| | | | | |
|---|---|---|---|---|
| NO | 30 | 30 | 29 | 11 |
| NE | 32 | 26 | 28 | 14 |
| C | 34 | 28 | 27 | 11 |
| S | 21 | 30 | 33 | 16 |

# Ain't No Mountains High Enough

Design: **Valerio Pellegrini**
Client: *Corriere della Sera*

The artwork shows ascents of the Everest and K2 in the last 20 years

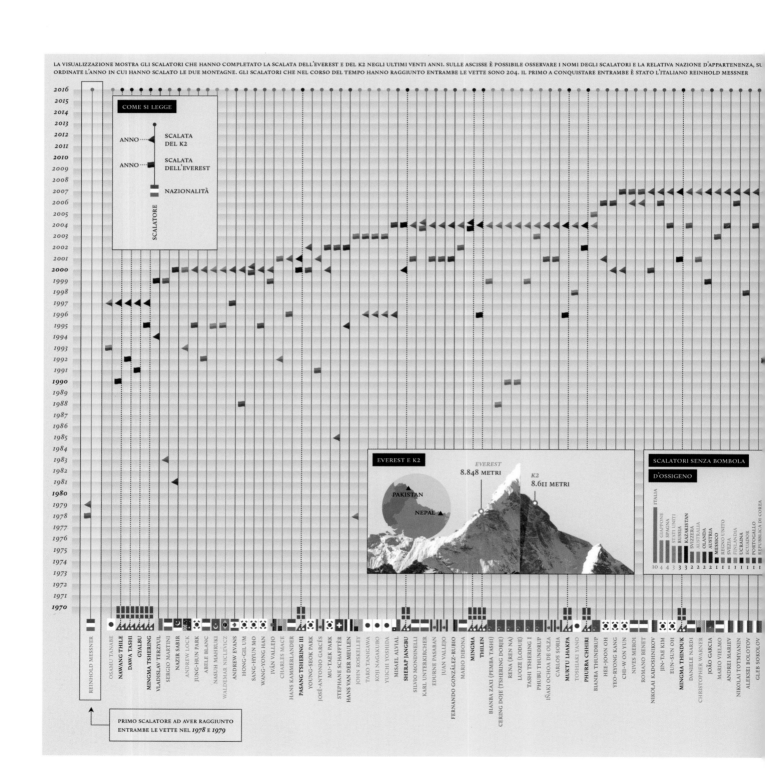

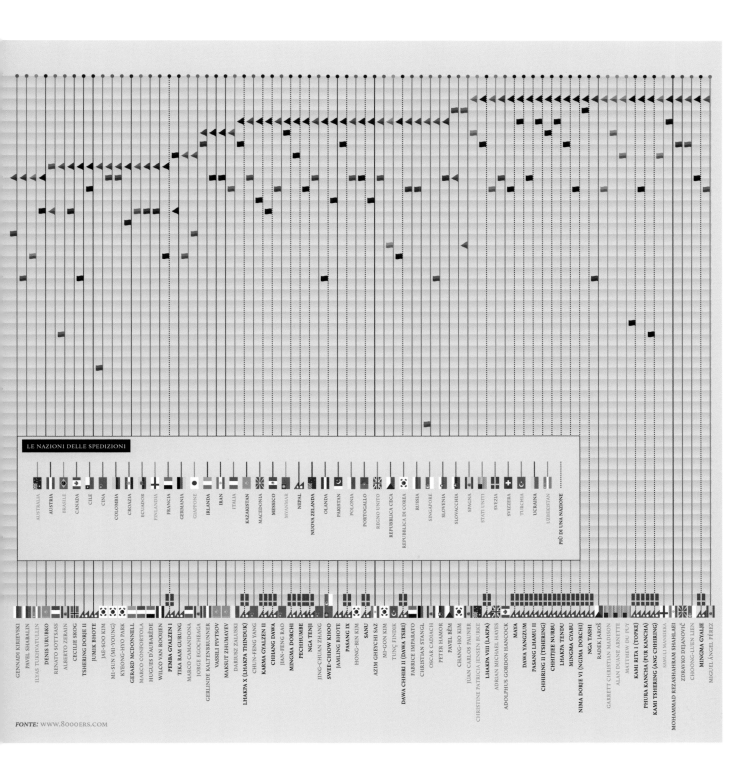

LE NAZIONI DELLE SPEDIZIONI

FONTE: WWW.8000ERS.COM

# PASTA!

..........................

Design: **Valerio Pellegrini**
Client: *Corriere della Sera*

The artwork is for *Corriere della Sera: La Lettura*, presenting the production and consumption of pasta in the world. The data is sourced from *The World Pasta Industry Status Report 2013* done by the International Pasta Organization.

# The Italian Job

Design: **Valerio Pellegrini**
Client: *Corriere della Sera*

The artwork shows data regarding foreign tourism in Italy in 2013 and 2014. In the middle, there is a comparison between the number of travelers in 2013 (yellow semi-circle) and that in 2014 ( blue semi-circle ), and the percentage of Italian and foreign tourists in 2014 for each Italian region. The outer circumference highlights the 15 main countries of origin and the respective number of tourists. In the bottom part, the tourists' spending in Italy from 2008 to 2015 is represented.

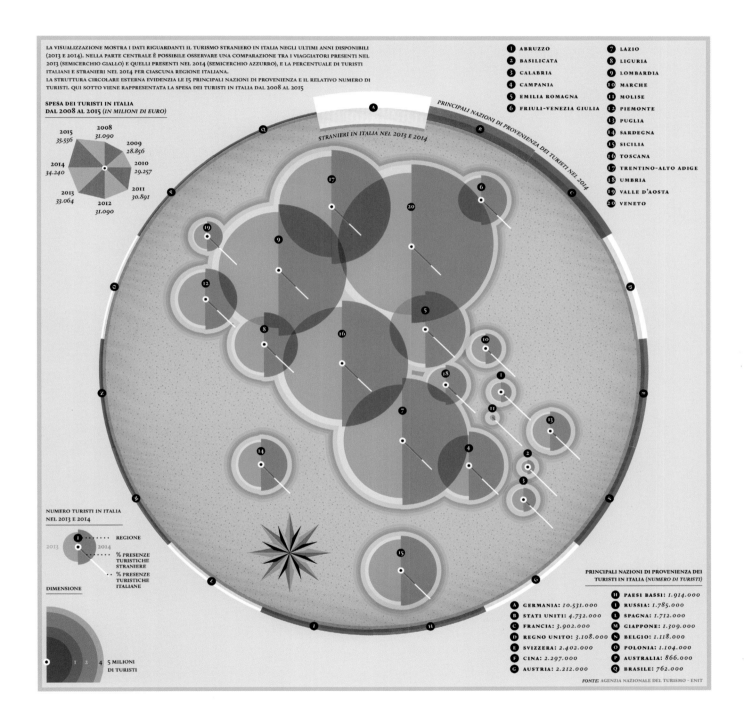

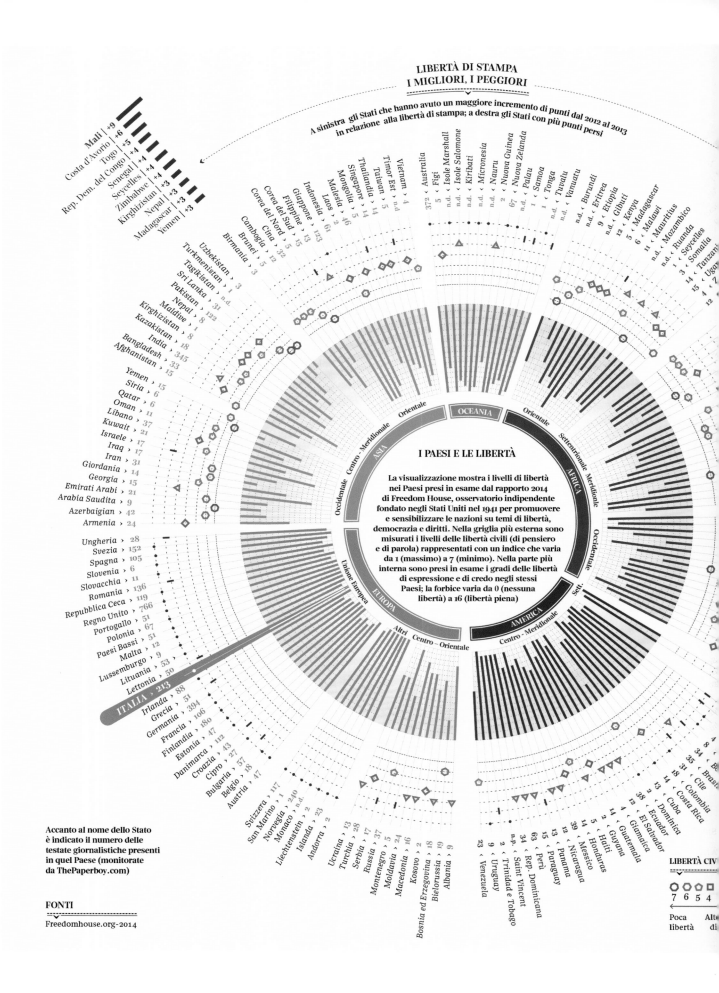

# LIBERTÀ DI STAMPA
## I MIGLIORI, I PEGGIORI

A sinistra gli Stati che hanno avuto un maggiore incremento di punti dal 2012 al 2013 in relazione alla libertà di stampa; a destra gli Stati con più punti persi

Mali | +9
Costa d'Avorio | +6
Togo | +5
Rep. Dem. del Congo | +5
Senegal | +4
Seychelles | +4
Zimbabwe | +4
Kirghizistan | +3
Nepal | +3
Madagascar | +3
Yemen | +3

## I PAESI E LE LIBERTÀ

La visualizzazione mostra i livelli di libertà nei Paesi presi in esame dal rapporto 2014 di Freedom House, osservatorio indipendente fondato negli Stati Uniti nel 1941 per promuovere e sensibilizzare le nazioni su temi di libertà, democrazia e diritti. Nella griglia più esterna sono misurati i livelli delle libertà civili (di pensiero e di parola) rappresentati con un indice che varia da 1 (massimo) a 7 (minimo). Nella parte più interna sono presi in esame i gradi delle libertà di espressione e di credo negli stessi Paesi; la forbice varia da 0 (nessuna libertà) a 16 (libertà piena)

Accanto al nome dello Stato è indicato il numero delle testate giornalistiche presenti in quel Paese (monitorate da ThePaperboy.com)

FONTI

Freedomhouse.org-2014

**LIBERTÀ CIV...**
7 6 5 4
Poca libertà  Alt... di...

-15 | Rep. Centrafricana
-6 | Egitto
-5 | Turchia
-5 | Grecia
-4 | Giordania
-4 | Kenya
-4 | Suriname
| Tanzania
| Stati Uniti
Montenegro
ozambico

# Freedom in Countries

............................................

Design: **Sara Piccolomini**
Client: *Corriere della Sera*

The visualization for *Corriere della Sera: La Lettura* explores the levels of freedom in countries according to *Freedom in the World*, Freedom House's flagship publication, which is the standard-setting comparative assessment of global political rights and civil liberties. Each country is assigned a numerical rating—from 1 to 7—for civil liberties, with "1" representing the freest and "7" the least free. The degrees of freedom in expression and belief (the gap varies from "0"—no freedom to "16"—complete freedom) are visualized with a circular histogram, and the number of newspapers for each country is reported near the name of the country.

udan
nisia
Angola
Botswana
Camerun
‹ Ciad
‹ Congo
‹ Gabon
.d. ‹ Lesotho
12 ‹ Namibia
n.d. ‹ Rep. Centrafricana
11 ‹ Rep. Dem. del Congo
‹ São Tomé e Príncipe
81 ‹ Sudafrica
1 ‹ Swaziland

1 ‹ Benin
5 ‹ Burkina Faso
n.d. ‹ Capo Verde
n.d. ‹ Costa d'Avorio
3 ‹ Gambia
13 ‹ Ghana
9 ‹ Guinea
2 ‹ Guinea Equatoriale
n.d. ‹ Guinea-Bissau
n.d. ‹ Liberia
.d. ‹ Mali
.d. ‹ Mauritania
‹ Niger
‹ Nigeria
Senegal
ierra Leone
go

da
niti
arbuda

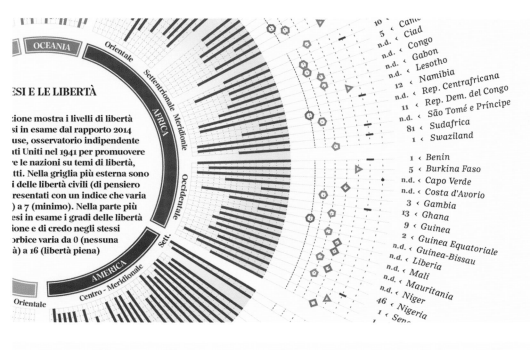

Within the illustration:

OCEANIA
Orientale
Settentrionale Meridionale
AFRICA
Occidentale
Sett.
AMERICA
Centro - Meridionale
Orientale

ESI E LE LIBERTÀ

ione mostra i livelli di libertà
si in esame dal rapporto 2014
use, osservatorio indipendente
ti Uniti nel 1941 per promuovere
e le nazioni su temi di libertà,
tti. Nella griglia più esterna sono
i delle libertà civili (di pensiero
resentati con un indice che varia
) a 7 (minimo). Nella parte più
esi in esame i gradi delle libertà
ione e di credo negli stessi
orbice varia da 0 (nessuna
à) a 16 (libertà piena)

10 ‹ Came
5 ‹ Ciad
n.d. ‹ Congo
n.d. ‹ Gabon
n.d. ‹ Lesotho
12 ‹ Namibia
n.d. ‹ Rep. Centrafricana
11 ‹ Rep. Dem. del Congo
n.d. ‹ São Tomé e Príncipe
81 ‹ Sudafrica
1 ‹ Swaziland

1 ‹ Benin
5 ‹ Burkina Faso
n.d. ‹ Capo Verde
n.d. ‹ Costa d'Avorio
3 ‹ Gambia
13 ‹ Ghana
9 ‹ Guinea
2 ‹ Guinea Equatoriale
n.d. ‹ Guinea-Bissau
n.d. ‹ Liberia
n.d. ‹ Mali
n.d. ‹ Mauritania
n.d. ‹ Niger
46 ‹ Nigeria
1 ‹ Sen

## COME SI LEGGE

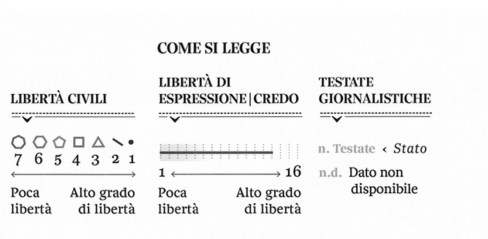

**LIBERTÀ CIVILI**

○ ○ ⬠ □ △ ＼ •
7 6 5 4 3 2 1

⟵⟶
Poca          Alto grado
libertà       di libertà

**LIBERTÀ DI ESPRESSIONE | CREDO**

1 ⟵⟶ 16
Poca          Alto grado
libertà       di libertà

**TESTATE GIORNALISTICHE**

n. Testate ‹ *Stato*

n.d. Dato non disponibile

SI LEGGE

À DI                TESTATE
SSIONE | CREDO      GIORNALISTICHE

                    n. Testate ‹ *Stato*
⟶ 16                n.d. Dato non
Alto grado              disponibile
di libertà

# Transfer

Design: **Matthew Benkert**
Art Direction: **Chris Hacker**

Over a four-day period, Matthew Benkert tracked and recorded three streams of data in a notebook. He collected data on how many times he switched devices (iPhone, iPad, MacBook), how long he used each device, and what programs or websites he used and for how long. Matthew used a sketchbook to track his data. Then he designed the layout and brought the data to life by using InDesign.

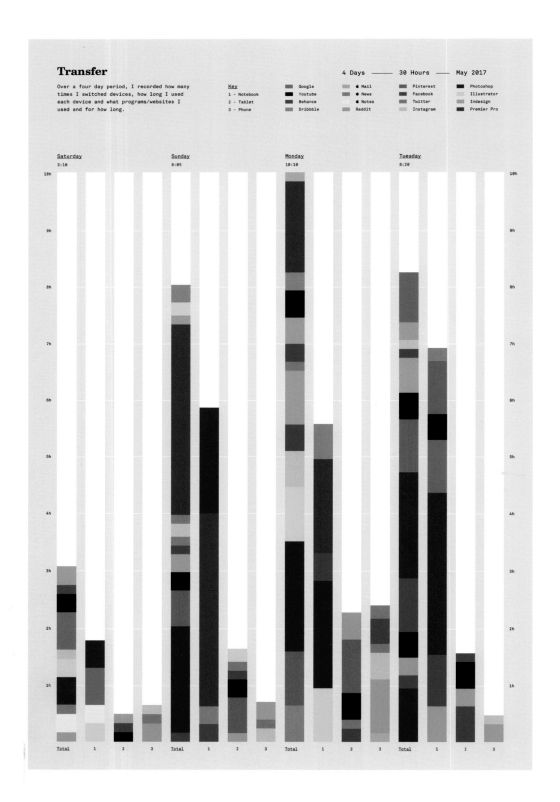

# World Ice Creams Consumption

..................................

Design: **Sara Piccolomini**
Client: *Corriere della Sera*

The visualization for *Corriere della Sera: La Lettura* shows the market value in euro for ice creams in the world. For each category of ice creams (single portion dairy ice cream, impulse ice cream, retail artisanal ice cream, ice-cream desserts, and multi-pack dairy ice cream), the 10 countries with the higher consumption of ice creams in 2015 have been reported. The data related to 2010 and data expected for 2020 have also been reported. The graphs at the bottom show the top 10 countries that consume more ice creams in 2015 and the data related to Italian consumption. Overall, according to the data provided by Euromonitor International, the consumption of ice creams in the world will increase until 2020.

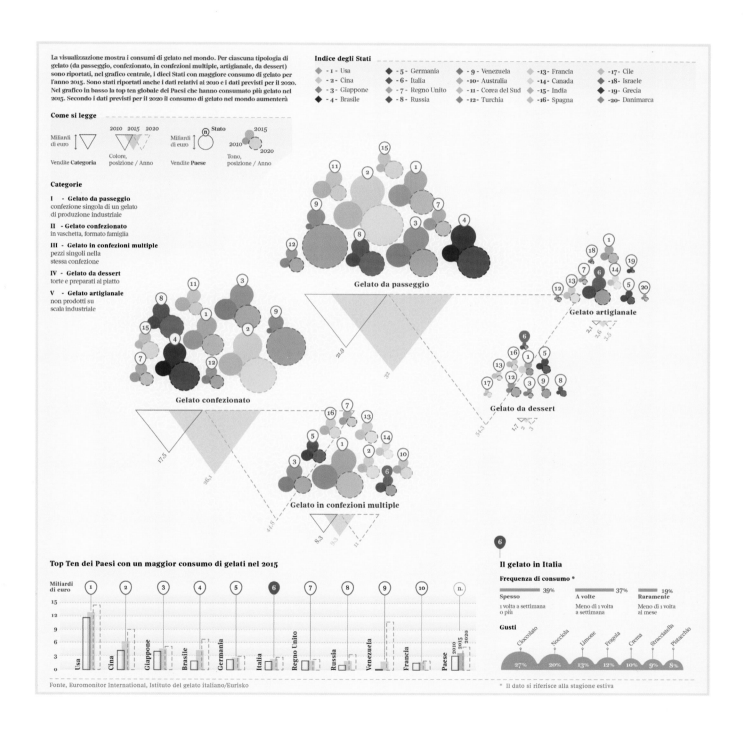

La visualizzazione mostra i consumi di gelato nel mondo. Per ciascuna tipologia di gelato (da passeggio, confezionato, in confezioni multiple, artigianale, da dessert) sono riportati, nel grafico centrale, i dieci Stati con maggiore consumo di gelato per l'anno 2015. Sono stati riportati anche i dati relativi al 2010 e i dati previsti per il 2020. Nel grafico in basso la top ten globale dei Paesi che hanno consumato più gelato nel 2015. Secondo i dati previsti per il 2020 il consumo di gelato nel mondo aumenterà

### Indice degli Stati

- 1 - Usa
- 2 - Cina
- 3 - Giappone
- 4 - Brasile
- 5 - Germania
- 6 - Italia
- 7 - Regno Unito
- 8 - Russia
- 9 - Venezuela
- 10- Australia
- 11 - Corea del Sud
- 12- Turchia
- 13- Francia
- 14- Canada
- 15- India
- 16- Spagna
- 17- Cile
- 18- Israele
- 19- Grecia
- 20- Danimarca

### Come si legge

Miliardi di euro — Vendite **Categoria**
2010 2015 2020 — Colore, posizione / Anno
Miliardi di euro — Vendite **Paese**
**n** Stato — Tono, posizione / Anno — 2015 2010 2020

### Categorie

**I - Gelato da passeggio**
confezione singola di un gelato di produzione industriale

**II - Gelato confezionato**
in vaschetta, formato famiglia

**III - Gelato in confezioni multiple**
pezzi singoli nella stessa confezione

**IV - Gelato da dessert**
torte e preparati al piatto

**V - Gelato artigianale**
non prodotti su scala industriale

Gelato da passeggio

Gelato artigianale

Gelato confezionato

Gelato da dessert

Gelato in confezioni multiple

### Top Ten dei Paesi con un maggior consumo di gelati nel 2015

Miliardi di euro
15
12
9
6
3
0

1 — Usa
2 — Cina
3 — Giappone
4 — Brasile
5 — Germania
6 — Italia
7 — Regno Unito
8 — Russia
9 — Venezuela
10 — Francia
n. — Paese (2010 2015 2020)

Fonte, Euromonitor International, Istituto del gelato italiano/Eurisko

### Il gelato in Italia

**Frequenza di consumo ***

| Spesso | A volte | Raramente |
|---|---|---|
| 39% | 37% | 19% |
| 1 volta a settimana o più | Meno di 1 volta a settimana | Meno di 1 volta al mese |

**Gusti**

| Cioccolato | Nocciola | Limone | Fragola | Crema | Stracciatella | Pistacchio |
|---|---|---|---|---|---|---|
| 27% | 20% | 13% | 12% | 10% | 9% | 8% |

* Il dato si riferisce alla stagione estiva

# Box Office Cinema

........................................

Design: **Sara Piccolomini**
Client: *Corriere della Sera*

The visualization for *Corriere della Sera: La Lettura* shows the box-office ranking for Italian movies of 2013, 2014, and 2015. On the left there is a global ranking for these three years in relation with the top 10 movies of each year; on the right there is a timeline showing the size of the audience who saw each movie according to the date of debut in theaters.

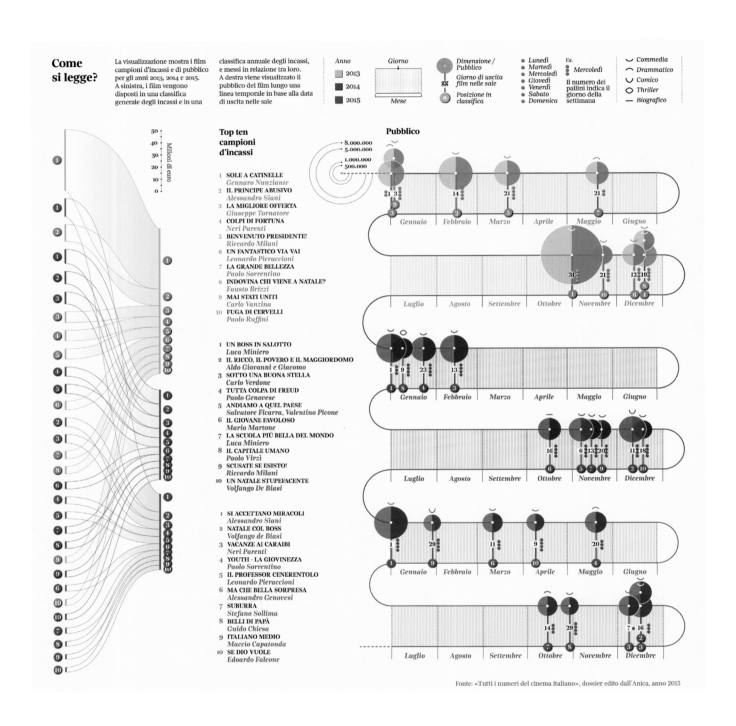

Fonte: «Tutti i numeri del cinema italiano», dossier edito dall'Anica, anno 2015

## Come si legge?

La visualizzazione mostra, nella parte in alto, i dieci film italiani con più pubblico disposti lungo una linea temporale; nel grafico centrale il pubblico totale relativo ai film italiani per ciascun mese dell'anno, in basso la top ten relativa agli incassi. L'analisi restituisce i dati relativi agli anni 2013, 2014 e 2015.

Anno: 2015 · 2014 · 2013

Dimensione / Pubblico

Giorno di uscita film nelle sale

Posizione in classifica

Lunedì · Martedì · Mercoledì · Giovedì · Venerdì · Sabato · Domenica

Es. → Mercoledì — Il numero delle palle indica il giorno della settimana

Commedia · Drammatico · Comico · Thriller · Biografico

### Top ten pubblico

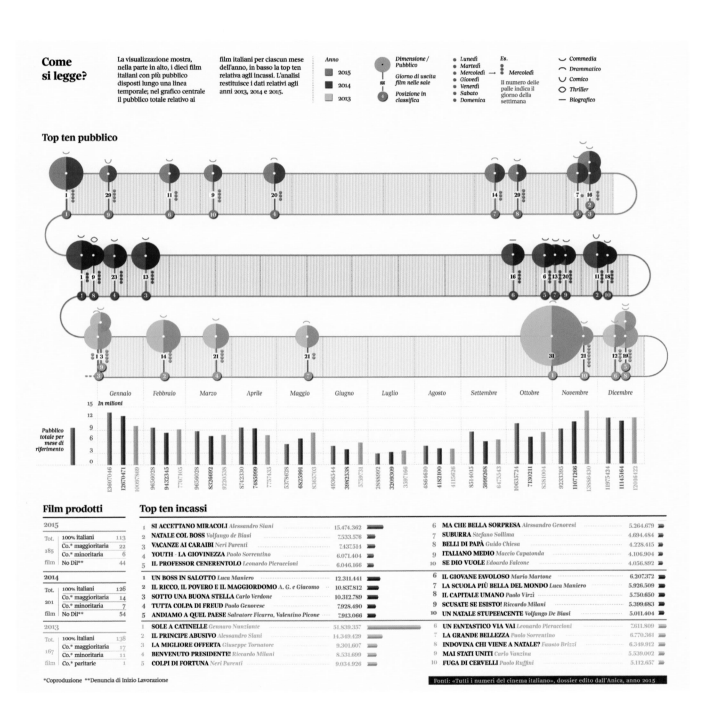

In milioni

Pubblico totale per mese di riferimento

Gennaio · Febbraio · Marzo · Aprile · Maggio · Giugno · Luglio · Agosto · Settembre · Ottobre · Novembre · Dicembre

### Film prodotti

**2015** — Tot. 185 film

| | |
|---|---|
| 100% italiani | 113 |
| Co.* maggioritaria | 22 |
| Co.* minoritaria | 6 |
| No Dil** | 44 |

**2014** — Tot. 201 film

| | |
|---|---|
| 100% italiani | 126 |
| Co.* maggioritaria | 14 |
| Co.* minoritaria | 7 |
| No Dil** | 54 |

**2013** — Tot. 167 film

| | |
|---|---|
| 100% italiani | 138 |
| Co.* maggioritaria | 17 |
| Co.* minoritaria | 11 |
| Co.* paritarie | 1 |

*Coproduzione  **Denuncia di Inizio Lavorazione

### Top ten incassi

**2015**

| | | |
|---|---|---|
| 1 | SI ACCETTANO MIRACOLI *Alessandro Siani* | 15.474.362 |
| 2 | NATALE COL BOSS *Volfango de Biasi* | 7.533.576 |
| 3 | VACANZE AI CARAIBI *Neri Parenti* | 7.437.514 |
| 4 | YOUTH - LA GIOVINEZZA *Paolo Sorrentino* | 6.071.404 |
| 5 | IL PROFESSOR CENERENTOLO *Leonardo Pieraccioni* | 6.046.166 |
| 6 | MA CHE BELLA SORPRESA *Alessandro Genovesi* | 5.264.679 |
| 7 | SUBURRA *Stefano Sollima* | 4.694.484 |
| 8 | BELLI DI PAPÀ *Guido Chiesa* | 4.228.415 |
| 9 | ITALIANO MEDIO *Maccio Capatonda* | 4.106.904 |
| 10 | SE DIO VUOLE *Edoardo Falcone* | 4.056.892 |

**2014**

| | | |
|---|---|---|
| 1 | UN BOSS IN SALOTTO *Luca Maniero* | 12.311.441 |
| 2 | IL RICCO, IL POVERO E IL MAGGIORDOMO *A. G. e Giacomo* | 10.837.812 |
| 3 | SOTTO UNA BUONA STELLA *Carlo Verdone* | 10.312.789 |
| 4 | TUTTA COLPA DI FREUD *Paolo Genovese* | 7.928.490 |
| 5 | ANDIAMO A QUEL PAESE *Salvatore Ficarra, Valentino Picone* | 7.913.066 |
| 6 | IL GIOVANE FAVOLOSO *Mario Martone* | 6.207.372 |
| 7 | LA SCUOLA PIÙ BELLA DEL MONDO *Luca Maniero* | 5.926.509 |
| 8 | IL CAPITALE UMANO *Paolo Virzì* | 5.750.650 |
| 9 | SCUSATE SE ESISTO! *Riccardo Milani* | 5.399.683 |
| 10 | UN NATALE STUPEFACENTE *Volfango De Biasi* | 5.011.404 |

**2013**

| | | |
|---|---|---|
| 1 | SOLE A CATINELLE *Gennaro Nunziante* | 51.839.357 |
| 2 | IL PRINCIPE ABUSIVO *Alessandro Siani* | 14.349.429 |
| 3 | LA MIGLIORE OFFERTA *Giuseppe Tornatore* | 9.301.607 |
| 4 | BENVENUTO PRESIDENTE! *Riccardo Milani* | 8.531.699 |
| 5 | COLPI DI FORTUNA *Neri Parenti* | 9.034.926 |
| 6 | UN FANTASTICO VIA VAI *Leonardo Pieraccioni* | 7.611.809 |
| 7 | LA GRANDE BELLEZZA *Paolo Sorrentino* | 6.770.361 |
| 8 | INDOVINA CHI VIENE A NATALE? *Fausto Brizzi* | 6.349.912 |
| 9 | MAI STATI UNITI *Carlo Vanzina* | 5.539.002 |
| 10 | FUGA DI CERVELLI *Paolo Ruffini* | 5.112.657 |

Fonti: «Tutti i numeri del cinema italiano», dossier edito dall'Anica, anno 2015

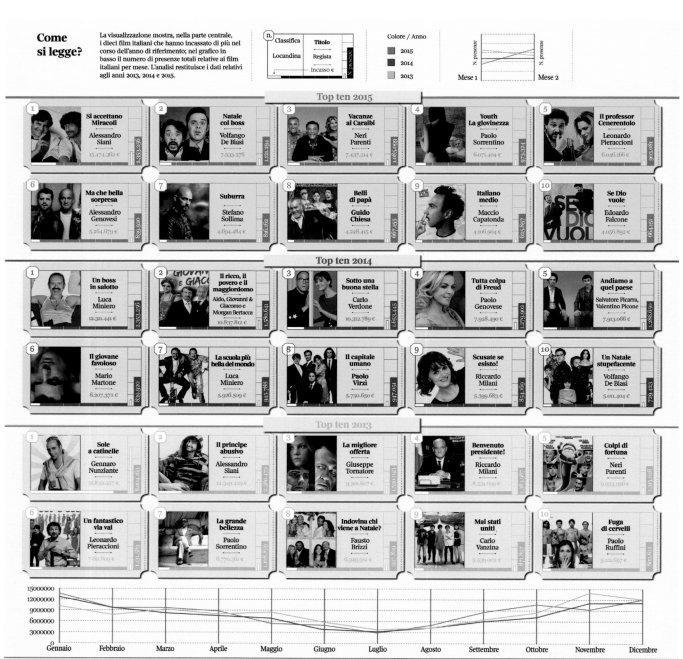

**Top ten 2015**

1. **Si accettano Miracoli** — Alessandro Siani — 15.474.362 €
2. **Natale col boss** — Volfango De Biasi — 7.533.576
3. **Vacanze ai Caraibi** — Neri Parenti — 7.437.514 €
4. **Youth La giovinezza** — Paolo Sorrentino — 6.071.404 €
5. **Il professor Cenerentolo** — Leonardo Pieraccioni — 6.046.166 €
6. **Ma che bella sorpresa** — Alessandro Genovesi — 5.264.679 €
7. **Suburra** — Stefano Sollima — 4.694.484 €
8. **Belli di papà** — Guido Chiesa — 4.228.415 €
9. **Italiano medio** — Maccio Capatonda — 4.106.904 €
10. **Se Dio vuole** — Edoardo Falcone — 4.056.892 €

**Top ten 2014**

1. **Un boss in salotto** — Luca Miniero — 12.311.441 €
2. **Il ricco, il povero e il maggiordomo** — Aldo, Giovanni & Giacomo e Morgan Bertacca — 10.837.812 €
3. **Sotto una buona stella** — Carlo Verdone — 10.312.789 €
4. **Tutta colpa di Freud** — Paolo Genovese — 7.928.490 €
5. **Andiamo a quel paese** — Salvatore Ficarra, Valentino Picone — 7.913.066 €
6. **Il giovane favoloso** — Mario Martone — 6.207.372 €
7. **La scuola più bella del mondo** — Luca Miniero — 5.926.509 €
8. **Il capitale umano** — Paolo Virzì — 5.750.650 €
9. **Scusate se esisto!** — Riccardo Milani — 5.399.683 €
10. **Un Natale stupefacente** — Volfango De Biasi — 5.011.404 €

**Top ten 2013**

1. **Sole a catinelle** — Gennaro Nunziante — 51.839.357 €
2. **Il principe abusivo** — Alessandro Siani — 14.349.139 €
3. **La migliore offerta** — Giuseppe Tornatore — 9.301.607 €
4. **Benvenuto presidente!** — Riccardo Milani — 8.531.699 €
5. **Colpi di fortuna** — Neri Parenti — 9.034.926 €
6. **Un fantastico via vai** — Leonardo Pieraccioni — 7.611.809 €
7. **La grande bellezza** — Paolo Sorrentino — 6.770.391 €
8. **Indovina chi viene a Natale?** — Fausto Brizzi — 6.349.912 €
9. **Mai stati uniti** — Carlo Vanzina — 5.539.002 €
10. **Fuga di cervelli** — Paolo Ruffini — 5.112.657 €

Colore / Anno: 2015, 2014, 2013

Gennaio — Febbraio — Marzo — Aprile — Maggio — Giugno — Luglio — Agosto — Settembre — Ottobre — Novembre — Dicembre

Fonti: «Tutti i numeri del cinema italiano», Anica Associazione Nazionale Industrie Cinematografiche Audiovisive e multimediali, anno 2015. Base dati: 1/1/2013-31/12/2015

# FLOW CHART

## 오므라이스

오므라이스**는 쌀 는 채소와 햄을 잘게 썰어 볶은 밥을
달걀로 싼 음식이다. '오므라이스'는 프랑스의 '오믈렛'**과
쌀을 의미하는 '라이스'**를 합해 만든 일본 특유의 요리다.

### 볶음밥 만들기

채소와 함께 밥을 볶아 준비한다.

밥    양파    당근

옥수수    완두콩    케첩

### 달걀 익히기

볼에 달걀, 우유, 소금, 후추를
넣고 섞은 후, 달군 팬에 올리브유
1/2큰술을 두르고 달걀물을 부어
30초 간 계속 저으면서 익힌다.

달걀    우유    소금

후추    올리브유

### 밥 올리기

아랫면이 익으면 볶음밥 1/2공기을
올리고 반으로 접어 붙여 익힌다.

달걀 지단    볶음밥

### 소스 만들기

밀가루와 버터로 루를 만들고,
물, 우스터소스, 케첩, 설탕을
넣어 섞어 끓인 뒤 후추를 넣어 준다.

버터    밀가루    우스터소스

케첩    설탕    물

우유    후추

### 완성

오므라이스에 소스를 곁들여서
맛있게 냠냠

# Hero: Process of Making Jam

..................................................

Agency: **Vormers'vuur**
Design: **Rutger Paulusse**
Client: **Hero**

Rutger Paulusse was asked by Hero, a manufacturer of jam, to create an infographic about the making process of jam. This poster, used for internal educational purposes, shows the breakdown on how to make jam.

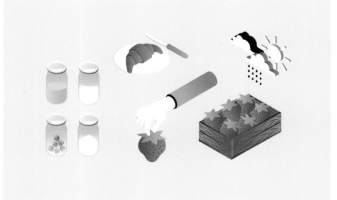

# Destination: Play Process Chart

Design: **Ella Zheng Meisi**

Destination: Play Process Chart shows how Ella Zheng Meisi started from having a number of design issues at hand to finally settling on one finalized design issue and how she conquered the fear of stepping out of the comfort zone.

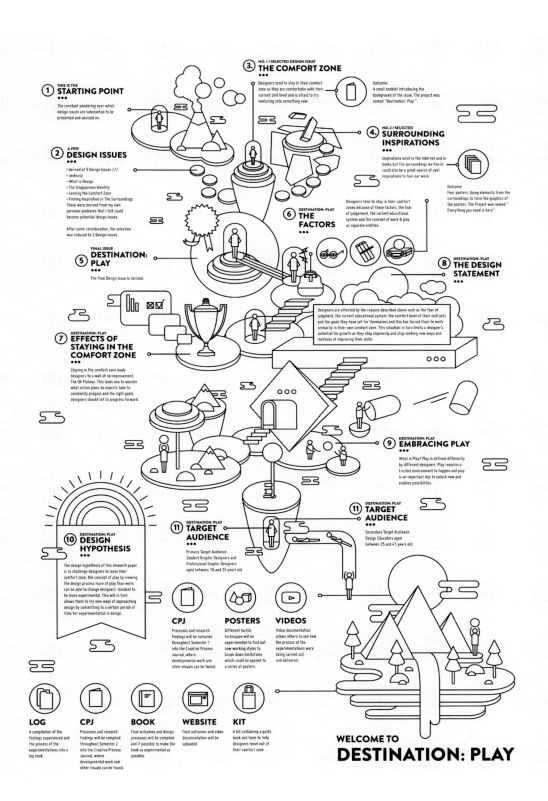

**THIS IS THE**
**① STARTING POINT**
•••
The constant pondering over which design issues are substantial to be presented and advised on.

**A FEW**
**② DESIGN ISSUES**
•••
I derived at 5 Design Issues ///
• Jealousy
• What is Design
• The Singaporean Identity
• Leaving the Comfort Zone
• Finding Inspiration in The Surroundings
These were derived from my own personal problems that I felt could become potential design issues.

After some consideration, the selection was reduced to 2 Design Issues.

**FINAL ISSUE**
**⑤ DESTINATION: PLAY**
•••
The final Design Issue is decided.

**NO. 1 / SELECTED DESIGN ISSUE**
**③ THE COMFORT ZONE**
•••
Designers tend to stay in their comfort zone as they are comfortable with their current skill level and is afraid to try venturing into something new.

Outcome:
A small booklet introducing the background of the issue. The project was named "Destination: Play".

**NO. 2 / SELECTED**
**④ SURROUNDING INSPIRATIONS**
•••
Inspirations exist in the internet and in books but the surroundings we live in could also be a great source of vast inspirations to fuel our work.

Outcome:
Four posters. Using elements from the surroundings to form the graphics of the posters. The Project was named "Everything you need is here".

**DESTINATION: PLAY**
**⑥ THE FACTORS**
•••
Designers tend to stay in their comfort zones because of these factors, the fear of judgement, the current educational system and the concept of work & play as separate entities.

**DESTINATION: PLAY**
**⑧ THE DESIGN STATEMENT**
•••
Designers are affected by the reasons described above such as the fear of judgment, the current educational system, the comfort level of their skill sets and the goals they have set for themselves and this has forced them to work primarily in their own comfort zone. This situation in turn limits a designer's potential for growth as they stop improving and stop seeking new ways and methods of improving their skills.

**DESTINATION: PLAY**
**⑦ EFFECTS OF STAYING IN THE COMFORT ZONE**
•••
Staying in the comfort zone leads designers to a wall of no improvement, The OK Plateau. This leads one to wonder what action plans do experts take to constantly progess and the right goals designers should set to progress forward.

**DESTINATION: PLAY**
**⑨ EMBRACING PLAY**
•••
What is Play? Play is defined differently by different designers. Play requires a trusted environment to happen and play is an important key to unlock new and endless possibilites.

**DESTINATION: PLAY**
**⑩ DESIGN HYPOTHESIS**
•••
The design hypothesis of this research paper is to challenge designers to leave their comfort zone, the concept of play by viewing the design process more of play than work can be able to change designers' mindset to be more experimental. This will in turn allows them to try new ways of approaching design by committing to a certain period of time for experimentation in design.

**DESTINATION: PLAY**
**⑪ TARGET AUDIENCE**
•••
Primary Target Audience:
Student Graphic Designers and Professional Graphic Designers aged between 16 and 35 years old

**DESTINATION: PLAY**
**⑪ TARGET AUDIENCE**
•••
Secondary Target Audience:
Design Educators aged between 25 and 45 years old.

**CPJ**
Processes and research findings will be compiled throughout Semester 1 into the Creative Process Journal, where developmental work and other visuals can be found.

**POSTERS**
Different tactile techniques will be experimented to find out new working styles to break down limitations which could be applied to a series of posters.

**VIDEOS**
Video documentation allows others to see how the process of the experimentations were being carried out and delivered.

**LOG**
A compilation of the feelings experienced and the process of the experimentations into a log book.

**CPJ**
Processes and research findings will be compiled throughout Semester 2 into the Creative Process Journal, where developmental work and other visuals can be found.

**BOOK**
Final outcomes and design processes will be compiled and if possible to make the book as experimental as possible.

**WEBSITE**
Final outcomes and video documentation will be uploaded.

**KIT**
A kit containing a guide book and tools to help designers move out of their comfort zone.

**WELCOME TO**
**DESTINATION: PLAY**

# Van Gansewinkel

Design: **Rutger Paulusse**
Art Direction: **Rutger Paulusse**
Client: **Van Gansewinkel**

Rutger Paulusse was asked to create an infographic for Van Gansewinkels's new website "Afval Bestaat Niet" (Waste Doesn't Exist), a website that takes the user through all the steps of recycling waste and Van Gansewinkel's workflow.

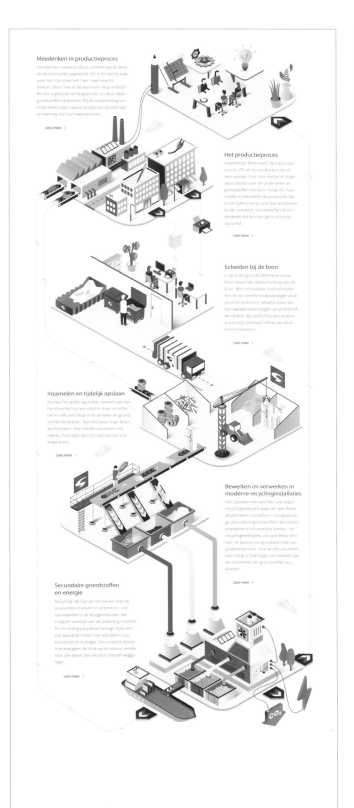
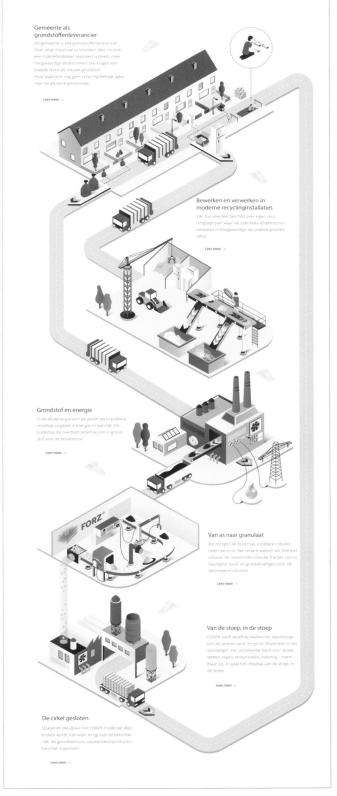

# Ecomobility: Electric Vehicle

Design: **Pablo Cabrera**

Ecomobility is a self-initiated project about the electric vehicles and renewable energies. The infographic story portrays the potential impact of transport on climate change due to the CO2 emissions to the atmosphere. The aim is to guide the viewer to different energy alternatives and to promote sustainable mobility. The visualization is supported by illustrations and infographics in a vector style. All data is sourced from Greenpeace, WWF, and Electric Vehicle Guides of the Community of Madrid.

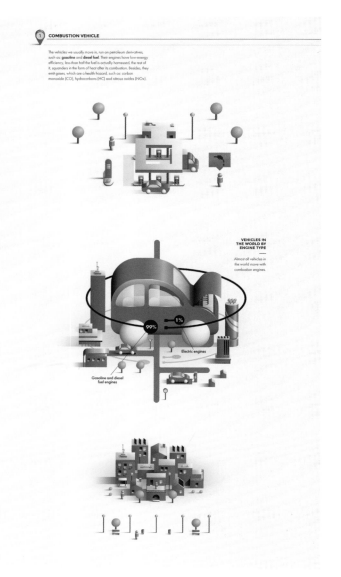

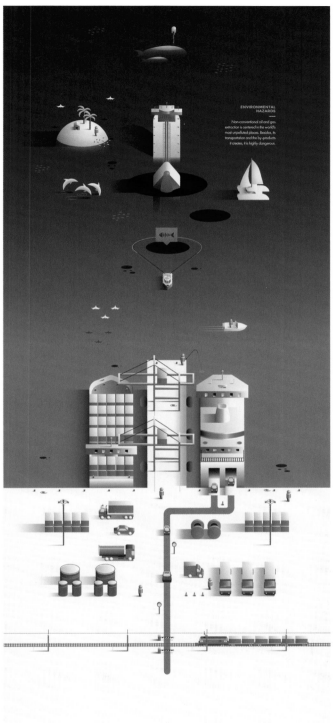

ENVIRONMENTAL
HAZARDS

Non-conventional oil and gas
extraction is centered in the world's
most unpolluted places. Besides, its
transportation and the by-products
it creates, it is highly dangerous.

## 2 FOSSIL FUELS

Grouped under this category, we have: carbon, petroleum and
natural gas, products, which, as a result of their chemical features,
are used as fuels. Albeit they gave way for productive
development in the history of humanity, they are also leaving a
highly-negative footprint in the environment. The combustion of
these type of fuels generates exhaust emissions that cause and
boost the greenhouse effect, acid rain, and pollution of the air,
soil and water.

**IF ALL THE PEOPLE IN THE WORLD
CONSUMED AT THE SAME PACE AS A
SAUDI-ARABIA, SINGAPORE OR USA INHABITANTS,
THE OIL-RESERVES WOULD BE DEPLETED
IN LESS THAN 10 YEARS**

## ③ CO₂ EMISSIONS

Energy needs to be procured from a source, be it for generating electrical energy or for a vehicle to run on. Most of this energy nowadays, is produced upon the **combustion of fossils**. These actions release CO₂ to the atmosphere and are the main cause for climate change.

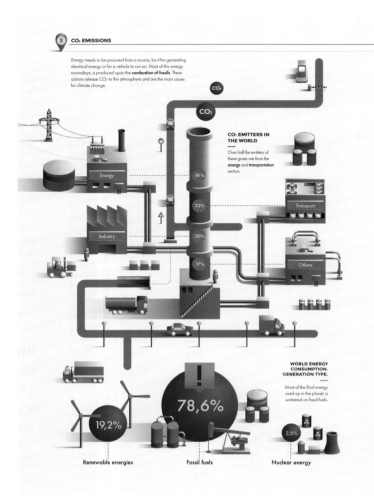

### CO₂ EMITTERS IN THE WORLD

Over half the emitters of these gases are from the **energy** and **transportation** sectors.

- 41% Energy
- 22% Transport
- 20% Industry
- 17% Others

### WORLD ENERGY CONSUMPTION. GENERATION TYPE.

Most of the final energy used-up in the planet, is sustained on fossil fuels.

- 19,2% Renewable energies
- 78,6% Fossil fuels
- 2,5% Nuclear energy

## ④ RENEWABLE ENERGIES

Renewable energies, which come from virtually inexhaustible **natural resources**, came to exist as a means to provide a solution for environmental problems. Their environmental footprint is null in the form of greenhouse-effect gas releases and the more mature technologies, are the photovoltaic and wind energies. We can find an assorted harnessing of natural resources to generate electricity.

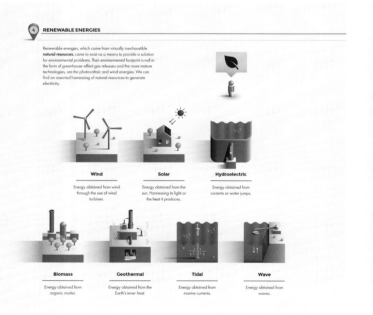

**Wind**
Energy obtained from wind through the use of wind turbines.

**Solar**
Energy obtained from the sun. Harnessing its light or the heat it produces.

**Hydroelectric**
Energy obtained from currents or water jumps.

**Biomass**
Energy obtained from organic matter.

**Geothermal**
Energy obtained from the Earth's inner heat.

**Tidal**
Energy obtained from marine currents.

**Wave**
Energy obtained from waves.

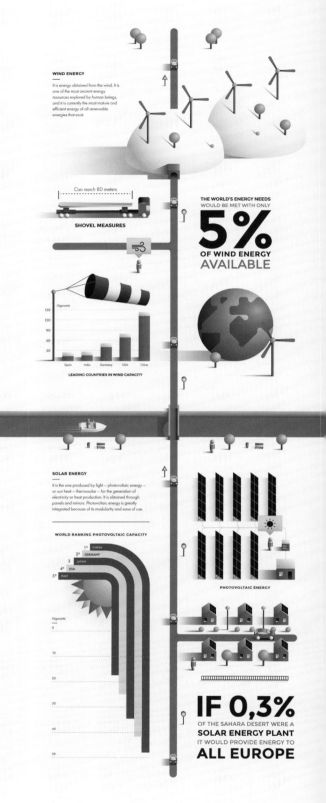

### WIND ENERGY

It is energy obtained from the wind. It is one of the most ancient energy resources explored by human beings, and it is currently the most mature and efficient energy of all renewable energies that exist.

Can reach 80 meters

**SHOVEL MEASURES**

### THE WORLD'S ENERGY NEEDS WOULD BE MET WITH ONLY

# 5%
## OF WIND ENERGY AVAILABLE

Gigawatts
- 150
- 120
- 90
- 60
- 30

Spain | India | Germany | USA | China

**LEADING COUNTRIES IN WIND CAPACITY**

### SOLAR ENERGY

It is the one produced by light – photovoltaic energy – or sun heat – thermosolar – for the generation of electricity or heat production. It is obtained through panels and mirrors. Photovoltaic energy is greatly integrated because of its modularity and ease of use.

**WORLD RANKING PHOTOVOLTAIC CAPACITY**

- 1º CHINA
- 2º GERMANY
- 3º JAPAN
- 4º USA
- 5º ITALY

Gigawatts
- 0
- 10
- 20
- 20
- 40
- 50

**PHOTOVOLTAIC ENERGY**

# IF 0,3%
## OF THE SAHARA DESERT WERE A SOLAR ENERGY PLANT IT WOULD PROVIDE ENERGY TO
# ALL EUROPE

# 5 ELECTRIC VEHICLE

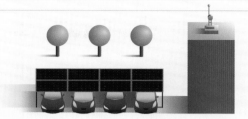

To cut greenhouse-effect exhaust emissions and other health-hazardous gases in the transportation sector, there is a solution which is, as feasible as it is real: the electric vehicle. These vehicles are powered by an **electrical engine** that moves with the aid of energy stored in a battery. They have started to be more present in our streets and now, they are not only viable options for the bold and innovative, but they have started to compete strongly with internal-combustion vehicles.

### 1- Charging pole
They are **electrical-network** accessing points where we can plug our electric vehicle. The length of the charge will depend on its power.

### 2- Charger
The element that absorbs energy directly from the network (1) in an alternate way and transforms it to direct current, so as to charge **the main battery**.

### 3- Batteries
Lithium-ion batteries **store energy** that comes from the charger (2) in the form of direct current. In cars that have a direct-current-powered electrical engine, this battery would be directly hooked to the engine. On the other hand, in alternate-current-powered electric cars, the battery would be hooked to an inverter.

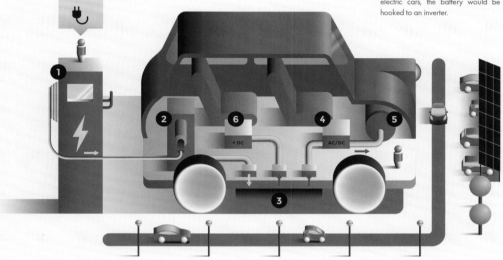

### 4- Inverters
They are in charge of **transforming direct current** that comes from the main battery (3), into alternate current. This component would not exist in the case of direct-current powered cars.

### 5- Electric Engine
An electric's car engine can be either alternate current or direct current. The **direct current** one, powers directly from the main battery, while the **alternate current** one powers through the energy emitted from the battery, previously transformed into alternate current by the inverter (4).

### 6- Converter
The converter transforms high-tension direct current, that the main battery (3) provides, into low-tension direct current. This type of current is the one that is used to power the vehicle's **auxiliary electrical components**.

**Gas-emission-free**

**Low-Maintenance**

**Low-noise**

**Great efficiency**

**6** BATTERIES

The most common and, the ones most manufacturers use are
**Lithium-ion** batteries, mostly known for their use in portable
devices and smartphones. These supply the energy that comes
from the charge through the cable or by harnessing the energy
that comes from the vehicle's braking. The greatest
inconveniences come in the form of the vehicle's autonomy and
the charging places, although as technology continues to
advance, manufacturers offer us better features.

# BATTERIES
## REPRESENT ABOUT
# 33%
#### AN ELECTRIC VEHICLE'S COST

### RANGE – ELECTRIC VS COMBUSTION VEHICLES

Electric
Combustion
300 kms   600 km   900 kms
Some manufacturers

**7** CHARGING AN ELECTRIC VEHICLE

Unlike combustion vehicles, that must pump fuel at gas stations,
the electric vehicle can do so at **multiple places**. From home, the
work place, shopping malls, garages and other places where
vehicles are parked for an extended period of time. We can
compare charging a vehicle to what we normally do every
evening, as we plug-in our **smartphone** charger. Thus, we only
need a charging point and a connector to link it to the vehicle.

| SMARTPHONE CHARGE | ELECTRIC VEHICLE CHARGE |
|---|---|
| 11:00 - 7:00 | 11:00 - 7:00 |

| Conventional charge | Semi-fast charge | Fast-charging |
|---|---|---|
| 3.7 Kw | 7.3 Kw | 50 Kw |
| alternate current | alternate current | direct current |
| **8-10 hours** | **4 hours** | **15 min - 65% battery** |
| It is an optimal solution for over-night charging at home garages. | It is an optimal solution for charging in places where the vehicle is parked for an extended period. | It is a solution for timely charges where the vehicle might run out of battery and need energy delivered quickly. |

# VEHICLES
## ARE PARKED
# 97%
## OF THE TIME

**8** PERKS TO AN ELECTRIC VEHICLE

Electric vehicles are starting to gain leverage in the automotive
industry, due to their advantages over traditional fueled vehicles,
in terms of saving in consumption and respect for the
**environment**. Due to the fact that it's not sufficiently implemented
in society and in light of the lack of information, the consumer
usually opts for a traditional one. The advantages that make the
electric vehicle, a competitive transportation means, are multiple
and even more so with the on-going development in technology.

**Gas-emission-free**
Does not emit gases that
are harmful, not only for
health, but for the
environment as well.

**Low-Maintenance**
An electrical engine does
not need refrigeration
circuitry nor oils.

**Low-noise**
Does not make noise while
circulating and its vibrations
are almost undiscernible.

**Great efficiency**
Almost double that of a
combustion engine.

**Fewer break-downs**
Due to the fact that an
electrical vehicle has fewer
mechanical elements.

**Priorities**
Transit and parking-wise, etc.

**Recovery**
Energy can be recovered
with the vehicle's braking.

# SUSTAINABLE CITY

An **intelligent transportation** system is able to satisfy mobility services with great reduction in energy consumption, thanks to the vehicle's efficiency and the occupancy that it achieves. The pedestrianization, bicycling, the electric vehicle and public transportation are complementary tools to an urban redesign that must take back the neighborhood as an essential core to urban life.

### MERCHANDISE
Trains, propelled by electricity from a renewable source, used to transport merchandise to large cities.

### COMPANIES
In turn, the merchandise is distributed in electric vans. Companies start to renew their fleets and work in a sustainable way.

### PRIVATE CHARGING
There are surfaces where vehicles are parked for a long time and that allow charging while customers do their shopping.

### PUBLIC TRANSPORTATION
High-capacity transportation means are powered by electrical energy from a renewable source.

### PUBLIC CHARGING
There are charging points, scattered all throughout the city. Electric-charging-stations are giving way to gas stations and new business models arise.

### CAR-SHARING
Rental services. From a smartphone, you can reserve an electrical vehicle at a 'per-minute' rate.

### ELECTRIC BICYCLES
The electric bicycle un-jams traffic in city centers and its battery aids in slopes.

### ELECTRIC TAXIS
Private transportation services also electrify, with prioritized transit routes.

### SELF-CONSUMPTION
Homes turn into self-sufficient systems, able to store and consume their own electrical energy. The electric vehicle usually charges at night-time.

### PUBLIC SERVICES
All vehicles with planned routes or narrowed-down areas are electrified, for instance: garbage disposal services.

---

# YOU DECIDE

If we want to preserve our planet, we don't need timely and isolated actions, but a world-wide strategy, molding our lifestyles and having a change of mind. We have seen alternatives in the energy and transportation sectors, now it's our turn to put our grain of sand. We would be deceiving ourselves if we used an electric vehicle and the electricity were generated by fossil fuels. For the **electric vehicle** integration to truly be clean, it must be linked to **renewable energies**.

Therefore, the future must be planned with a greater presence of renewable energies in mind, and a strong development of the electric vehicle.

**+ COMBUSTION VEHICLE**
**FOSSIL FUELS**

**+ ELECTRIC VEHICLE**
**RENEWABLE ENERGIES**

very low — **Sustainability**

very high — **Sustainability**

**Sources:**

Greenpeace - Energía 3.0
WWF - El informe de la energía renovable
Comunidad de Madrid - Guía del vehículo eléctrico

**Thanks for scrolling!**

# How the Chickens Are Bred

.................................................................

Design: **Justyna Sikora**

The infographics show the industrial way of breeding chickens. The whole infographics include 11 charts. The data is sourced from the documentary series on the Discovery Channel called *How It's Made*.

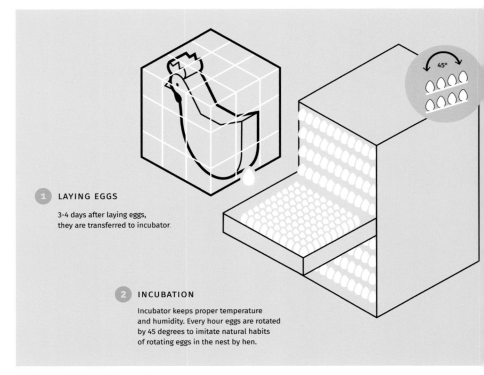

**1** LAYING EGGS

3-4 days after laying eggs, they are transferred to incubator.

**2** INCUBATION

Incubator keeps proper temperature and humidity. Every hour eggs are rotated by 45 degrees to imitate natural habits of rotating eggs in the nest by hen.

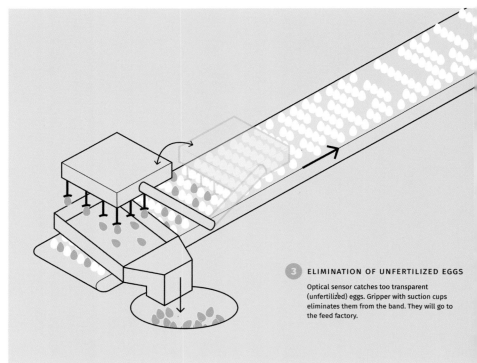

**3** ELIMINATION OF UNFERTILIZED EGGS

Optical sensor catches too transparent (unfertilized) eggs. Gripper with suction cups eliminates them from the band. They will go to the feed factory.

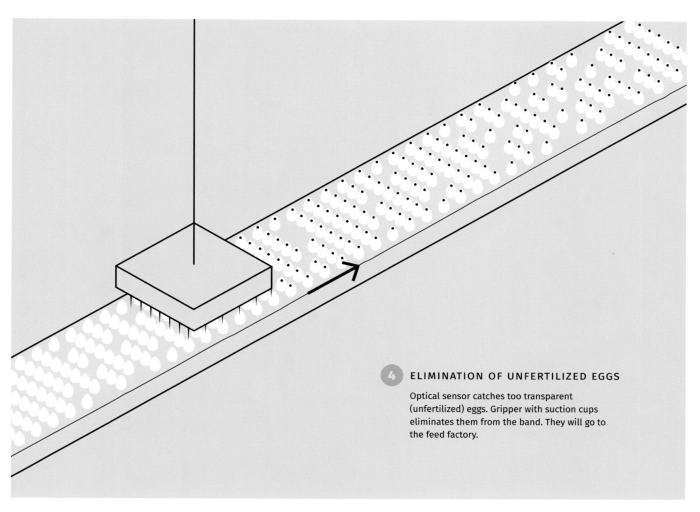

**4** ELIMINATION OF UNFERTILIZED EGGS

Optical sensor catches too transparent
(unfertilized) eggs. Gripper with suction cups
eliminates them from the band. They will go to
the feed factory.

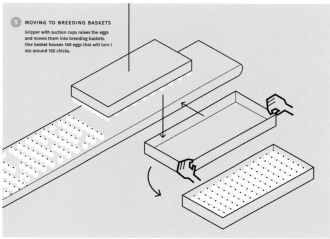

**5** MOVING TO BREEDING BASKETS

Gripper with suction cups raises the eggs
and moves them into breeding baskets.
One basket houses 168 eggs that will turn i
nto around 150 chicks.

**6** HATCHING

At 19th day chick makes hole in a shell.
Within next 6-8 hours it gets rid of the rest
of the shell. It hatch out covered with
short feather called fluff. After next 4 hours
it becomes dry.

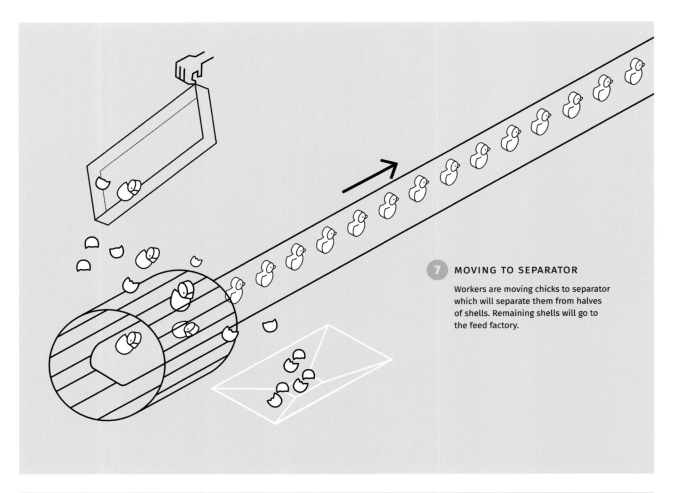

**7  MOVING TO SEPARATOR**

Workers are moving chicks to separator which will separate them from halves of shells. Remaining shells will go to the feed factory.

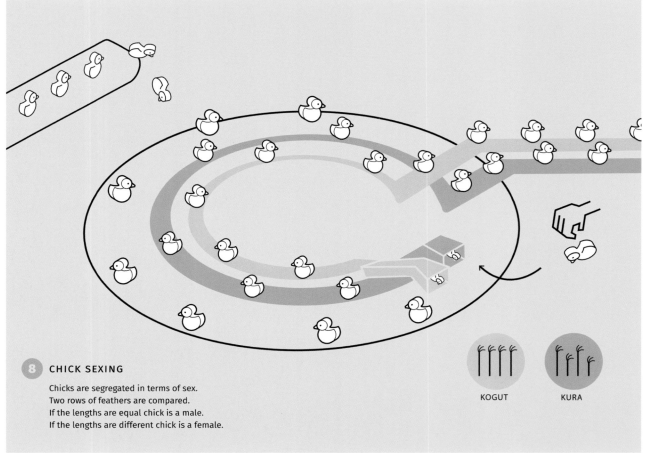

**8  CHICK SEXING**

Chicks are segregated in terms of sex.
Two rows of feathers are compared.
If the lengths are equal chick is a male.
If the lengths are different chick is a female.

KOGUT

KURA

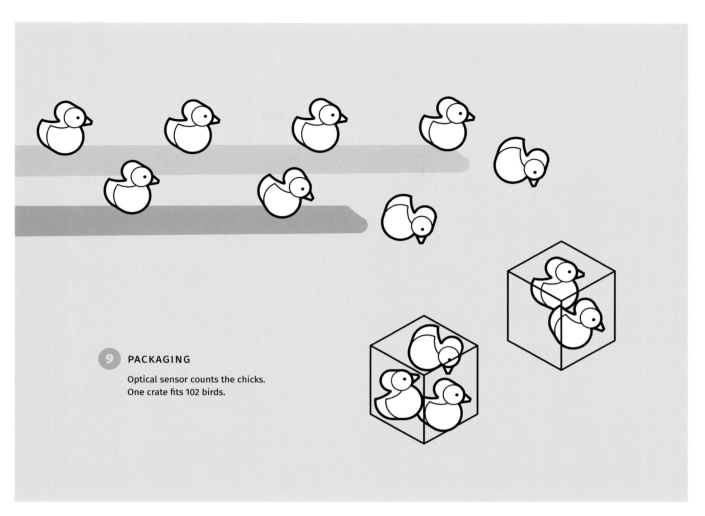

### 9 PACKAGING

Optical sensor counts the chicks.
One crate fits 102 birds.

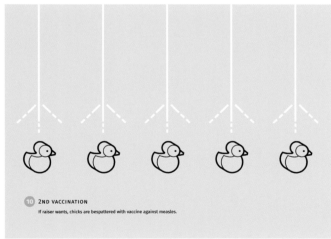

### 10 2ND VACCINATION

If raiser wants, chicks are bespattered with vaccine against measles.

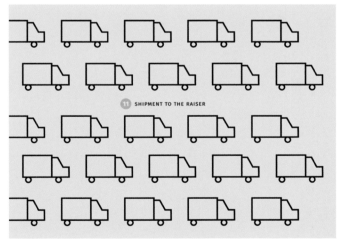

### 11 SHIPMENT TO THE RAISER

# Hankook Coffee: Journey

........................................................................

Agency: **DAEKI & JUN Studio**
Design: **Daeki Shim, Hyojun Shim, Juyoung Shin**
Art Direction: **Daeki Shim, Hyojun Shim**
Client: **Hankook Coffee**

These infographic posters illustrate how Hankook Coffee selects, imports, and processes high-quality coffee beans by visiting coffee plantations. The project focused on researching and analyzing all information covering the process of cultivation, production of coffee beans, transportation, roasting, and distribution to consumers. The overall design challenge of this project might be how to enable the consumers who do not have much knowledge of coffee to easily understand how coffee beans are cultivated, selected, and produced to be distributed to consumers by unraveling every aspect visually through illustrations and infographics. The size of the poster is 420mm x 594mm.

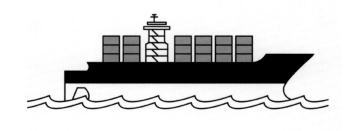

한국커피는 세계 7%의 최상급 스페셜티 생두와 차별화된 로스팅 시스템으로 다양한 맛과 풍부한 향을 전합니다.

한국커피는 85점 이상 되는 커피만을 산지에서 직접 구매해서, 자체 개발한 컴퓨터 시스템으로 로스팅 기계를 정밀하게 조절 하면서 로스팅합니다.

한국커피는 1992년부터 좋은 원료의 커피만을 까다롭게 골라 수십 번의 컵테스트를 통해 한국커피만의 다채롭고 다양한 맛과 향으로 완성된 한 잔의 커피를 만듭니다.

a 7

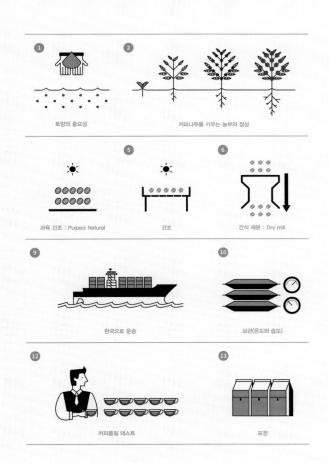

1 토양의 중요성
2 커피나무를 키우는 농부의 정성
5 과육 건조 : Pulped Natural
6 건조
6 건식 제분 : Dry mill

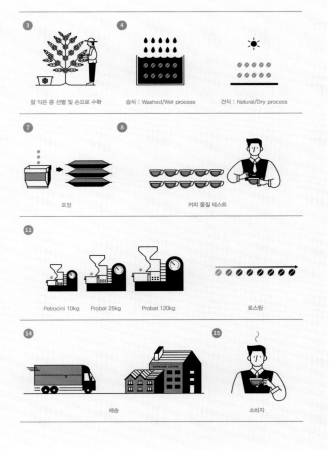

3 잘 익은 콩 선별 및 손으로 수확
4 습식 : Washed/Wet process
4 건식 : Natural/Dry process
7 포장
8 커피 품질 테스트
9 한국으로 운송
10 보관(온도와 습도)
11 Petrocini 10kg  Probat 25kg  Probat 120kg  로스팅
12 커피품질 테스트
13 포장
14 배송
15 소비자

## Disaster Survival Manual

Design: **Bunkyo Gakuin University**

"Disaster Survival Manual" was specially created for foreign residents who live in Bunkyo, Tokyo to get prepared for earthquakes. By using infographics, foreign residents who have never experienced an earthquake can easily understand how to evacuate. The design guides them on what to do for the first five minutes after an earthquake occurs and provides information including shelters.

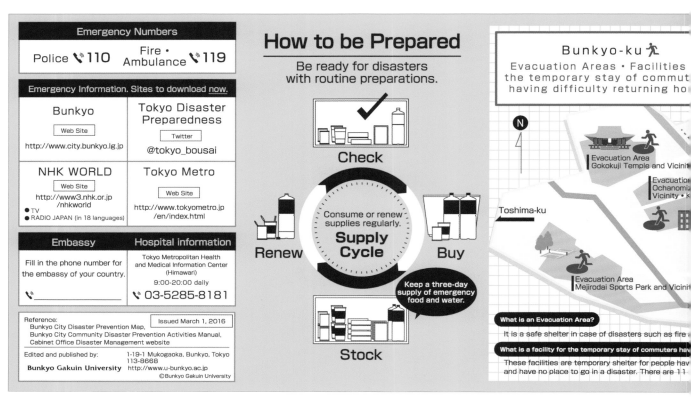

### Emergency Numbers

Police 📞110    Fire・Ambulance 📞119

**Emergency Information. Sites to download now.**

| Bunkyo | Tokyo Disaster Preparedness |
|---|---|
| Web Site | Twitter |
| http://www.city.bunkyo.lg.jp | @tokyo_bousai |

| NHK WORLD | Tokyo Metro |
|---|---|
| Web Site | Web Site |
| http://www3.nhk.or.jp /nhkworld | http://www.tokyometro.jp /en/index.html |
| ● TV ● RADIO JAPAN (in 18 languages) | |

| Embassy | Hospital information |
|---|---|
| Fill in the phone number for the embassy of your country. 📞_____ | Tokyo Metropolitan Health and Medical Information Center (Himawari) 9:00-20:00 daily 📞 03-5285-8181 |

Reference:
Bunkyo City Disaster Prevention Map,        Issued March 1, 2016
Bunkyo City Community Disaster Prevention Activities Manual,
Cabinet Office Disaster Management website

Edited and published by:        1-19-1 Mukogaoka, Bunkyo, Tokyo
**Bunkyo Gakuin University**    113-8668
                                http://www.u-bunkyo.ac.jp
                                ©Bunkyo Gakuin University

### How to be Prepared

Be ready for disasters with routine preparations.

**Check**

Consume or renew supplies regularly.
**Supply Cycle**

**Renew**    **Buy**

Keep a three-day supply of emergency food and water.

**Stock**

### Bunkyo-ku 🏃

Evacuation Areas・Facilities [for] the temporary stay of commut[ers] having difficulty returning ho[me]

N

Toshima-ku

Evacuation Area
Gokokuji Temple and Vicini[ty]

Evacuation [Area]
Ochanomi[zu] Vicinity・[k]

Evacuation Area
Mejirodai Sports Park and Vicinit[y]

**What is an Evacuation Area?**
It is a safe shelter in case of disasters such as fire [...]

**What is a facility for the temporary stay of commuters hav[...]**
These facilities are temporary shelter for people hav[ing] and have no place to go in a disaster. There are 11 [...]

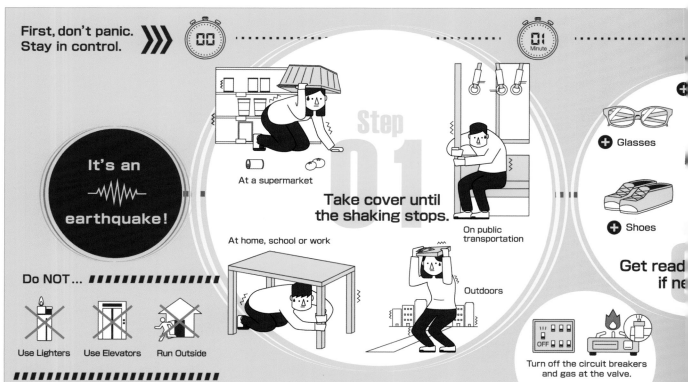

**First, don't panic. Stay in control.** ▶▶▶

00

01 Minute

**It's an earthquake!**

Step 01

At a supermarket

**Take cover until the shaking stops.**

On public transportation

At home, school or work

Outdoors

Glasses

Shoes

Get read[y] if ne[...]

**Do NOT...**

Use Lighters    Use Elevators    Run Outside

Turn off the circuit breakers and gas at the valve.

OFF

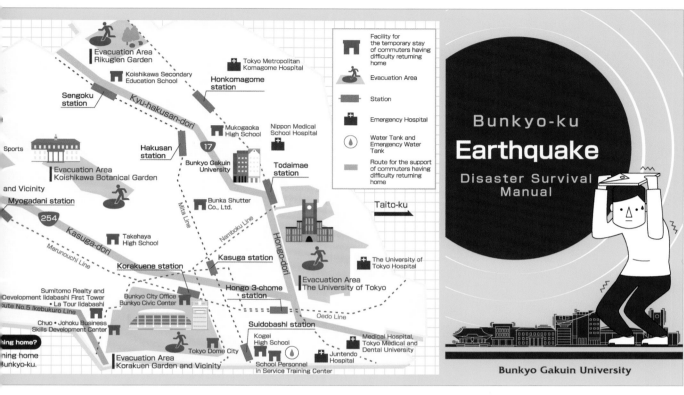

Facility for the temporary stay of commuters having difficulty returning home

Evacuation Area

Station

Emergency Hospital

Water Tank and Emergency Water Tank

Route for the support of commuters having difficulty returning home

Evacuation Area
Rikugien Garden

Tokyo Metropolitan Komagome Hospital

Koishikawa Secondary Education School

Honkomagome station

Sengoku station

Kyu-hakusan-dori

Mukogaoka High School

Nippon Medical School Hospital

Sports

Hakusan station

17

Evacuation Area
Koishikawa Botanical Garden

Bunkyo Gakuin University

Todaimae station

and Vicinity

Myogadani station

254

Bunka Shutter Co., Ltd.

Mita Line

Nanboku Line

Hongo-dori

Taito-ku

Kasuga-dori

Takehaya High School

Marunouchi Line

Korakuene station

Kasuga station

The University of Tokyo Hospital

Hongo 3-chome station

Evacuation Area
The University of Tokyo

Sumitomo Realty and Development Iidabashi First Tower
• La Tour Iidabashi

ute No.5 Ikebukuro Line

Bunkyo City Office
Bunkyo Civic Center

Oedo Line

Suidobashi station

Chuo • Johoku Business Skills Development Center

Kogei High School

Medical Hospital, Tokyo Medical and Dental University

ing home?

ning home
unkyo-ku.

Evacuation Area
Korakuen Garden and Vicinity

Tokyo Dome City

School Personnel in Service Training Center

Juntendo Hospital

Bunkyo-ku
**Earthquake**
Disaster Survival Manual

**Bunkyo Gakuin University**

---

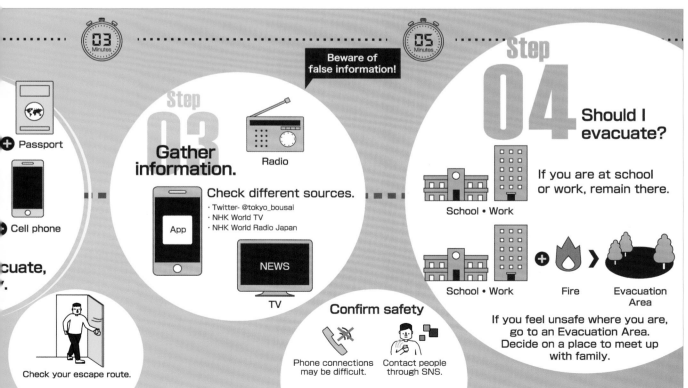

03 Minutes

05 Minutes

Beware of false information!

Passport

Step
**03**

**Gather information.**

Radio

Cell phone

App

**Check different sources.**
· Twitter- @tokyo_bousai
· NHK World TV
· NHK World Radio Japan

NEWS

TV

cuate,

Check your escape route.

**Confirm safety**

Phone connections may be difficult.

Contact people through SNS.

Step
**04**

**Should I evacuate?**

School • Work

If you are at school or work, remain there.

School • Work       Fire       Evacuation Area

If you feel unsafe where you are, go to an Evacuation Area.
Decide on a place to meet up with family.

# Leaning Tower of Pizza

Design: **Joey Ng**

This is a fun visualization of the Leaning Tower of Pisa. The tower is illustrated into a pizza-making factory that also serves as an infographic on the process of making a pizza, ingredients, and other interesting facts including a recipe. Sketches were initially drawn on paper and brought into Adobe Photoshop and Adobe Illustrator to be illustrated part-by-part and colored digitally.

**DOUGH**

*The dough is the most fundamental ingredient of the pizza.*

Mix flour, yeast and water in a mixing bowl.

Knead the dough for 5-10 minutes.

Add olive oil and leave the dough to rise.

Split dough into two. Cover with moist cloth till ready for use.

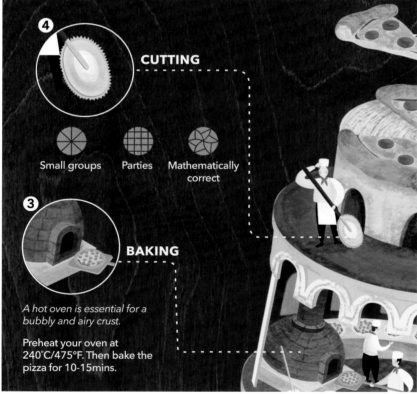

**CUTTING**

Small groups — Parties — Mathematically correct

**BAKING**

*A hot oven is essential for a bubbly and airy crust.*

Preheat your oven at 240°C/475°F. Then bake the pizza for 10-15mins.

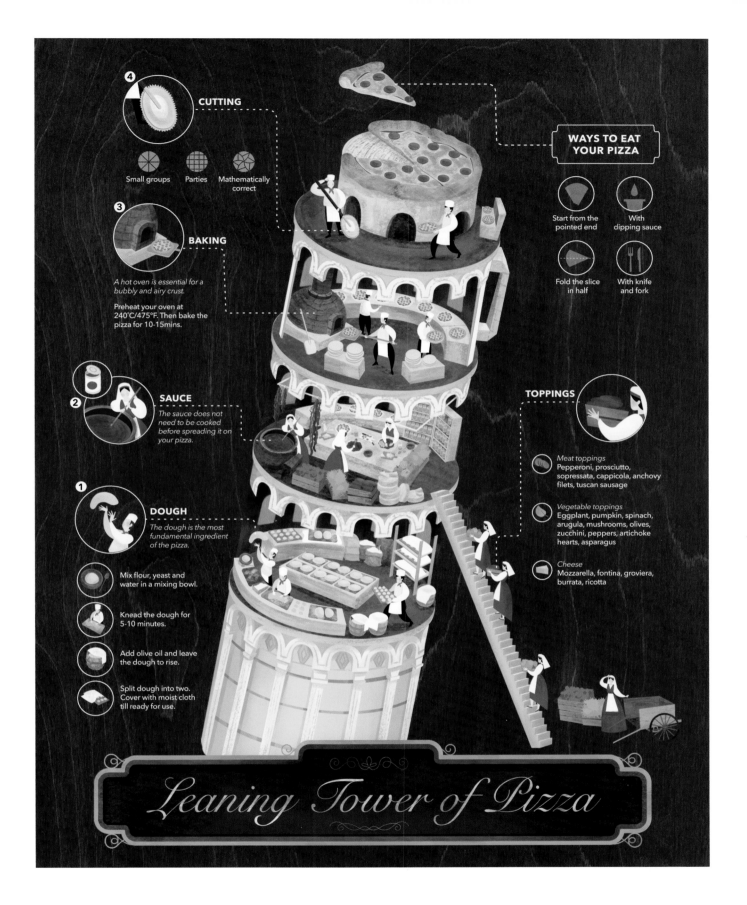

**WAYS TO EAT YOUR PIZZA**

**④ CUTTING**

Small groups

Parties

Mathematically correct

**③ BAKING**

A hot oven is essential for a bubbly and airy crust.

Preheat your oven at 240°C/475°F. Then bake the pizza for 10-15mins.

Start from the pointed end

With dipping sauce

Fold the slice in half

With knife and fork

**② SAUCE**

The sauce does not need to be cooked before spreading it on your pizza.

**TOPPINGS**

*Meat toppings*
Pepperoni, prosciutto, sopressata, cappicola, anchovy filets, tuscan sausage

*Vegetable toppings*
Eggplant, pumpkin, spinach, arugula, mushrooms, olives, zucchini, peppers, artichoke hearts, asparagus

*Cheese*
Mozzarella, fontina, groviera, burrata, ricotta

**① DOUGH**

The dough is the most fundamental ingredient of the pizza.

Mix flour, yeast and water in a mixing bowl.

Knead the dough for 5-10 minutes.

Add olive oil and leave the dough to rise.

Split dough into two. Cover with moist cloth till ready for use.

*Leaning Tower of Pizza*

# Black Tea

Agency: **203 × Infographics Lab**

Black tea is known as the epitome of tea worldwide. Due to the distinct characteristics of each producing area, it evolved into various teas depending on how it is mixed. In addition, various ingredients are enjoyed in each country. Black tea reminds the viewers of a luxurious and elegant image, but it is also a popular drink loved by a wide variety of people. Everything about black tea was placed in this infographic.

# Egg

Eggs are known as perfect food along with milk. People scarcely pass the days without having eggs in any form—eggs are an important part of one's diet. Food that can be made with eggs is also inexhaustible. The interesting facts about eggs were included in this infographic.

Agency: **203 × Infographics Lab**

# Risograph Printing

Agency: **203 × Infographics Lab**

Risograph is one of the printing types that are similar to the silk screen printing technique. The ink is ejected from the small holes of the preprinted master paper and printed on paper. It is a printing method that automates the principle of stencil through digital technology. Everything about the risograph can be seen in this infographic at one glance.

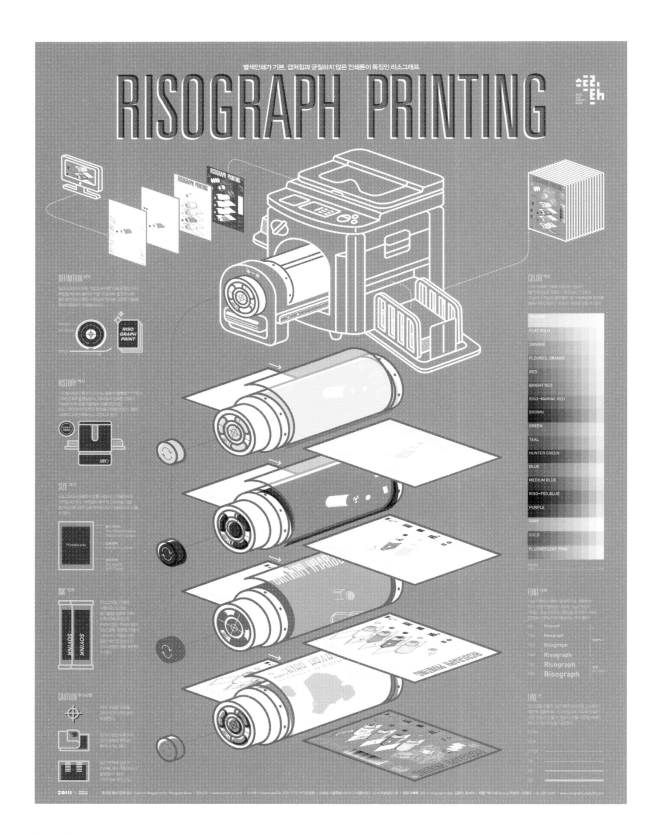

# Silk Screen Printing

Agency: **203 × Infographics Lab**

It has not a long history, but due to its convenient, versatile, and simple way of using, silk screen printing is now widely used. Even if the user is not an expert, it is relatively easy to print what he/she wants by applying silk screen printing. Everything about silk screen printing is included in this infographic.

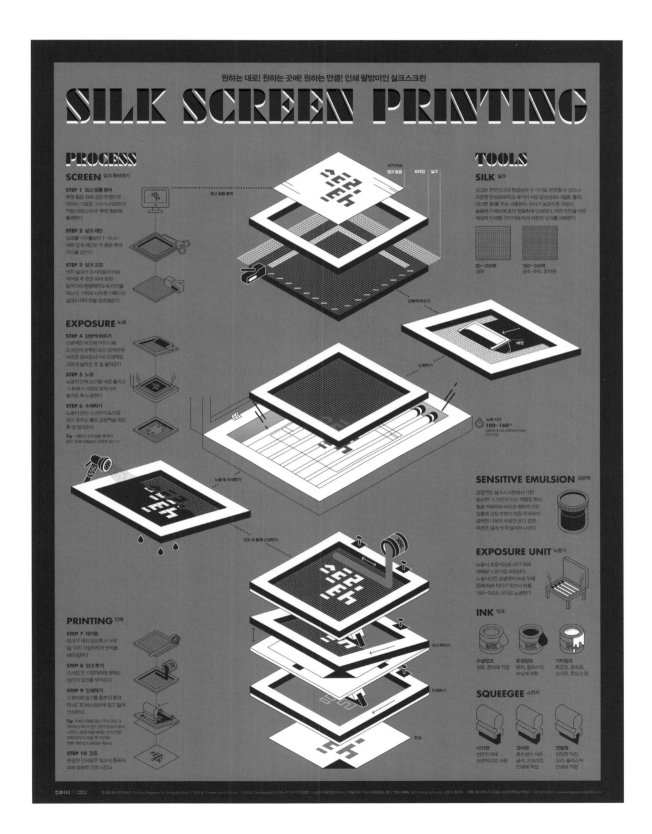

# Process of Shoe Creation

..................................................

The infographic shows the process of footwear manufacturing of a small company located in London.

Design: **Anton Yermolov**
Art Direction: **Anton Yermolov**

# Game of Thrones Season 6 Map

Agency: **relajaelcoco**
Edition: **EW staff**
Client: *Entertainment Weekly* **(USA)**

The project consists of a double-page map representing the lands of the TV series *Game of Thrones* for *Entertainment Weekly*, an American magazine about TV and cinema. The challenge was to make an extreme synthesis of the whole visual content and to create icons that could be read at a very small size.

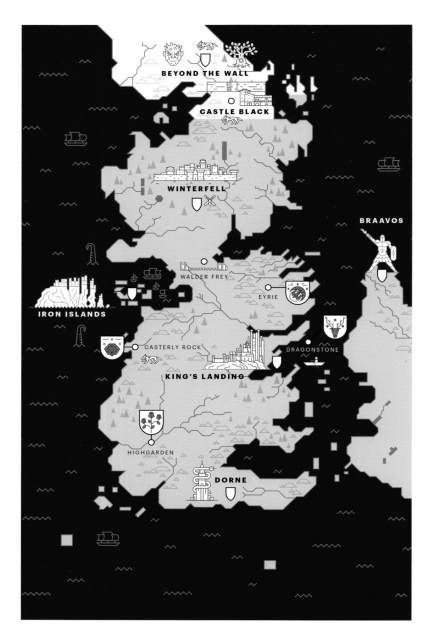

DORNE

CASTLE BLACK

WALDER FREY

KING'S LANDING

WINTERFELL

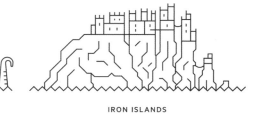

IRON ISLANDS

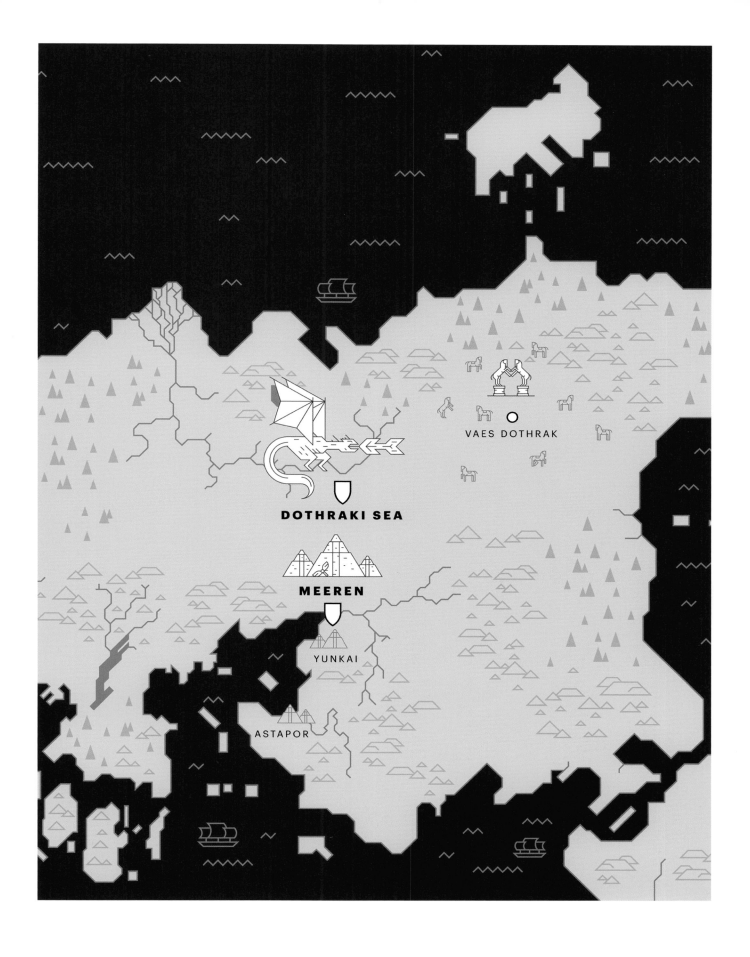

DOTHRAKI SEA

VAES DOTHRAK

MEEREN

YUNKAI

ASTAPOR

# Illustrated Map of Ashgabat

Design: **Alexandra Erkaeva**

This is a map of Ashgabat, the capital and the largest city of Turkmenistan in Central Asia. The city is situated between the Karakum Desert and the Kopet Dag mountain range. Alexandra Erkaeva has visited all of the places illustrated in this map. The map portrays the things that visitors can do during their stay in this city.

# Colombia Map Illustration

Design: **Kürşat Ünsal**
Client: *The Business Year*

This is one of the ten cover illustrations that Kürşat Ünsal has designed for *The Business Year* magazine in 2017. The design stands out from the monotonous covers for most publications on business with its simplicity and minimalism. Kürşat has illustrated Colombia's economic, industrial, and cultural icons, and combined them with the geographically detailed map illustration.

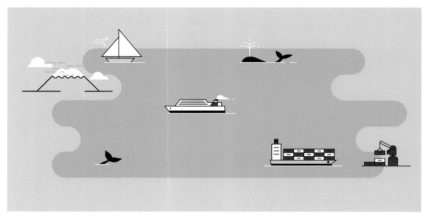

Barranquilla

Cartagena

Barrancabermeja

Medellin

BOGOTÃ

Buenaventura

Cali

Tumaco

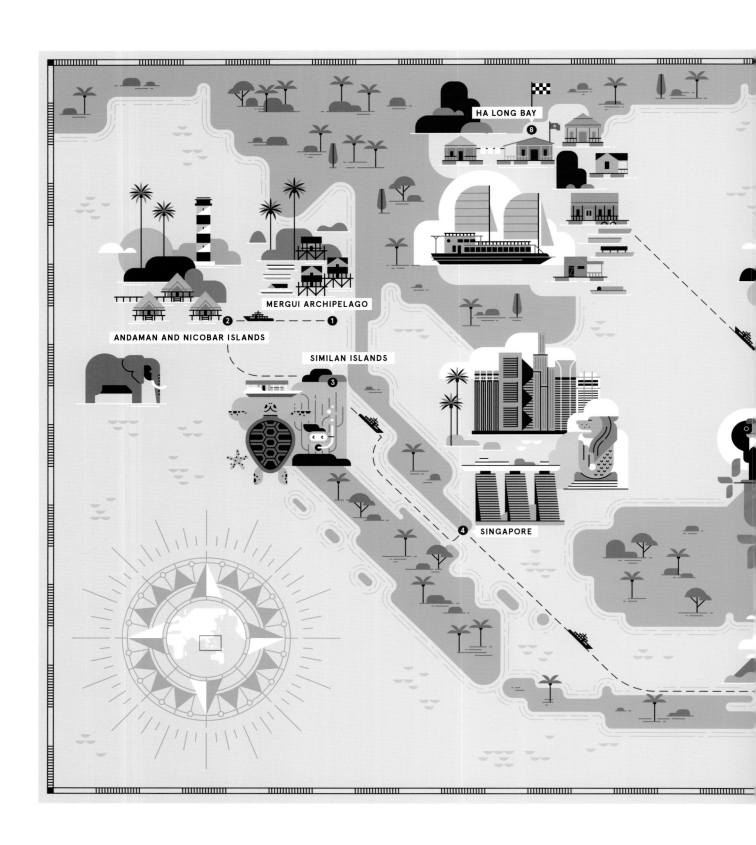

HA LONG BAY

8

MERGUI ARCHIPELAGO

2 ——— 1

ANDAMAN AND NICOBAR ISLANDS

SIMILAN ISLANDS

3

4 SINGAPORE

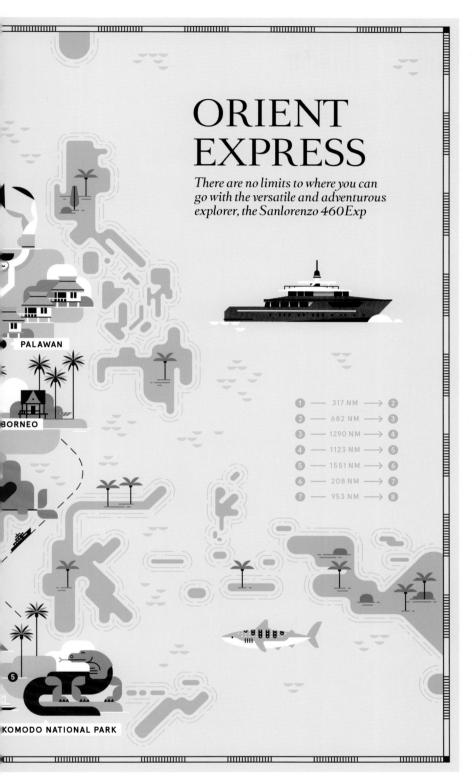

# ORIENT EXPRESS

*There are no limits to where you can go with the versatile and adventurous explorer, the Sanlorenzo 460Exp*

PALAWAN

BORNEO

KOMODO NATIONAL PARK

| ① | — 317 NM → | ② |
| ② | — 682 NM → | ③ |
| ③ | — 1290 NM → | ④ |
| ④ | — 1123 NM → | ⑤ |
| ⑤ | — 1551 NM → | ⑥ |
| ⑥ | — 208 NM → | ⑦ |
| ⑦ | — 953 NM → | ⑧ |

## Orient Express

Design: **Olga Günther**
Art Direction: **Nina Hundt**
Client: ***BOAT International***

This infographic is created for *BOAT International* magazine to promote Sanlorenzo's superyacht 460Exp, which is designed specifically for long-range cruises. This time Sanlorenzo's superyacht goes on an orient adventure. The infographic with iconic illustrations of the cities introduces the itinerary and the stops of the cruise around Southeast Asia.

# Empire Building

Design: **Olga Günther**
Art Direction: **Mia Lily Johnson**
Client: ***BOAT International***

The infographic created for *BOAT International* magazine's issue *"Viva Italia!"* is about Italian boat yards—their location and the number of boats that they are currently working on. The infographic also includes information about some fashion designers' yachts, connected to the yards where they were built.

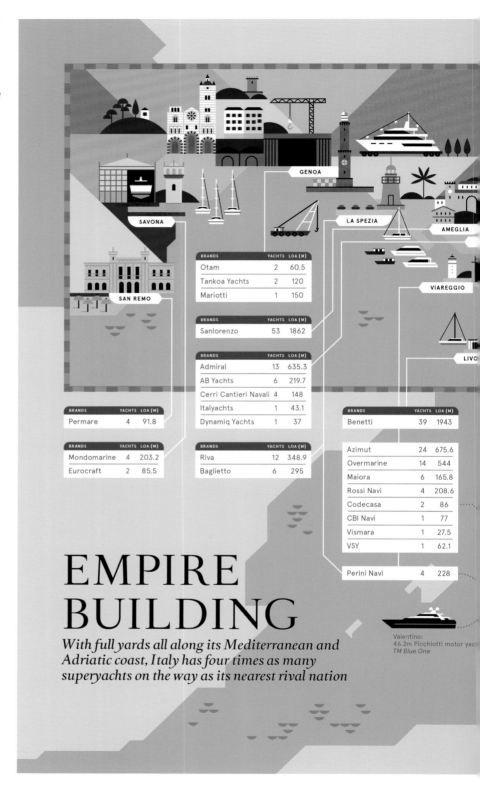

| BRANDS | YACHTS | LOA (M) |
|---|---|---|
| Otam | 2 | 60.5 |
| Tankoa Yachts | 2 | 120 |
| Mariotti | 1 | 150 |

| BRANDS | YACHTS | LOA (M) |
|---|---|---|
| Sanlorenzo | 53 | 1862 |

| BRANDS | YACHTS | LOA (M) |
|---|---|---|
| Admiral | 13 | 635.3 |
| AB Yachts | 6 | 219.7 |
| Cerri Cantieri Navali | 4 | 148 |
| Italyachts | 1 | 43.1 |
| Dynamiq Yachts | 1 | 37 |

| BRANDS | YACHTS | LOA (M) |
|---|---|---|
| Permare | 4 | 91.8 |

| BRANDS | YACHTS | LOA (M) |
|---|---|---|
| Mondomarine | 4 | 203.2 |
| Eurocraft | 2 | 85.5 |

| BRANDS | YACHTS | LOA (M) |
|---|---|---|
| Riva | 12 | 348.9 |
| Baglietto | 6 | 295 |

| BRANDS | YACHTS | LOA (M) |
|---|---|---|
| Benetti | 39 | 1943 |
| Azimut | 24 | 675.6 |
| Overmarine | 14 | 544 |
| Maiora | 6 | 165.8 |
| Rossi Navi | 4 | 208.6 |
| Codecasa | 2 | 86 |
| CBI Navi | 1 | 77 |
| Vismara | 1 | 27.5 |
| VSY | 1 | 62.1 |
| Perini Navi | 4 | 228 |

# EMPIRE BUILDING

*With full yards all along its Mediterranean and Adriatic coast, Italy has four times as many superyachts on the way as its nearest rival nation*

Valentino:
46.2m Picchiotti motor yacht
*TM Blue One*

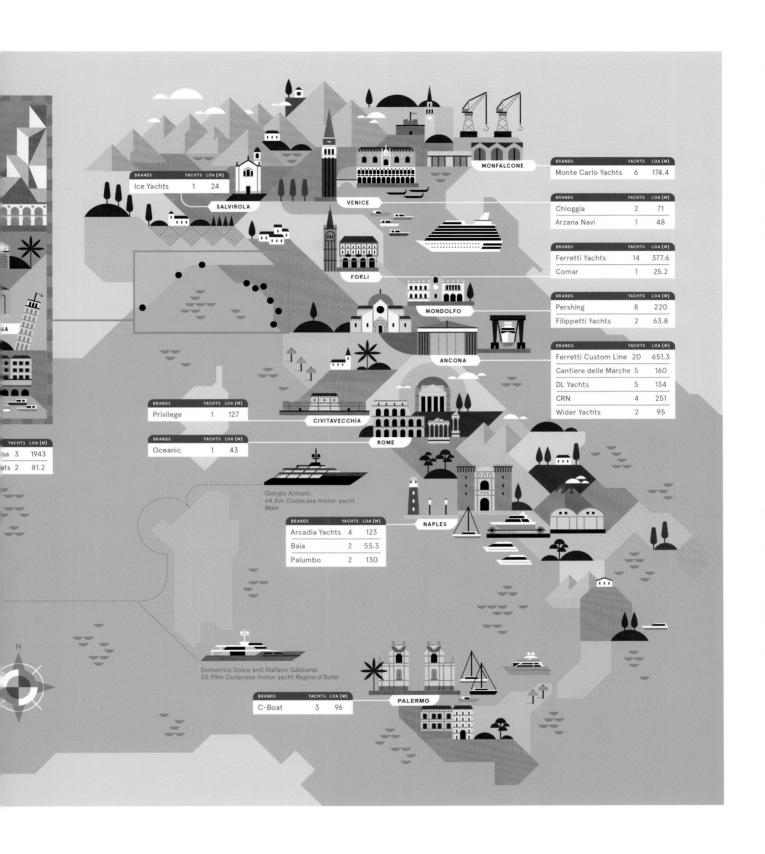

| BRANDS | YACHTS | LOA (M) |
| --- | --- | --- |
| Ice Yachts | 1 | 24 |

SALVIROLA

VENICE

MONFALCONE

| BRANDS | YACHTS | LOA (M) |
| --- | --- | --- |
| Monte Carlo Yachts | 6 | 174.4 |

| BRANDS | YACHTS | LOA (M) |
| --- | --- | --- |
| Chioggia | 2 | 71 |
| Arzana Navi | 1 | 48 |

FORLI

| BRANDS | YACHTS | LOA (M) |
| --- | --- | --- |
| Ferretti Yachts | 14 | 377.6 |
| Comar | 1 | 25.2 |

MONDOLFO

| BRANDS | YACHTS | LOA (M) |
| --- | --- | --- |
| Pershing | 8 | 220 |
| Filippetti Yachts | 2 | 63.8 |

ANCONA

| BRANDS | YACHTS | LOA (M) |
| --- | --- | --- |
| Ferretti Custom Line | 20 | 651.3 |
| Cantiere delle Marche | 5 | 160 |
| DL Yachts | 5 | 134 |
| CRN | 4 | 251 |
| Wider Yachts | 2 | 95 |

| BRANDS | YACHTS | LOA (M) |
| --- | --- | --- |
| Privilege | 1 | 127 |

CIVITAVECCHIA

| BRANDS | YACHTS | LOA (M) |
| --- | --- | --- |
| Oceanic | 1 | 43 |

ROME

Giorgio Armani:
64.8m Codecasa motor yacht
*Main*

| BRANDS | YACHTS | LOA (M) |
| --- | --- | --- |
| Arcadia Yachts | 4 | 123 |
| Baia | 2 | 55.3 |
| Palumbo | 2 | 130 |

NAPLES

| YACHTS | LOA (M) |
| --- | --- |
| 3 | 1943 |
| 2 | 81.2 |

Domenico Dolce and Stefano Gabbana:
50.99m Codecasa motor yacht *Regina d'Italia*

| BRANDS | YACHTS | LOA (M) |
| --- | --- | --- |
| C-Boat | 3 | 96 |

PALERMO

GREENLAND

ICELAND

# NORTHERN
# HIGHLIGHTS

*With Sanlorenzo's go-anywhere 460Exp,
you can cruise wherever the mood and your green,
efficient engines take you*

# Northern Highlights

Design: **Olga Günther**
Art Direction: **Nina Hundt**
Client: ***BOAT International***

This infographic created for *BOAT International* magazine features the adventures of Sanlorenzo's superyacht 460Exp in the Northern Europe. The map illustrates places explored by the superyacht on a luxury cruise in the Baltic, Scandinavia, and the Arctic, from the historic city of St. Petersburg to the coast of Iceland.

# Google × Dufan Information Map

. . . . . . . . . . . . . . . . . . . . . . . . . . . . .

Agency: **Bujukrayu**
Design: **Jumping Space Studio**
Client: **Google Indonesia, Dufan**

Dunia Fantasi, more popularly known as Dufan, first opened to the public in Jakarta on August 29, 1985, and became the first and the largest outdoor theme park in Indonesia. Dufan is the largest edutainment place in Indonesia that provides experience to visitors to fantasize around the world through high-tech rides. Dufan is divided into eight regions namely Indonesia, Jakarta, Asia, Eropa, Amerika, Yunani, Hikayat, and Kalila.

In cooperation with Dufan, Google Indonesia tries to re-create an information map that provides information and guidance to visitors about places and a variety of interesting rides in Dufan.

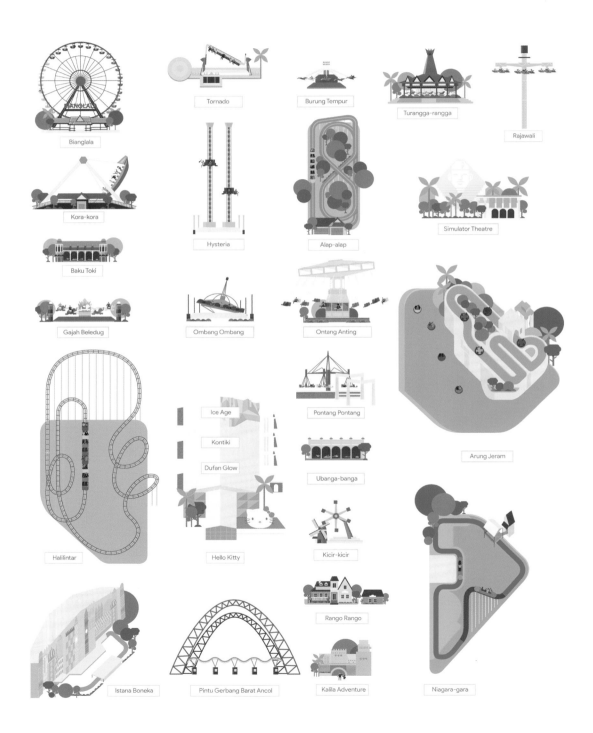

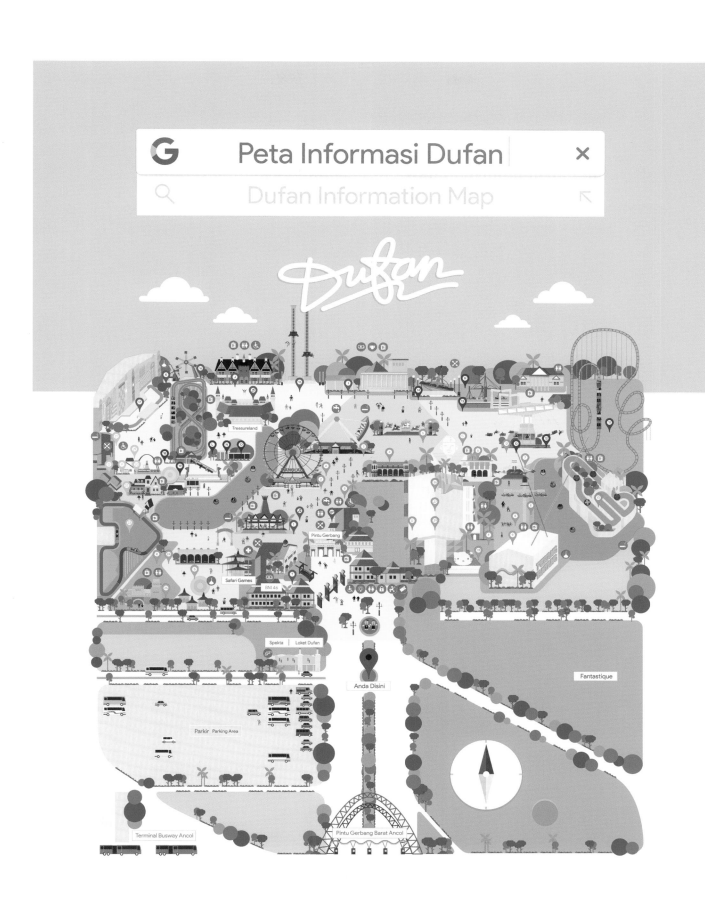

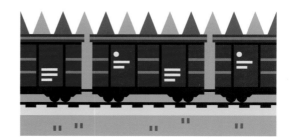

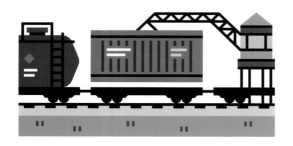

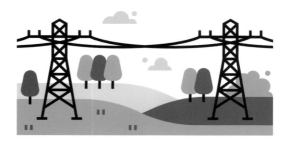

# Latvia in EXPO 2017 Astana

Design: **Agris Bobrovs**
Art Direction: **Agris Bobrovs**
Creative Direction: **Ansis Egle**
Client: **Latvian Chamber of Commerce and Industry**

World Expo 2017 was taking place in Astana, Kazakhstan and the Expo's theme was "Future Energy." The idea of the Latvian Pavilion "Energy in Our Nature" bears a dual significance: the "nature" can refer to the environment where Latvian people live and derive energy; it can also refer to the nature of the Latvian—very energetic and laborious—this nature is in their genes and sometimes it helps them to achieve the impossible. It is the story about the future energy of Latvia, about the Latvian people and events, and about what makes Latvians what they are. Agris has created the illustrated map of Latvia and a set of spot illustrations representing the companies from Latvia that have participated in the Expo.

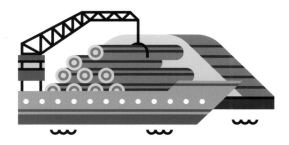

# Game of Thrones Flat Illustrations

......................................................................

Design: **Laura Palumbo**

This is Laura Palumbo's personal project—her own interpretation of Westeros—the main place in the first books of *Game of Thrones*. She wanted to interpret the saga as if it was written and illustrated for children, with a lighter vision of the whole concept.

# Great Places of Amsterdam Map

Agency: **in60seconds**
Design: **Lienke Raben**

This visualization of Amsterdam is a true treasure map containing all of these hidden gems on which seasoned Amsterdam locals can discover their favorite places and be proud of the city they love. But it is also a treasure map which helps tourists to avoid the tourist traps and discover what Amsterdam can really be like. The designers wanted the map to be full of illustrations and names, so that every time the viewer checks it, he/she will discover new places. The map is hand-drawn on Wacom Cintiq and printed in A2 size. It is available as a poster and as a handy foldable mini-map, with all the locations and addresses on the back.

# London Property Development Brochure

Design: **Saskia Rasink**
Art Direction: **Socrates Communications, Oliver Dadak**

A map with building illustrations for a luxury property development brochure at 130 Jermyn Street in London.

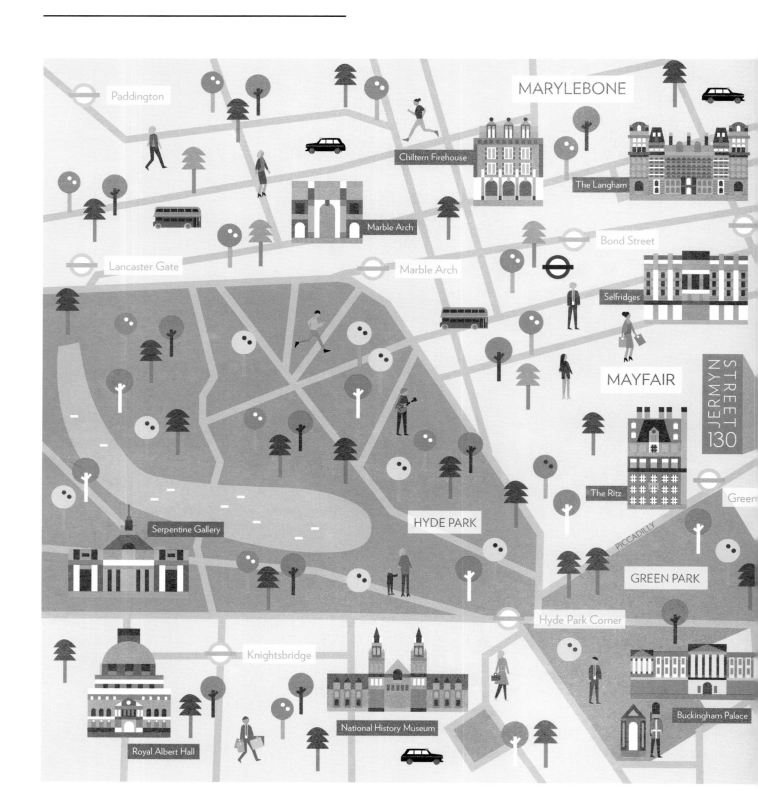

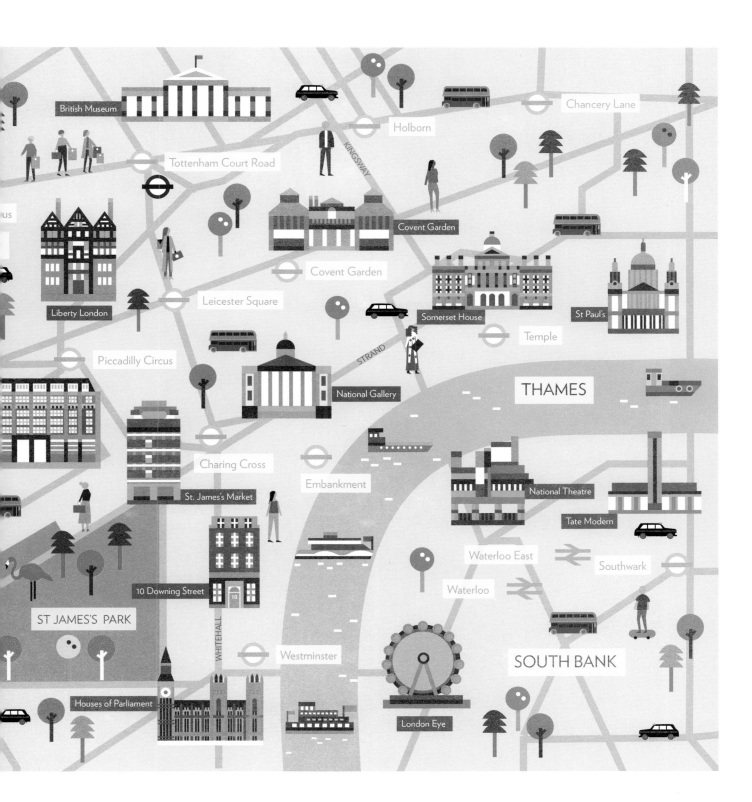

British Museum

Holborn

Chancery Lane

KINGSWAY

Tottenham Court Road

Covent Garden

Covent Garden

Liberty London

Leicester Square

Somerset House

St Paul's

Temple

Piccadilly Circus

STRAND

National Gallery

THAMES

Charing Cross

Embankment

National Theatre

Tate Modern

St. James's Market

Waterloo East

Southwark

Waterloo

10 Downing Street

WHITEHALL

ST JAMES'S PARK

Westminster

SOUTH BANK

Houses of Parliament

London Eye

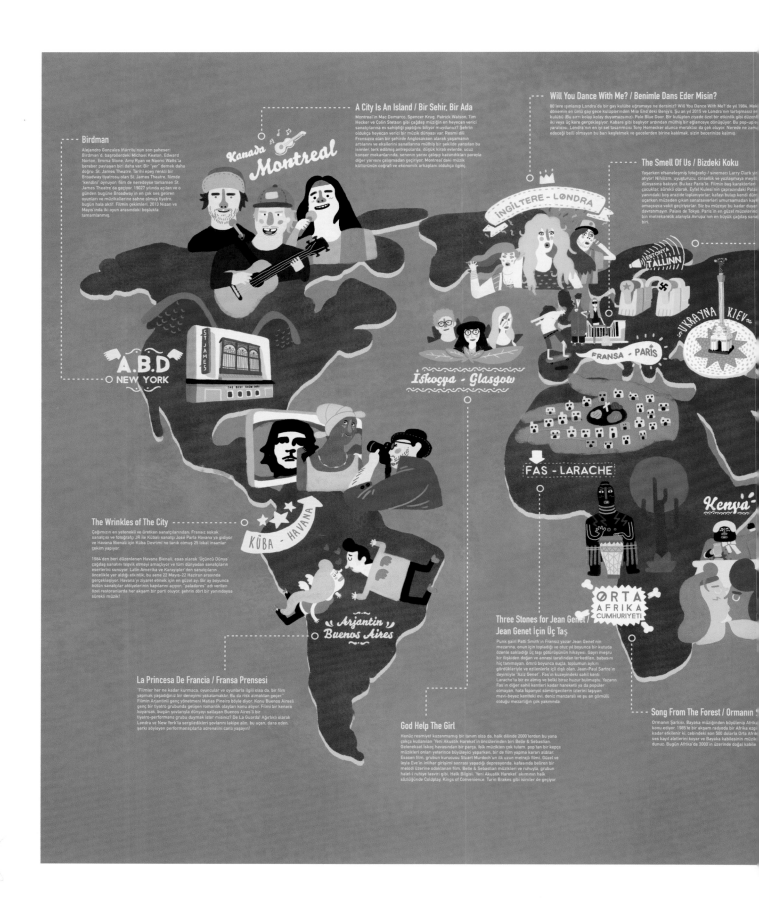

### Birdman

Alejandro Gonzales Iñárritu'nun son şaheseri Birdman d, başrollerdeki Michael Keaton, Edward Norton, Emma Stone, Amy Ryan ve Naomi Watts'la beraber paylaşan biri daha var. Bir "yer" demek daha doğru. St. James Theatre. Tarihi epey renkli bir Broadway tiyatrosu olan St. James Theatre, filmde "kendini" oynuyor. film de neredeyse tamamen St. James Theatre'da geçiyor. 1927 yılında açılan ve o günden bugüne Broadway'in en çok ses getiren oyunları ve müzikallerine sahne olmuş tiyatro, bugün hala aktif. Filmin çekimleri, 2013 Nisan ve Mayıs'ında iki oyun arasındaki boşlukta tamamlanmış.

### A City Is An Island / Bir Şehir, Bir Ada

Montreal'in Mac Demarco, Spencer Krug, Patrick Watson, Tim Hecker ve Colin Stetson gibi çağdaş müziğin en heyecan verici sanatçılarına ev sahipliği yaptığını biliyor muydunuz? Şehrin oldukça heyecan verici bir müzik dünyası var. Resmi dili Fransızca olan bir şehirde Anglosakson olarak yaşamanın artılarını ve eksilerini sanatlarına müthiş bir şekilde yansıtan bu isimler, terk edilmiş antrepolarda, düşük kiralı evlerde, ucuz konser mekanlarında, senenin yarısı çalışıp kazandıkları parayla diğer yarısını çalışmadan geçiriyor. Montreal'daki müzik kültürünün coğrafi ve ekonomik arkaplanı oldukça ilginç.

### Will You Dance With Me? / Benimle Dans Eder Misin?

80 lere ışınlanıp Londra'da bir gay kulübe uğramaya ne dersiniz? Will You Dance With Me? de yıl 1984. Mekan dönemin en ünlü gay gece kulüplerinden Mile End'deki Benjy's. Şu an yıl 2015 ve Londra'nın tartışmasız en kulübü (Bu sırrı kolay kolay duyamazsınız). Pale Blue Door. Bir kulüpten ziyade özel bir etkinlik gibi düzenlenen iki veya üç kere açılan bu barı gizli tutuyorlar. Kabare gibi başlıyor ardından müthiş bir eğlenceye dönüşüyor. Bu pop-up'ın yaratıcısı, Londra'nın en iyi set tasarımcısı Tony Homecker olunca meraklısı da çok oluyor. Nerede ne zaman açacağı belli olmayan bu barı keşfetmek ve gecelerden birine katılmak, sizin becerinize kalmış.

### The Smell Of Us / Bizdeki Koku

Yaşarken efsaneleşmiş fotoğrafçı / sinemacı Larry Clark yine atıyor! Nihilizm, uyuşturucu, cinsellik ve yozlaşmaya meyilli dünyasına bakıyor. Bu kez Paris'te. Filmin baş karakterleri çocuklar, sürekli olarak, Eyfel Kulesi'nin çaprazındaki Palais yanındaki boş arazide toplanıyorlar. kafayı bulup kendi dünyalarında uçarken müzeden çıkan sanatseverleri umursamadan kayıtsızca amaçsızca vakit geçiriyorlar. Siz bu müzeye bu kadar duyarsız davranmayın. Palais de Tokyo. Paris'in en güzel müzelerinden biri. bin metrekarelik alanıyla Avrupa'nın en büyük çağdaş sanat merkezi.

### The Wrinkles of The City

Çağımızın en yetenekli ve üretken sanatçılarından. Fransız sokak sanatçısı ve fotoğrafçı JR ile Kübalı sanatçı José Parla Havana'ya gidiyor ve Havana Bienali için Küba Devrimi'ne tanık olmuş 25 lokal insanın çekim yapıyor.

1984'den beri düzenlenen Havana Bienali, esas olarak 'Üçüncü Dünya' çağdaş sanatını teşvik etmeyi amaçlıyor ve tüm dünyadan sanatçıların eserlerini sunuyor. Latin Amerika ve Karayipler'den sanatçıların öncelikle yer aldığı etkinlik, bu sene 22 Mayıs–22 Haziran arasında gerçekleşiyor. Havana'yı ziyaret etmek için en güzel ay. Bir ay boyunca bütün sanatçılar atölyelerinin kapılarını açıyor. 'paladares' adı verilen özel restoranlarda her akşam bir parti oluyor, şehrin dört bir yanındaysa sürekli müzik!

### La Princesa De Francia / Fransa Prensesi

"Filmler her ne kadar kurmaca, oyuncular ve oyunlarla ilgili olsa da, bir film yapmak yaşadığınız bir deneyimi yakalamaktır. Bu da risk almaktan geçer." Filmin Arjantinli genç yönetmeni Matias Pineiro böyle diyor. Konu Buenos Aires'li genç bir tiyatro grubunda gelişen romantik olaylar konu alıyor. Filmi bir kenara koyarsak, bugün oyunlarıyla dünyayı sallayan Buenos Aires'li bir tiyatro-performans grubu duymak ister misiniz? De La Guarda! Ağırlıklı olarak Londra ve New York'ta sergiledikleri şovlarını takibe alın, bu uçan, dans eden, şarkı söyleyen performanslarla adrenalini canlı yaşayın!

### God Help The Girl

Henüz resmiyet kazanmamış bir tanım olsa da, halk dilinde 2000'lerden bu yana çokça kullanılan 'Yeni Akustik Hareket'in öncülerinden biri Belle & Sebastian. Geleneksel folk havasından bir parça. folk müzikten çok tutam, pop'tan bir kepçe müzikleri onları yeterince büyüleyici yaparken, bir de film yapma kararı aldılar. Esasen film, grubun kurucusu Stuart Murdoch'un ilk uzun metrajlı filmi. Güzel ve leyla Eve'in intihar girişimi sonrası yaşadığı depresyonda, kafasında beliren bir melodi üzerine odaklanan film. Belle & Sebastian müzikleri ve ruhuyla, grubun halet-i ruhiye tasviri gibi. Halk Bilgisi: Yeni Akustik Hareket' akımının halk sözlüğünde Coldplay, Kings of Convenience, Turin Brakes gibi isimler de geçiyor.

### Three Stones for Jean Genet / Jean Genet İçin Üç Taş

Punk şairi Patti Smith'in Fransız yazar Jean Genet'nin mezarına, onun için topladığı ve otuz yıl boyunca bir kutuda özenle sakladığı üç taşı götürüşünün hikayesi. Gayri meşru bir ilişkiden doğan ve annesi tarafından terkedilen, babasını hiç tanımayan, ömrü boyunca suçla, toplumun aykırı gördükleriyle ve ezilenlerle içli dışlı olan, Jean-Paul Sartre'in deyimiyle "Aziz Genet". Fas'ın kuzeyindeki sahil kenti Larache'a bir ev almış ve belki biraz huzur bulmuştu. Yazarın Fas'ın diğer sahil kentleri kadar hareketli ya da popüler olmayan, hala İspanyol sömürgecilerin izlerini taşıyan mavi-beyaz kentleri evi, deniz manzaralı ve şu an gömülü olduğu mezarlıktan çok yakınında.

### Song From The Forest / Ormanın Şarkısı

Ormanın Şarkısı, Bayaka müziğinden büyülenip Afrika konu ediyor. 1985'te bir akşam radyoda bir Afrika ezgisi kadar etkilenir ki, cebindeki son 500 dolarla Orta Afrika ses kayıt aletlerini koyar ve Bayaka kabilesinin müzik dunusi. Bugün Afrika'da 3000'in üzerinde doğal kabil...

# !F Map Poster

Agency: **Dükkan Creative**
Design: **Murat Kalkavan**
Creative Direction: **Orkun Demirelli**
Copywriter: **Zeynep Erekli**

!f Istanbul International Independent Film Festival was founded in 2001. In every February and March, it hosts some 80,000 film buffs and celebrated filmmakers from around the world.

### ttuules / Rüzgarların Arasında

garların Arasında 1941 Haziran ında, Alman işgaline karşılık Rusya tarafından evlerinden zorla çıkarılarak Sibirya'ya trenlere bindirilen. ilarca açlığa, soğuğa, zor çalışma koşullarına ve ölüme göğüs germek durumunda kalan yüz binleri anmak için yazılmış bir şiir. iki ateş nda kalan Tallinn in öyküsü. Bir yanda Nazi ordusu, diğer yanda Rus totalitarizmiyle bu arada kalmışlık Tallinn sokaklarında hissediliyor. n şehirdeki işgal müzesinde "işgal" kelimesi çoğul kullanılmış. Museum of Occupations. Ziyaretçileri biri Nazi işareti, diğeri kızıl yıldız an iki tren karşılıyor ve müzeye bunların arasından geçerek giriliyor.

### Maïdan / Meydan

Sergei Loznitsa imzalı Meydan, Ukrayna'yı 2013-2014 boyunca dönüştüren devrimin başlangıç sürecini gözler önüne seriyor. Kievli yönetimenin gözünden, önce 500 bin kişinin katıldığı barışçıl gösterilere sonra da polisle çatışmalara uzanarak, sokaklara sıçrayan isyanın gelişimini büyük Meydan ın etrafından izliyoruz. İstanbul için Taksim Meydanı, Londra için Piccadilly Circus ne ise, Kiev için Maïdan o. İkinci Dünya Savaşı nda Ruslar, işgale gelen Alman askerlerinin şehrin kalbinin atığı bu noktada toplanacağını biliyorlardı ve önceden meydana düşecikleri yüksek miktarda patlayıcıyı doğru zamanda harekete geçirip hem Alman ordusuna, hem de meydana büyük zarar vermişlerdi. 1986 öğrenci eylemleri. 1999 seçimlerinin ardından gelen dev protesto dalgası ve Turuncu Devrim, hepsi bu meydanda gerçekleşti. Türkçe adıyla 'Bağımsızlık Meydanı' yani Maïdan Nezalezhnosti, meydan gibi meydan.

### Tomorrow We Disappear / Yarın Yok Olacağız

1950'lerden günümüze gelmiş belki de dünyanın en büyük sanatçı kolonisi. 3000 bin aileden oluşuyor. Aralarında, dünyanın dört bir yanında geleneksel Hint sanatını temsil edenler de var, sihirbazlar da, akrobatlar da... Yoksullar, donsuzlar ve gecekondu insanları. Bu tarz hikayelerde ilk önce "yoksullar" sonra "sanatçılar" gelir. Bu filmde ise alt metin bolca ilham olmak üzere kurulu. Hindistan'ın başkenti Yeni Delhi'de yaşayan Kathputli Kolonisi, biz Türkiye vatandaşları için çok şaşırılmayacak bir tehdit ile karşı karşıya. Yaşadıkları mahalle bir gökdelen ve alışveriş merkezi inşaatı için müteahhitlere satılmak üzere. Tanıdık geldi, değil mi?

### The Dark Horse / Kayıp Şampiyon

Yaşam boyu depresyon oranının %12.6 olduğu Yeni Zelanda'da geçen film, çağ yangını manik depresif hastalıkla uğraşan eski yerli satranç şampiyonu Genesis Potini'nin hayatını anlatıyor. Psikiyatri kliniğinden salıverildikten sonra, kardeşi Ariki'nin suçla haşır neşir hayatına dahil olan Potini, huzuru kendisine benzer sorunlu çocukların bulunduğu bir satranç kulübünde buluyor.

### yo Tribe / Tokyo Çetesi

lle kendi kuşağının en gözüpek yönetmenlerinden olan ono. Yakuza filmi gibi başlayıp hip-hop resitaline bir filmle Tokyo'yu ayağımıza getiriyor. Ama bu listopik bir Tokyo. Şehir mahallelere bölünmüş, bu ar Yakuza çeteleri tarafından kontrol ediliyor. ığı un adeta filmin bir karakteri gibi olduğu, muazzam koreografileriyle aklınızı başınızdan alacak Tokyo hem gözler hem de kulaklar için bir şölen! nüzün gerçek Tokyo'sunda Yakuza nın mevzilendiği ise Kabukicho. Kentin 'red light district'i, aşkın ın, şimdi satıldığı, silahların patladığı, sert ve karanlık halle.

### ies Of Our Lives / Yaşamımızdan Hikayeler

Of Our Lives ın konusu, Kenya'da gay olmak. Nairobili multidisipliner bir kolektifi, kendilerini homoseksüel, lezbiyen, biseksüel, trans ve interseks gören bireylerin deneyimlerini ve tanıklıklarını arşivlemeye başlar. nımızdan Hikayeler adını verdikleri projeyle Kenya da eşcinsel olma minin ne demek olduğunu araştırmaya koyulurlar. Bunu biliyor muydunuz, 'da eşcinsellik halen bir "suç" olarak kabul ediliyor ve kendi cinsiyetinden cinsel temas suçuna, 5 ila 14 yıl arasında hapis cezası veriliyor.

dığı hikayesini uğu müzikten o t alır. Çantasına nu biliyor muy-

### 52 Tuesdays

Sıradan bir gün, uyanıyorsunuz, anneniz size gülümsüyor ve "Ben transım." diyor. Muhtemelen gün, sıradanlıktan çıkardı değil mi? Bu geçiş döneminde, annesini haftada bir gedece Salı günleri görmeye başlayacak Billie'nin kendi cinsel araştırma sürecinde de başlayacağı aşikar. Avustralya sinemasının genç ve yetenekli isimlerinden Sophie Hyde'ın son filmi 52 Tuesdays / 52 Salı trans psikolojisine derin ve samimi bir perspektiften bakmayı başarmış filmlerden. Yönetmenin geçtiğimiz sene Berlin Altın Ayı ve Sundance En İyi Yönetmen ödülünü aldığını eklemeyi unutmayalım. Bir trans olacaksanız Adelaide'de yaşamak iyi bir fikir olabilir zira Adelaide çeşitli dergiler ve araştırma kurumları tarafından düzenlenen Dünyanın En Yaşanabilir Şehirleri anketlerinde kültürel nitelik, iklim, yaşama ücreti, ve sağlık, suç oranı gibi sosyal koşullar bakımından sürekli ilk 3 veya 5'te...

# Amzei Map

Design: **Paula Rusu**
Client: **Ion Creangă Children's Theatre in Bucharest**

Ion Creangă Children's Theatre in Bucharest needed an illustrated map to highlight the route between their two venues. This was an extremely fun project as Paula Rusu loves drawing maps. She has spent quite a lot of hours in Google Maps investigating the buildings in the area. She can now say that she knows that part of Bucharest by heart.

# Compass Quarterly Luxury Winter Holiday

........................................

Design: **Saskia Rasink**
Art Direction: **Jeff Lai**
Client: **Campass**, *Compass Quarterly*

*Compass Quarterly* is the magazine of a tech-driven real estate platform called Compass. In this issue, real estate agents show their favorite Winter get-aways in different parts of the USA. In Luxury Winter Holiday maps, the viewer can find the top six cities: Miami, Washington DC, Aspen, San Francisco, New York City, and the Hamptons.

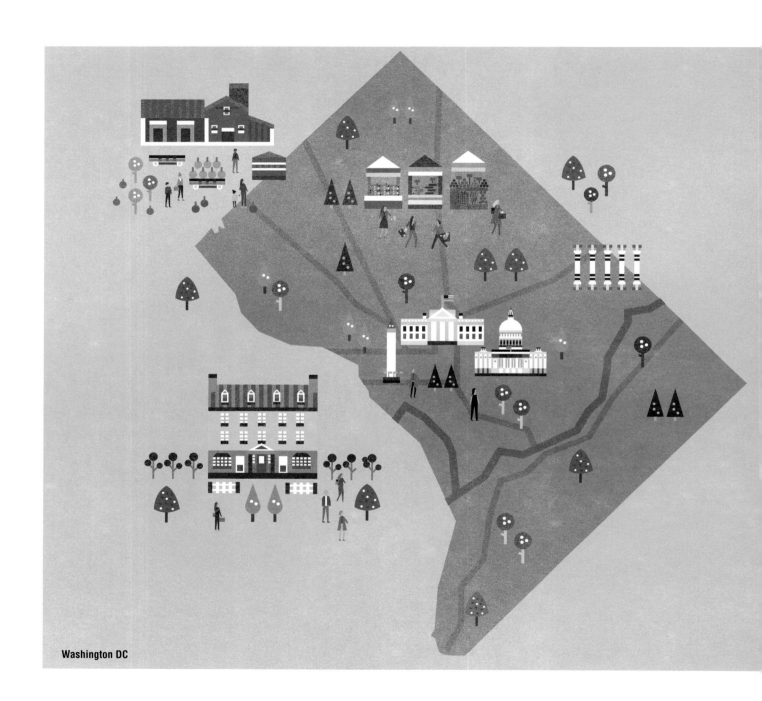

Washington DC

New York City

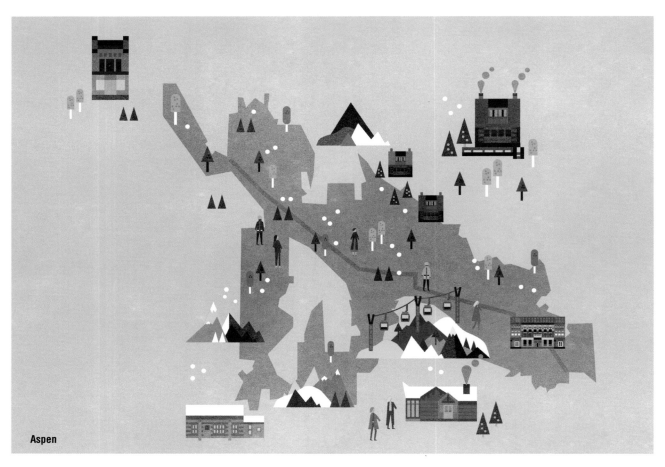

Aspen

San Francisco

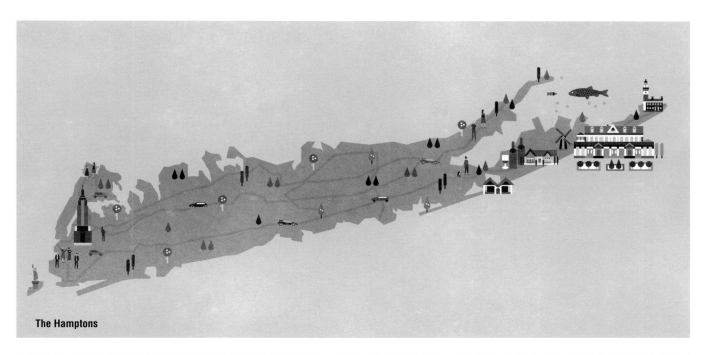

The Hamptons

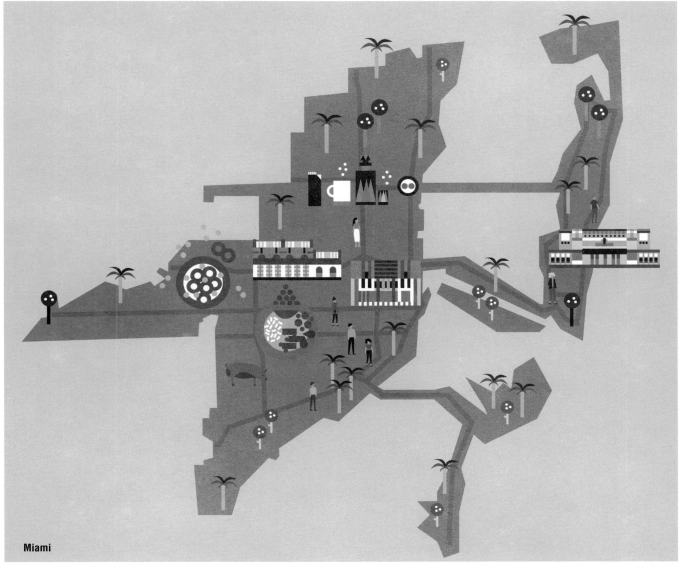

Miami

# Illustrated Map of Osaka

Design: **Ngooi Su Hwa**
Client: **Malaysia Airlines**

This is an illustration for an in-flight magazine of Malaysia Airlines, depicting the hearty street food, architectures, historical landmarks, and the blooms of cherry blossoms in the lively city of Osaka, Japan.

# Illustrated Map of Hong Kong

Design: **Ngooi Su Hwa**
Client: **Malaysia Airlines**

This is an illustration for an in-flight magazine of Malaysia Airlines, depicting the typical scenes of Hong Kong—a city that combines the nostalgic old-world charm and cutting-edge modernity.

# Fuel My City Map Illustration

Design: **Ngooi Su Hwa**
Client: **Caltex Malaysia**

At Caltex, they do not just fuel vehicles; they fuel people too by inspiring them to experience fun road trips in Malaysia. This is an illustration for Fuel My City Campaign, a platform driven by Caltex for various road trippers, to unravel the hidden gem locations and exciting things to do in Malaysia.

NG HAN

2 ·· ·· ··

Restoran
OK Seafood

3 CALTEX

4 ·· 5 ··

l & Rojak

myBurgerLab

Nasi Lemak
Bambung

HANEEF

1 ··

Hard Rock Cafe

2 ··

Hang Tuah Mall

4 ··

Grind Shack
@ AEON

5 ··

Kampung Baru

3 ··

The Shore
@ Malacca River

6 ··

Cameron Highlands

BRIAN

1 LEVAIN

Levain Boulangerie
& Patisserie

2 ··

Bank Negara
Malaysia Museum
and Art Gallery

3 美真林
MERCHANT'S LANE

Merchant's Lane

4 ··

View Rooftop Bar

5 CALTEX

LED Show

pang

NADEA

1 ··

2 ··

Rekreasi Air Terjun
Serendah

DENNIS

1 CALTEX

2 ··

Bukit Gasing

3 ··

Jim Xuan
Dim Sum

4 OREGI

3 ··

Panasonic National
Spot Centre

Linggi Beach

OREGI

5 CALTEX

6 ··

Jumpstreet

ERRIE

2 CALTEX

3 awesome
canteen

Awesome Canteen

ANA ABU

1 ··

Fuga Village

2 ··

Ayer Keroh

5 ··

Jonker Street

4 ·· BRATS

Brats

5 ··

Barlai Bar

3 ··

Klebang
Original

4 CALTEX

# Sky Map

Design: **Federica Fragapane**
Art Direction: **Federica Fragapane**
Client: *Corriere della Sera*

This is a piece of artwork for the column Visual Data on *La Lettura*, the cultural supplement of *Corriere Della Sera*. The project is a representation of the world, seen through the eyes of a pilot, inspired by Mark Vanhoenacker's book *Skyfaring: A Journey with a Pilot*. On the map are indicated the airports and the regions of airspace. For each continent, the 10 countries with the highest number of airline passengers have been selected. For each country are indicated: the total number of passenger and number of waypoints (the reference points used to create the routes). Each waypoint is defined by a name and the most interesting ones have been illustrated.

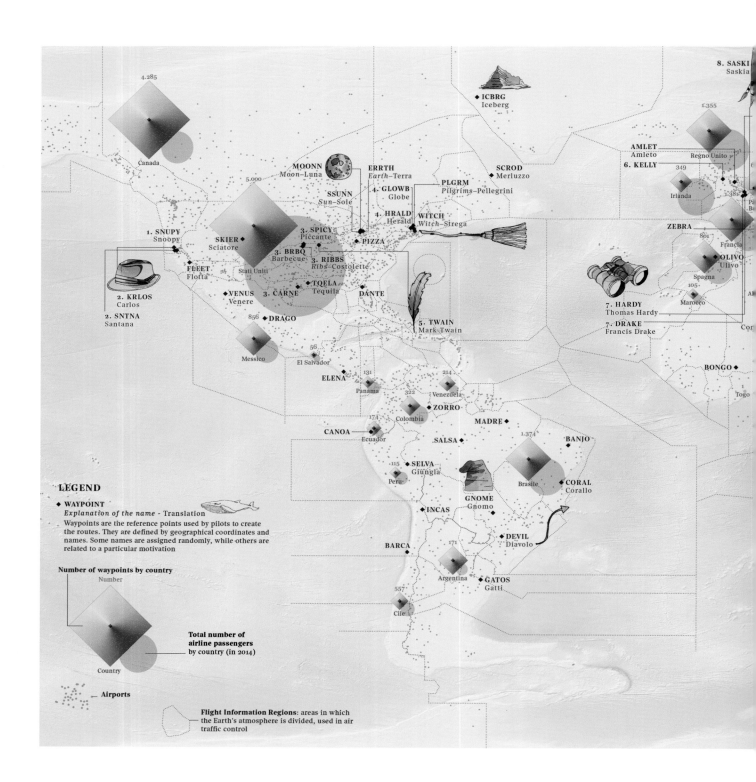

LEGEND

◆ **WAYPOINT**
*Explanation of the name* - Translation
Waypoints are the reference points used by pilots to create the routes. They are defined by geographical coordinates and names. Some names are assigned randomly, while others are related to a particular motivation.

**Number of waypoints by country**
Number

Country

**Total number of airline passengers by country (in 2014)**

Airports

**Flight Information Regions:** areas in which the Earth's atmosphere is divided, used in air traffic control

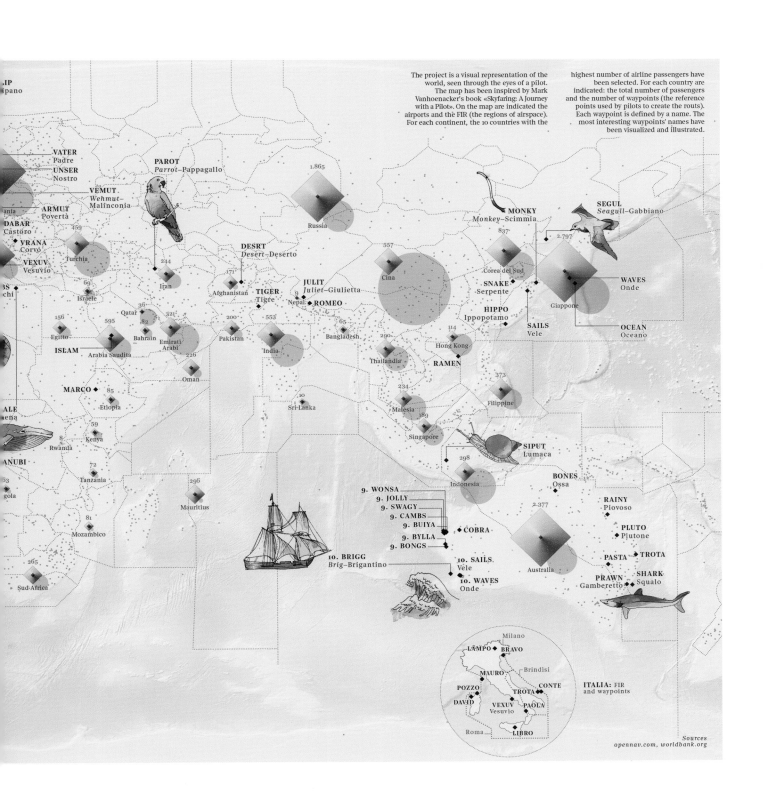

The project is a visual representation of the world, seen through the eyes of a pilot. The map has been inspired by Mark Vanhoenacker's book «Skyfaring: A Journey with a Pilot». On the map are indicated the airports and the FIR (the regions of airspace). For each continent, the 10 countries with the highest number of airline passengers have been selected. For each country are indicated: the total number of passengers and the number of waypoints (the reference points used by pilots to create the routs). Each waypoint is defined by a name. The most interesting waypoints' names have been visualized and illustrated.

**VATER** Padre
**UNSER** Nostro
**VEMUT** Wehmut–Malinconia
**ARMUT** Povertà
**DABAR** Castoro
**VRANA** Corvo
**VEXUV** Vesuvio
**ISLAM**

**PAROT** Parrot–Pappagallo

**DESRT** Desert–Deserto

**JULIT** Juliet–Giulietta
**ROMEO**

**TIGER** Tigre

**MONKY** Monkey–Scimmia

**SEGUL** Seagull–Gabbiano

**SNAKE** Serpente
**HIPPO** Ippopotamo
**SAILS** Vele
**WAVES** Onde
**OCEAN** Oceano
**RAMEN**

**MARCO**

**ALE**
**ANUBI**

**SIPUT** Lumaca

**BONES** Ossa

**RAINY** Piovoso
**PLUTO** Plutone
**PASTA**
**TROTA**
**PRAWN** Gamberetto
**SHARK** Squalo

1.865 Russia
459
Turchia
69 Israele
36 Qatar
156 Egitto
595
82 Bahrain
321
Emirati Arabi
226 Oman
244 Iran
171 Afghanistan
9 Nepal
200 Pakistan
553 India
65 Bangladesh
290 Thailandia
10 Sri-Lanka
234 Malesia
189 Singapore
85 Etiopia
59 Kenya
8 Rwanda
72 Tanzania
296 Mauritius
81 Mozambico
265 Sud-Africa
557 Cina
837 Corea del Sud
2.797
Giappone
114 Hong Kong
373 Filippine
298 Indonesia
2.377 Australia

9. WONSA
9. JOLLY
9. SWAGY
9. CAMBS
9. BUIYA
9. BYLLA
9. BONGS
10. BRIGG Brig–Brigantino
COBRA
10. SAILS Vele
10. WAVES Onde

ITALIA: FIR and waypoints
Milano
LAMPO ◆ BRAVO
MAURO
Brindisi
POZZO
CONTE
TROTA
DAVID
VEXUV PAOLA
Vesuvio
Roma
LIBRO

Sources
opennav.com, worldbank.org

# The Atlas of Innovation

Agency: **La Tigre**
Art Direction: **Massimo Pitis, David Moretti**
Client: **Wired Italia**

"(R)Evolution," *Wired* Italia No.76 issue, is about the altas of innovation (the place of innovation). The series includes the designs of 6 maps, 6 illustrations, and 8 covers. Chapter 1 relates to Marina di Pisa, Italy—the country transforms the force of the sea waves into electricity. Chapter 2 depicts Europe (Paris, France)—Facebook gathers and categorizes a big amount of data with the aim of predicting the user's needs. Chapter 3 refers to America (Key Largo, Florida)—a laboratory anchored underwater used for training astronauts. Chapter 4 portrays Africa (Port Louis, Mauritius)—the first woman president of the Mauritius is also a biodiversity scientist who is changing the nature of her country. Chapter 5 pictures Asia (Guangzhou, China)—the rising of the new Chinese enterprises. Chapter 6 represents Oceania (Wollongong, Australia)—"Geldom," a new condom made of water.

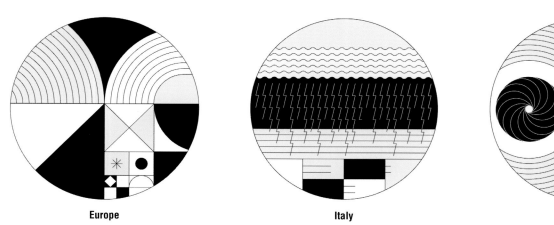

Europe

Italy

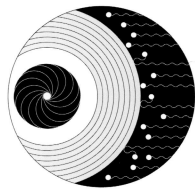

Oceania

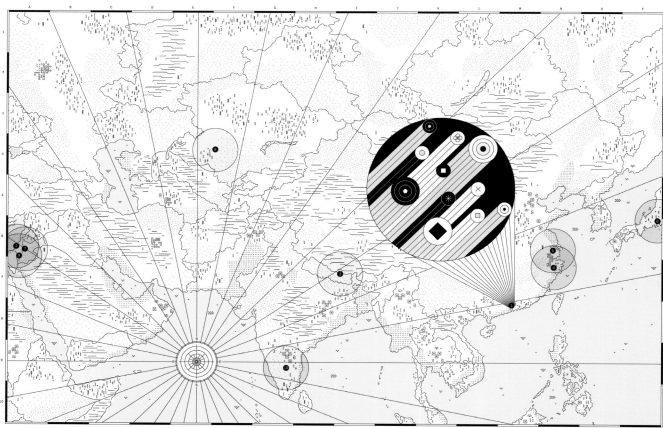

Asia

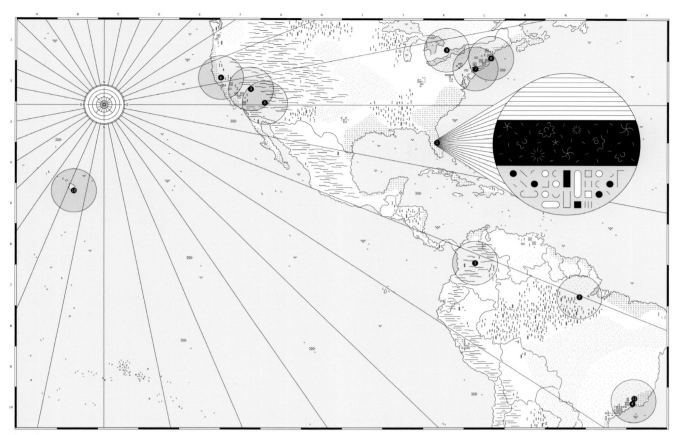

**Ameria**

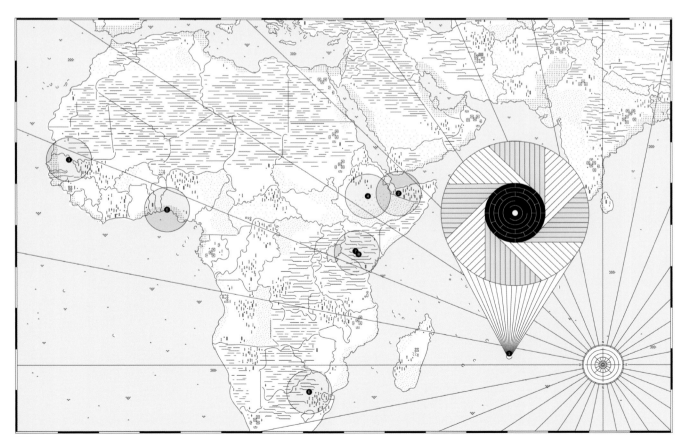

**Africa**

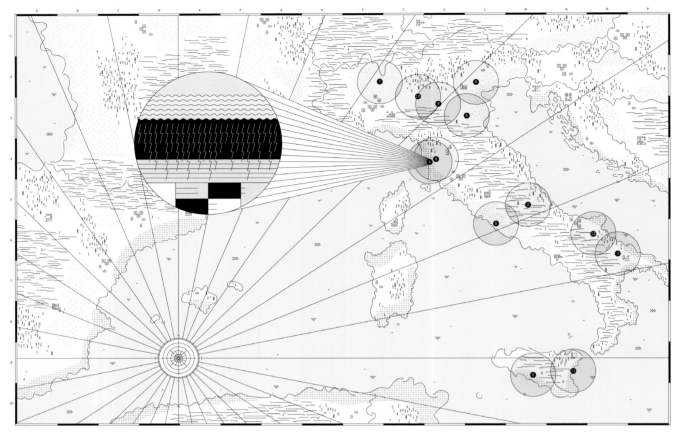

**Italia**

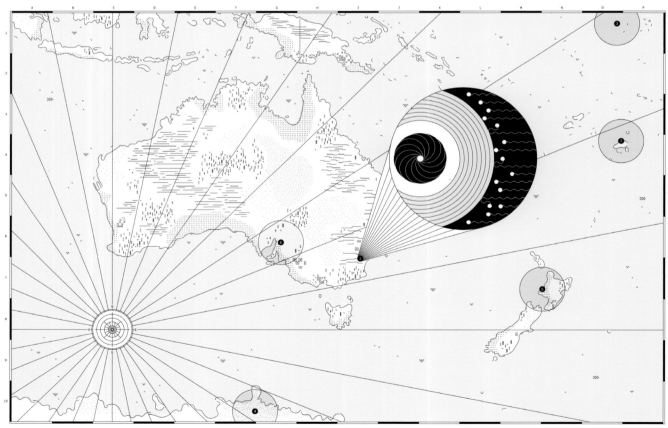

**Oceania**

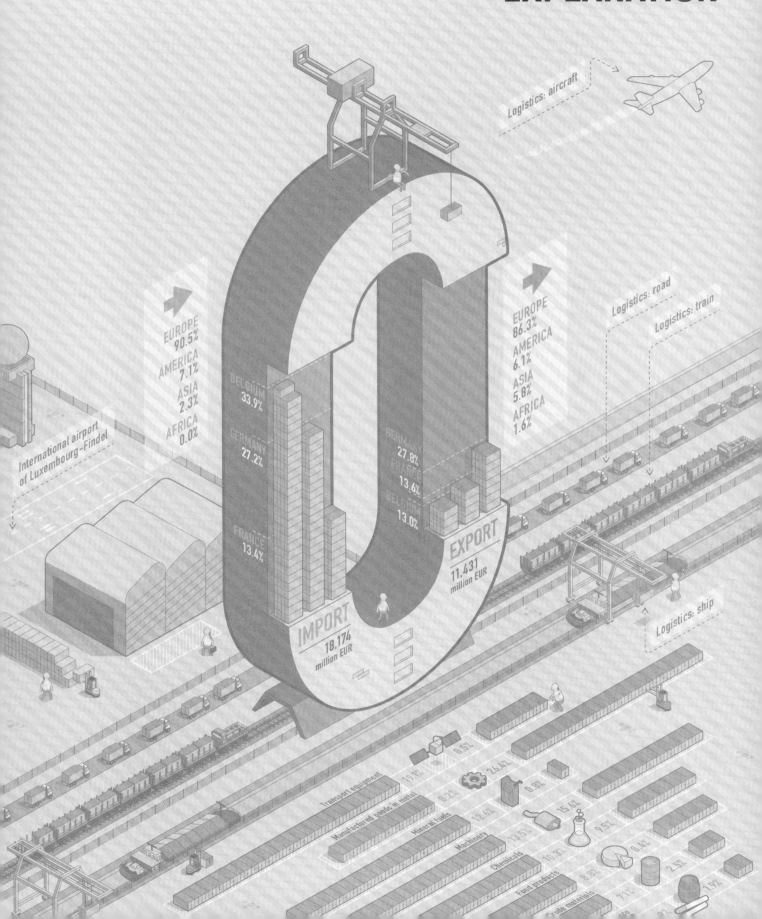

Logistics: aircraft

Logistics: road

Logistics: train

Logistics: ship

International airport
of Luxembourg-Findel

EUROPE
90.5%

AMERICA
7.1%

ASIA
2.3%

AFRICA
0.0%

EUROPE
86.3%

AMERICA
6.1%

ASIA
5.8%

AFRICA
1.6%

BELGIUM
33.9%

GERMANY
27.2%

FRANCE
13.4%

GERMANY
27.8%

FRANCE
13.6%

BELGIUM
13.0%

IMPORT
18,174
million EUR

EXPORT
11,431
million EUR

Transport equipment

Manufactured goods in metal

Mineral fuels

Machinery

Chemicals

Food Products

Crude materials

8.5%

19.1%

26.4%

0.8%

8.2%

15.6%

12.6%

9.5%

13.5%

0.6%

10.3%

2.5%

8.9%

7.1%

1.9%

........................................

Design: **Ana Cuna**
Art Direction: **Mia Johnson**
Client: *Boat International*

The infographic is designed for *Boat International* magazine's special issue of Monaco, which illustrates the marking tips and essential places of Port Hercules, the only deep-water port in Monaco. If you are one of those fortunate persons who have a yacht and want to make a stop there, this will be useful for you.

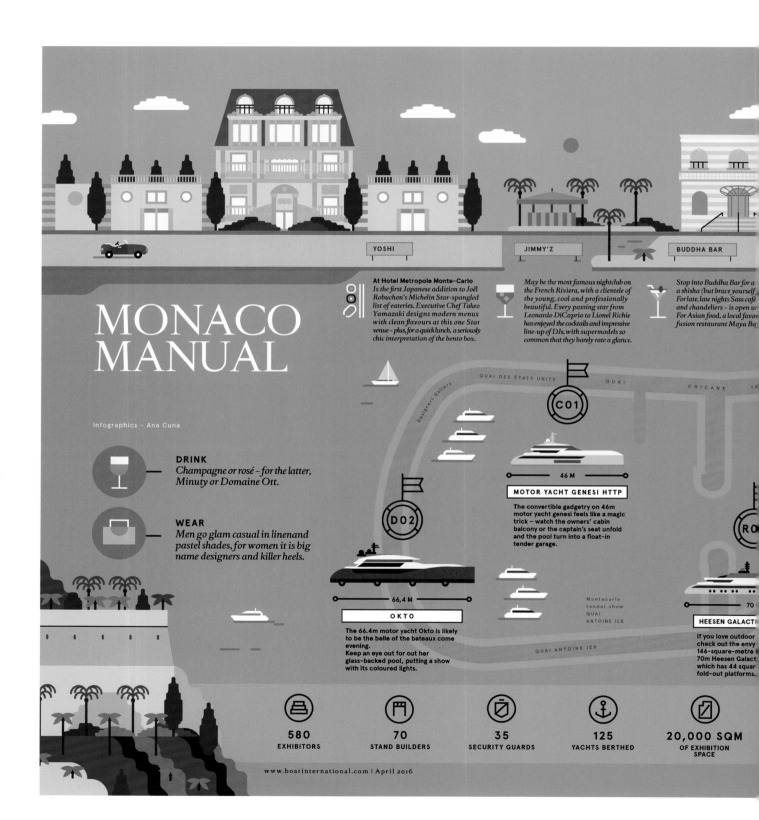

YOSHI

**At Hotel Metropole Monte-Carlo**
*Is the first Japanese addition to Joël Robuchon's Michelin Star-spangled list of eateries. Executive Chef Takeo Yamazaki designs modern menus with clean flavours at this one Star venue - plus, for a quick lunch, a seriously chic interpretation of the bento box.*

JIMMY'Z

*Maybe be the most famous nightclub on the French Riviera, with a clientele of the young, cool and professionally beautiful. Every passing star from Leonardo DiCaprio to Lionel Richie has enjoyed the cocktails and impressive line-up of DJs, with supermodels so common that they barely rate a glance.*

BUDDHA BAR

*Stop into Buddha Bar for a a shisha (but brace yourself For late, late nights Sass café and chandeliers - is open ur For Asian food, a local favo fusion restaurant Maya Ba*

# MONACO MANUAL

Infographics - Ana Cuna

**DRINK**
*Champagne or rosé - for the latter, Minuty or Domaine Ott.*

**WEAR**
*Men go glam casual in linenand pastel shades, for women it is big name designers and killer heels.*

QUAI DES ÉTATS UNITS        QUAI        CHICANE        Y

C01

46 M

**MOTOR YACHT GENESI HTTP**

The convertible gadgetry on 46m motor yacht genesi feels like a magic trick – watch the owners' cabin balcony or the captain's seat unfold and the pool turn into a float-in tender garage.

D02

RO

66,4 M

**OKTO**

The 66.4m motor yacht Okto is likely to be the belle of the bateaux come evening.
Keep an eye out for out her glass-backed pool, putting a show with its coloured lights.

Montecarlo tender show
QUAI
ANTOINE IER

70

**HEESEN GALACT**

If you love outdoor check out the envy 146-square-metre 70m Heesen Galact which has 44 squar fold-out platforms.

QUAI ANTOINE IER

**580**
EXHIBITORS

**70**
STAND BUILDERS

**35**
SECURITY GUARDS

**125**
YACHTS BERTHED

**20,000 SQM**
OF EXHIBITION SPACE

www.boatinternational.com | April 2016

MOTOR YACHT GENESI HTTP

C 01

45 M

HEESEN GALACTICA SUPERNOVA

R 01

70 M

O K T O

D 02

66,4 M

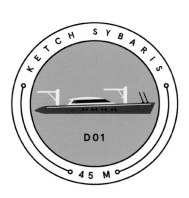

K E T C H   S Y B A R I S

D 01

45 M

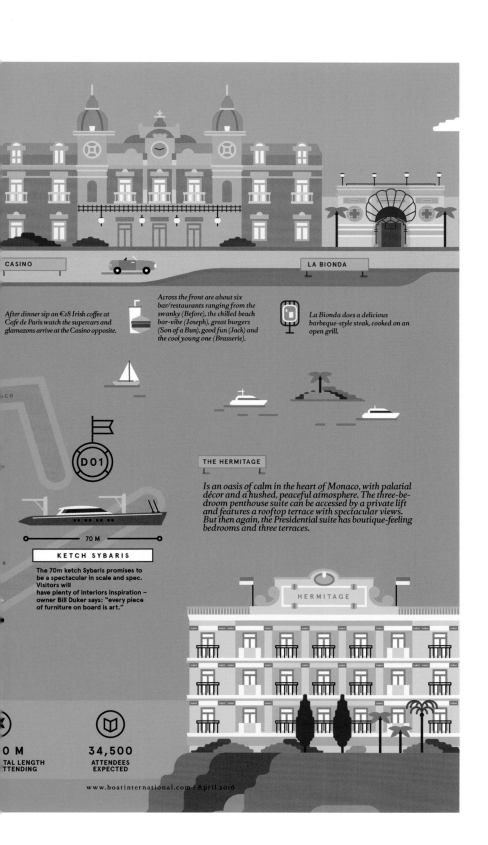

CASINO

LA BIONDA

*After dinner sip an €18 Irish coffee at Café de Paris watch the supercars and glamazons arrive at the Casino opposite.*

*Across the front are about six bar/restaurants ranging from the swanky (Before), the chilled beach bar-vibe (Joseph), great burgers (Son of a Bun), good fun (Jack) and the cool young one (Brasserie).*

*La Bionda does a delicious barbeque-style steak, cooked on an open grill.*

D 01

70 M

**KETCH SYBARIS**

The 70m ketch Sybaris promises to be a spectacular in scale and spec. Visitors will
have plenty of interiors inspiration – owner Bill Duker says: "every piece of furniture on board is art."

THE HERMITAGE

*Is an oasis of calm in the heart of Monaco, with palatial décor and a hushed, peaceful atmosphere. The three-bedroom penthouse suite can be accessed by a private lift and features a rooftop terrace with spectacular views. But then again, the Presidential suite has boutique-feeling bedrooms and three terraces.*

HERMITAGE

0 M
**TAL LENGTH TTENDING**

**34,500**
**ATTENDEES EXPECTED**

# Los Festivales del Mañana

Design: **Ana Cuna**
Art Direction: **Artur Galocha**
Contents: **Guillermo Arenas**
Client: *El País*

This is a virtual visualization for the publication *Tentaciones* of *El País*. The report wanted to represent the music festivals of the future, with artists in the hologram, VIPs' zones with the seat of *Game of Thrones*, absurd tastings, and many more things that people could see in the festivals of the future, perhaps in the Summer of 2030. Ana Cuna came up with isometric illustrations in a fresh style to show all the parts of the festival in detail.

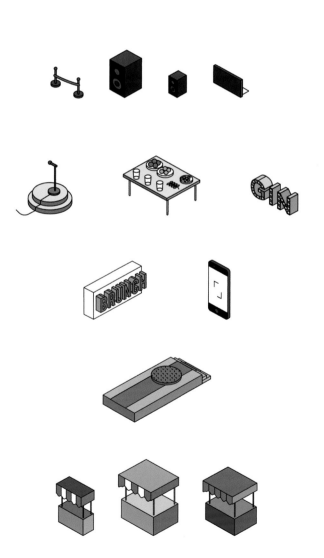

# Todos los festivales del mañana

**Verano de 2030. Los más viejos del lugar recuerdan la época en la que una ardilla podía cruzar la península de macrofestival en macrofestival para acabar muriendo extenuada (y sin blanca), pero nadie les hace caso. Unos están participando en una yincana, otros esperan para subirse al globo de un *sponsor*, y en la zona VIP se reparten gafas de realidad virtual para ver cualquier concierto desde primerísima fila. Comienza la actuación estrella: Amy Winehouse, recién salida de la tumba gracias a la tecnología. ¿Ciencia ficción? No tanto; los festivales del futuro bien podrían parecerse bastante a todo esto**

CARPA KARAOKE
La estrella eres tú.

ATRACCIONES
Añade un poco de emo a los conciertos má muermos.

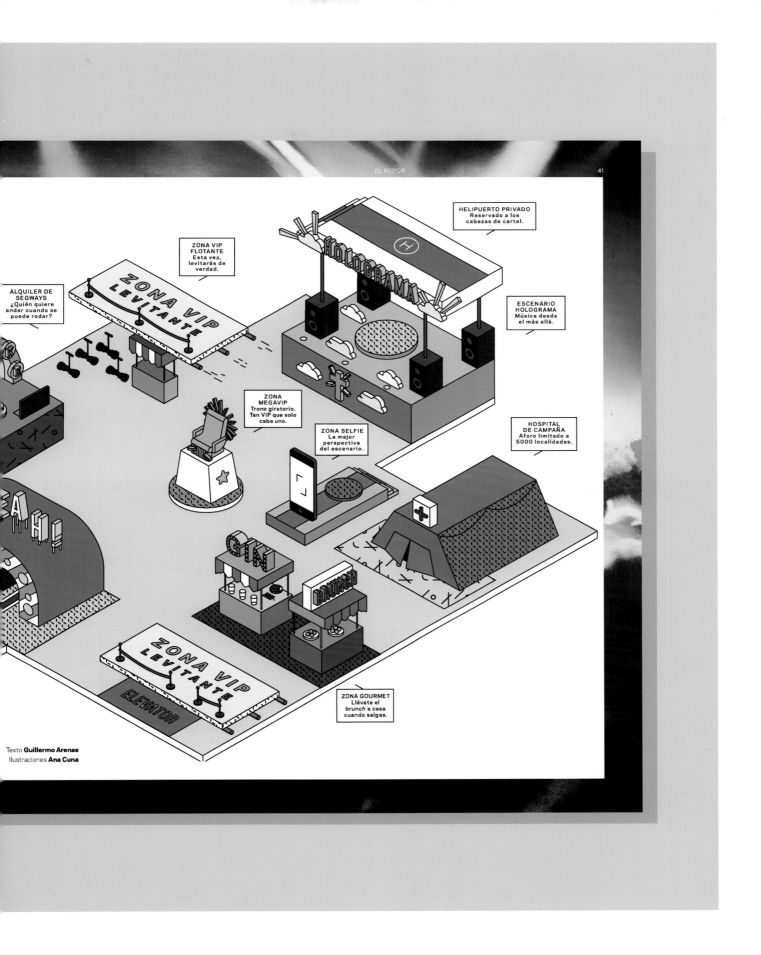

HELIPUERTO PRIVADO
Reservado a los
cabezas de cartel.

ZONA VIP
FLOTANTE
Esta vez,
levitarás de
verdad.

ALQUILER DE
SEGWAYS
¿Quién quiere
andar cuando se
puede rodar?

ESCENARIO
HOLOGRAMA
Música desde
el más allá.

ZONA
MEGAVIP
Trono giratorio.
Tan VIP que solo
cabe uno.

ZONA SELFIE
La mejor
perspectiva
del escenario.

HOSPITAL
DE CAMPAÑA
Aforo limitado a
5000 localidades.

ZONA GOURMET
Llévate el
*brunch* a casa
cuando salgas.

Texto **Guillermo Arenas**
Ilustraciones **Ana Cuna**

# Las Vegas Galactic Hands 2017

Agency: **GumGum**
Design: **Ana Cuna**
Art Direction: **Vanessa Sanoja**
Client: **GumGum**

GumGum needed to create a visual universe that portrayed Las Vegas as the most luminous city on Earth, and at the same time, they wanted it to look like a theme park. Ana Cuna then created a map that serves as a guide for the events and activities held in different locations of the city. In addition, the design was involved in the concept of exploring the Outer Space.

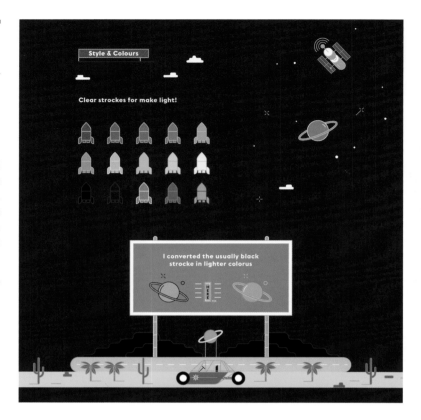

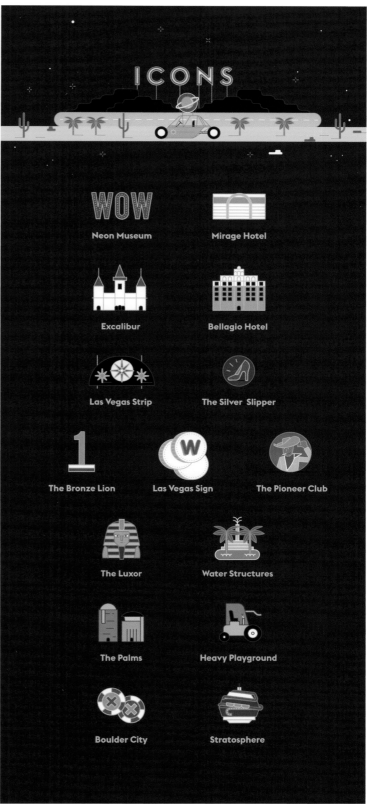

## JEANNE BARET

Realizó la mayor parte del trabajo botánico de la expedición del conde de Bougainville, para lo cual tuvo que hacerse pasar por un hombre. Fue la primera mujer en circunnavegar el mundo.

| ⛵ La Boudeuse | ⊢m⊣ 40 m | ⏱ 1766 - 1769 |
|---|---|---|

ISLA ASCENSIÓN — **BREST** — MONTEVIDEO

ISLA MAURICIO — RIO DE JANEIRO

AUSTRALIA

INDONESIA — MALVINAS

1 🍃 Buganvilla (*Bougainvillea*) / Brasil

## JOSEPH BANKS

Botánico del primer viaje de James Cook, entre otras muchas expediciones, describió por primera vez la flora de Australia.
En este viaje también se observó el tránsito de Venus.

| ⛵ Endeavour | ⊢m⊣ 30 m | ⏱ 1768 - 1771 |
|---|---|---|

CIUDAD DEL CABO — **PLYMOUTH** — RÍO DE JANEIRO

BATAVIA — CABO DE HORNOS

NUEVA ZELANDA

AUSTRALIA — TAHITÍ

2 🍃 Araucaria australiana (*Araucaria cunninghammii*) / Australia

## THADDÄUS

Se unió a la Ex[...]
na en Santiago[...]
tras un largo pe[...]
de plantas en A[...]
buyó al desarro[...]
la viruela.

| ⛵ Descubierta | | |
|---|---|---|

PER[...]

AUST[...]

NUEVA ZELAND[...]

3 🍃 Encina [...]

# MARES DE FAUNA Y FLORA

## ALEXANDER VON HUMBOLDT

Humboldt se financió su propio viaje de exploración científica en América. Su obra tuvo un impacto incalculable y revolucionó la interpretación de la naturaleza.

| ⛵ Múltiples naves | ⏱ 1789 - 1794 |
|---|---|

**BURDEOS** — **A CORUÑA**

ESTADOS UNIDOS — VENEZUELA

MÉXICO — CUBA

ECUADOR

PERÚ — COLOMBIA

5 🐾 Mono lanudo gris (*Lagothrix lagotricha*) / Sudamérica

## CHARLES ROBERT DARWIN

Se unió a la expedición del Beagle como naturalista aficionado (no formaba parte de la tripulación oficial), sus observaciones de biogeografía y variación de las especies inspiró el descubrimiento de la selección natural.

| ⛵ Beagle | ⊢m⊣ 27 m | ⏱ 1831 - 1836 |
|---|---|---|

AZORES — **PLYMOUTH** — CABO VERDE

BRASIL — BRASIL

CIUDAD DEL CABO — MONTEVIDEO

ISLA MAURICIO — GALÁPAGOS — MALVINAS

AUSTRALIA — PERÚ — CHILE

6 🐾 Ñandú de Darwin (*Rhea pennata*) / Brasil

## JOSEPH DA[...]

Participó en n[...]
de exploració[...]
destacamos a[...]
Malvinas, Antá[...]
y Australia, y d[...]
una parte de l[...]

| ⛵ Erebus y T[...] | | |
|---|---|---|

IN[...]

M[...]

MALVINAS

7 🐾 Foca d[...]

## ARCHIBALD MENZIES

Circunnavegó el globo por segunda vez en la expedición de George Vancouver. Menzies descubrió animales y plantas desde Australia a California y ascendió al volcán Mauna Loa.

⛵ Discovery | ⊢m⊣ 30 m | ⏱ 1790 - 1795

CABO VERDE — **LONDRES** — CIUDAD DEL CABO

MÉXICO — AUSTRALIA

HAWAI — TAHITÍ

CALIFORNIA — NUEVA ZELANDA

| 4 | 🍃 | Abeto Douglas (*Pseudotsuga menziesii*) / Columbia Británica

---

⊢m⊣ 3 m | ⏱ 1789 - 1794

CÁDIZ — MONTEVIDEO

CHILE

CALIFORNIA

ALASKA

*grifolia*) / California

---

Mientras el mundo se sumerge en la mayor revolución económica, tecnológica y social de la historia desde el Neolítico, intrépidos exploradores se disponían a llegar hasta los últimos confines del mundo.

Los naturalistas de estas grandes expediciones (que a menudo eran los médicos de la tripulación) fueron pioneros descubriendo la biodiversidad más exótica y catalizando también una revolución científica

| LEYENDA | | | |
|---|---|---|---|
| ⛵ Embarcación | ⊢m⊣ Eslora | ⏱ Duración del viaje | |
| 🐾 Animal | 🍃 Vegetal | 0 Numeración especie | |

---

## ALFRED RUSSELL WALLACE

Se embarcó por su cuenta en dos grandes viajes de exploración, primero en el Amazonas y después en el archipiélago indo-malayo. Descubrió la selección natural y estableció las bases de la biogeografía.

⛵ Múltiples naves | ⏱ 1854 - 1862

BOMBAY — **INGLATERRA** — SRI LANKA

CÉLEBES — SINGAPUR

BORNEO

JAVA — SUMATRA

| 8 | 🐾 | Rana voladora de Wallace (*Rhacophorus nigropalmatus*)

---

⏱ 1839 - 1843

**TASMANIA**

TIERRA VICTORIA

NDA

BARRERA DE ROSS

*ssii*) / Ártico

Infografía creada por *El Abrelatas* a partir de la información facilitada por Rafael para *Principia Magazine*.

---

# Mares de Fauna y Flora

Design: **el abrelatas**
Client: *Principia Magazine*

"Mares de Fauna y Flora," which is translated as "Seas of Fauna and Flora" in English, is an infographic that approaches the routes, history, and some species discovered by the intrepid naturalists, biologists, geologists, and scientists of the 18th and 19th centuries. All information was summed up in a double-page and published in the 4th issue of *Principia Magazine*.

# SOS4.8 Map Festival

Design: **Samu Coronado**
Client: **SOS4.8 Festival**

This is a map for the music festival SOS4.8, both digital and in print. The idea was creating a map where the audience could quickly find each corner of the festival. It was a functional map full of small funny elements and paired with a fresh and current chromatic palette in fluorescent and bright colors.

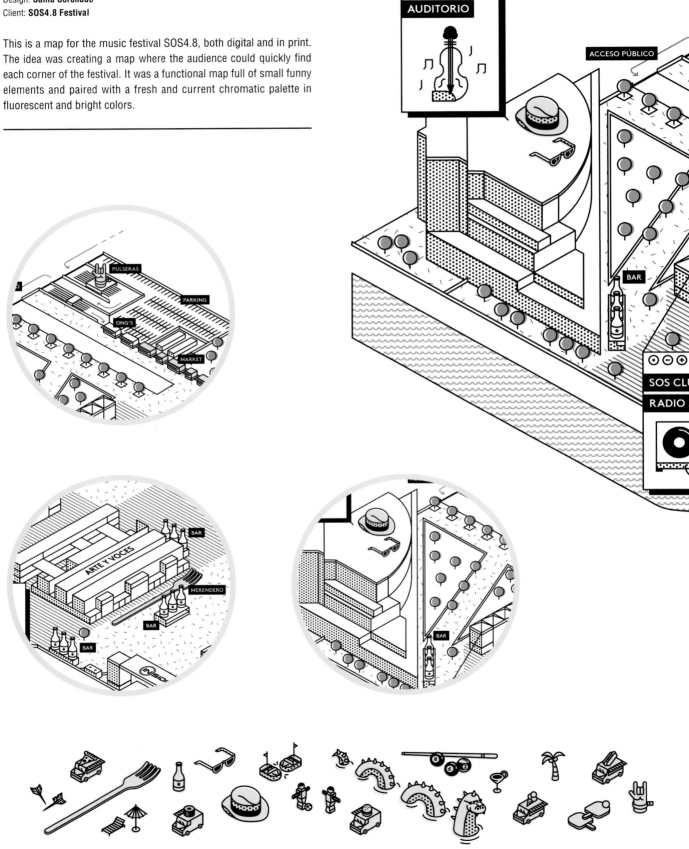

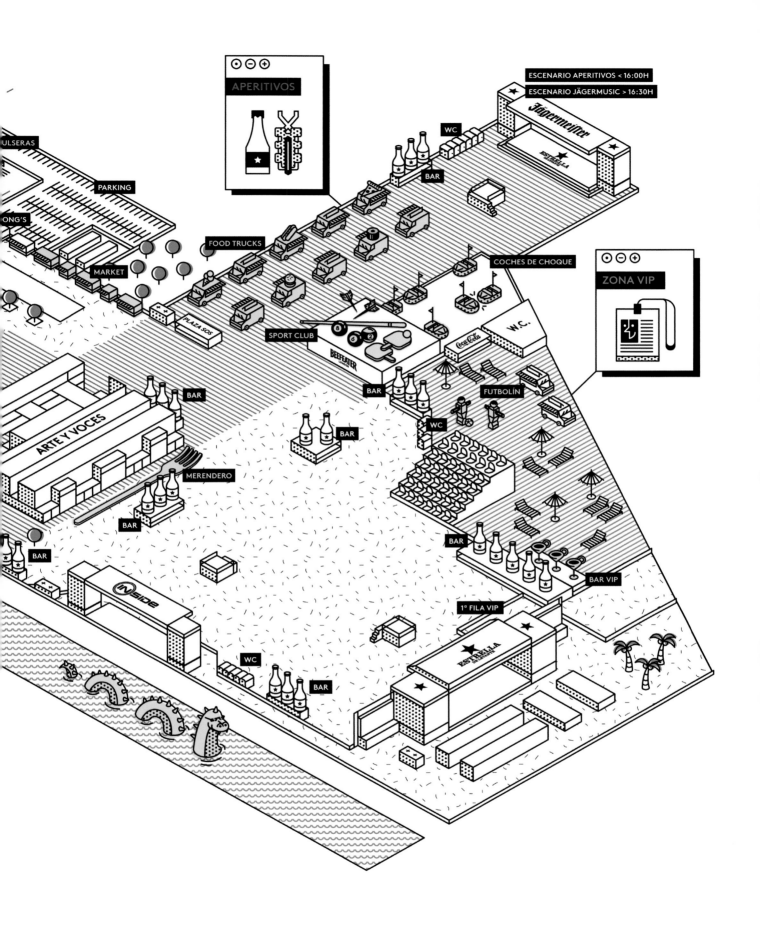

APERITIVOS

ESCENARIO APERITIVOS < 16:00H
ESCENARIO JÄGERMUSIC > 16:30H

Jägermeifter

WC

ULSERAS

PARKING

ONG'S

MARKET

FOOD TRUCKS

BAR

COCHES DE CHOQUE

ZONA VIP

PLAZA SOS

SPORT CLUB

BEEFEATER

Coca-Cola

W.C.

BAR

FUTBOLÍN

WC

ARTE Y VOCES

BAR

BAR

MERENDERO

BAR

BAR

BAR

BAR VIP

BAR

1º FILA VIP

INSIDE

ESTRELLA

WC

BAR

# Pacha Festival Infographic

Agency: **Brands&Roses**
Design: **Ana Cuna**
Art Direction: **Tema Barcelona**
Client: *Pacha*

*Pacha* was looking for a way to represent Pacha Festival, one of the most important events in the world, using a bunch of numbers and illustrations. During the 3rd of June in 2016, more than 5,000 spectators have participated in this biggest event held in the Harumi with an area of more than 25,000 m$^2$.

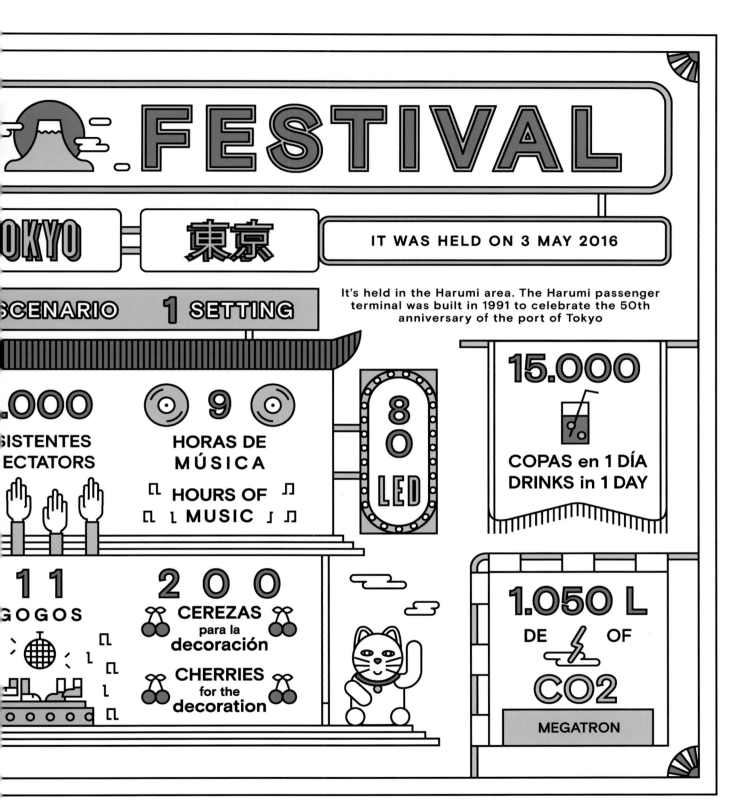

# FESTIVAL

OKYO | 東京 | IT WAS HELD ON 3 MAY 2016

It's held in the Harumi area. The Harumi passenger terminal was built in 1991 to celebrate the 50th anniversary of the port of Tokyo

SCENARIO | 1 SETTING

.000
SISTENTES
ECTATORS

9
HORAS DE MÚSICA
♫ HOURS OF MUSIC ♪

8 0 LED

15.000
COPAS en 1 DÍA
DRINKS in 1 DAY

1 1
GOGOS

2 0 0
CEREZAS
para la
decoración
CHERRIES
for the
decoration

1.050 L
DE ⚡ OF
$CO_2$
MEGATRON

# ING: Frankfurt

Design: **Rutger Paulusse**
Art Direction: **United State Of Fans\TBWA**
Concept: **United State Of Fans\TBWA**
Client: **ING**

United State Of Fans approached Rutger Paulusse to make an infographic about Frankfurt. The illustration was part of a concept for ING who launched an international marketing campaign named "World, Here I Come" at Amsterdam Airport Schiphol. The infographic is 250cm × 135cm. The viewers could photograph it, so that they had a guide with all the hotspots of Frankfurt on their mobile phones.

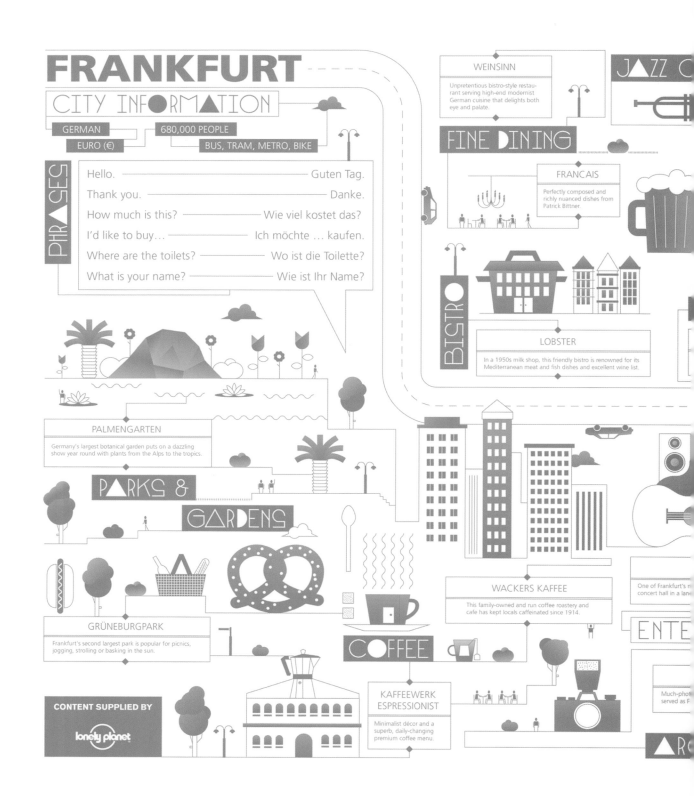

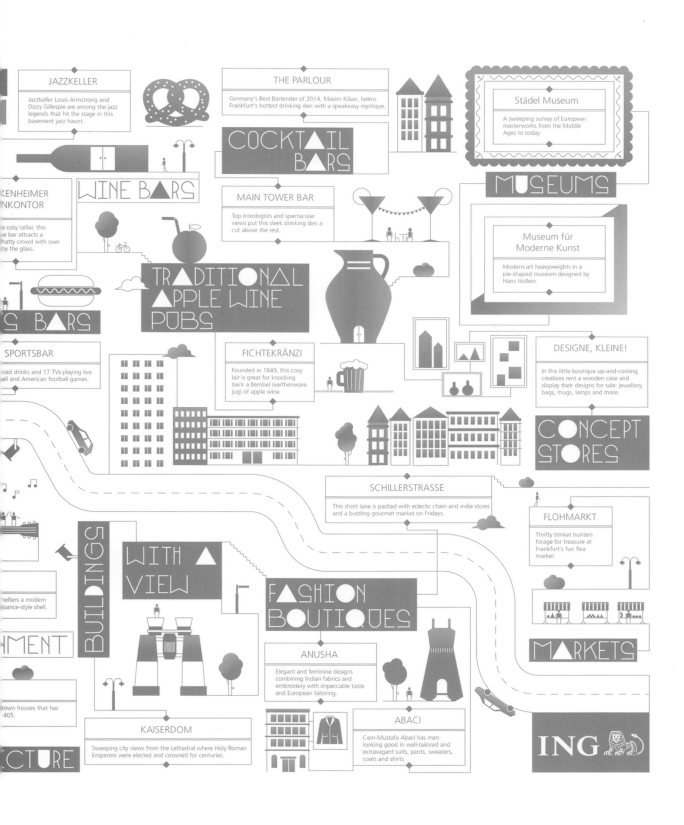

### JAZZKELLER

Jazzkeller Louis Armstrong and Dizzy Gillespie are among the jazz legends that hit the stage in this basement jazz haunt.

### THE PARLOUR

Germany's Best Bartender of 2014, Maxim Kilian, helms Frankfurt's hottest drinking den with a speakeasy mystique.

### Städel Museum

A sweeping survey of European masterworks from the Middle Ages to today.

## COCKTAIL BARS

## WINE BARS

...KENHEIMER
...NKONTOR

...a cosy cellar, this
...e bar attracts a
...hatty crowd with over
...by the glass.

## MUSEUMS

### MAIN TOWER BAR

Top mixologists and spectacular views put this sleek drinking den a cut above the rest.

### Museum für Moderne Kunst

Modern-art heavyweights in a pie-shaped museum designed by Hans Hollein.

## TRADITIONAL APPLE WINE PUBS

## ...S BARS

### SPORTSBAR

...ced drinks and 17 TVs playing live
...all and American football games.

### FICHTEKRÄNZI

Founded in 1849, this cosy lair is great for knocking back a Bembel (earthenware jug) of apple wine.

### DESIGNE, KLEINE!

In this little boutique up-and-coming creatives rent a wooden case and display their designs for sale: jewellery, bags, mugs, lamps and more.

## CONCEPT STORES

### SCHILLERSTRASSE

This short lane is packed with eclectic chain and indie stores and a bustling gourmet market on Fridays.

### FLOHMARKT

Thrifty trinket hunters forage for treasure at Frankfurt's fun flea market.

## BUILDINGS WITH A VIEW

## FASHION BOUTIQUES

...MENT

...helters a modern
...ssance-style shell.

### ANUSHA

Elegant and feminine designs combining Indian fabrics and embroidery with impeccable taste and European tailoring.

## MARKETS

...town houses that has
...405.

### KAISERDOM

Sweeping city views from the cathedral where Holy Roman Emperors were elected and crowned for centuries.

### ABACI

Cem-Mustafa Abaci has men looking good in well-tailored and extravagant suits, pants, sweaters, coats and shirts

...CTURE

ING

# History of Jawsfood

Design: **Hong Sungwoo**

It is an infographic of the history of Jawsfood. Since its establishment in 2007, the main events of Jawsfood have been listed in a chronological order. Each event was depicted directly or figuratively. Pastel tone colors and simple shapes are used to make the brand look more friendly. The infographic was printed on canvas (5000mm × 1000mm).

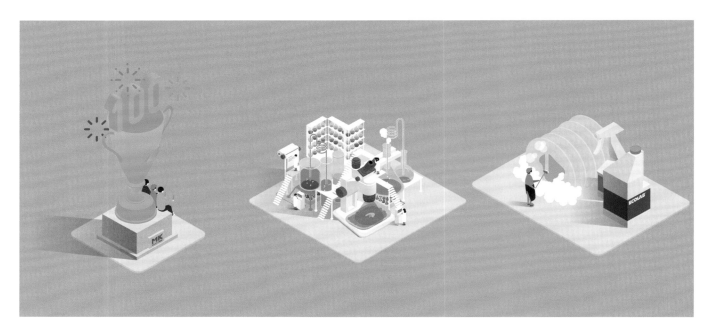

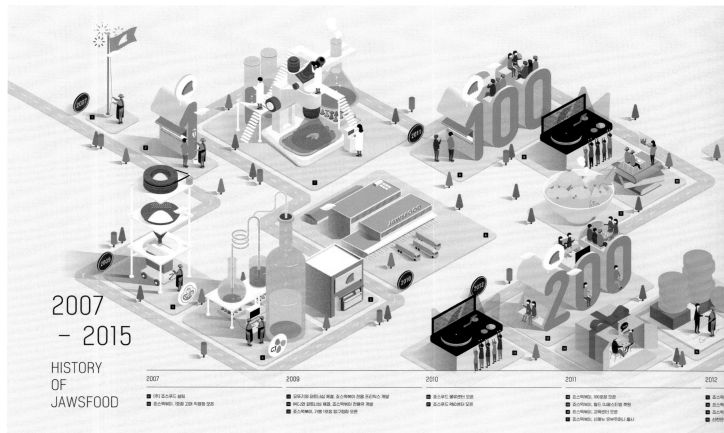

2007
– 2015

HISTORY
OF
JAWSFOOD

| 2007 | 2009 | 2010 | 2011 | 2012 |
|---|---|---|---|---|
| ㈜ 죠스푸드 설립 | 오뚜기와 파트너십 체결, 죠스떡볶이 전용 프리믹스 개발 | 죠스푸드 물류센터 오픈 | 죠스떡볶이, 100호점 오픈 | 죠스떡 |
| 죠스떡볶이, 1호점 고대 직영점 오픈 | ㈜CJ와 파트너십 체결, 죠스떡볶이 전용유 개발 | 죠스푸드 R&D센터 오픈 | 죠스떡볶이, 월드 DJ페스티벌 후원 | 죠스떡 |
| | 죠스떡볶이, 가맹 1호점 입구정점 오픈 | | 죠스떡볶이, 교육센터 오픈 | 죠스떡 |
| | | | 죠스떡볶이, 신메뉴 유부주머니 출시 | 신한은 |

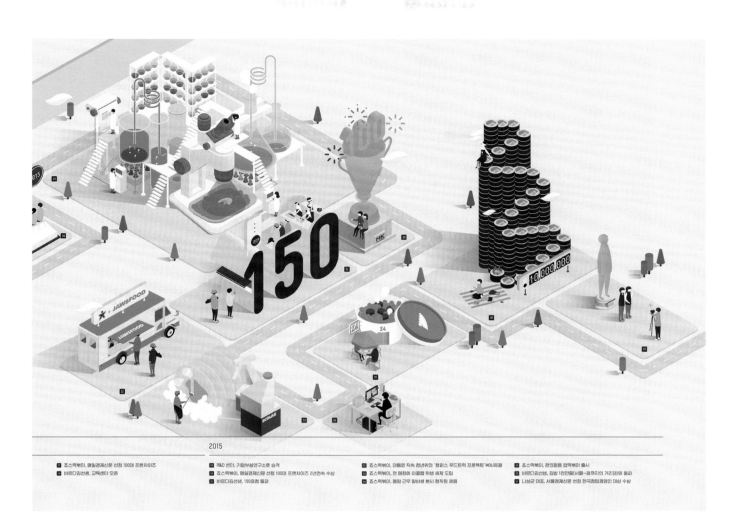

2015

① 죠스떡볶이, 매일경제신문 선정 100대 프랜차이즈          ⑥ R&D 센터, 기업부설연구소로 승격               ⑨ 죠스떡볶이, 대통령 직속 청년위와 '캠퍼스 푸드트럭 프로젝트' MOU체결        ⑫ 죠스떡볶이, 관의점용 컵떡볶이 출시
② 바르다김선생, 교육센터 오픈                    ⑦ 죠스떡볶이, 매일경제신문 선정 100대 프랜차이즈 2년연속 수상     ⑩ 죠스떡볶이, 전 매장에 이콜랩 위생 세제 도입              ⑬ 바르다김선생, 김밥 1천만줄(서울~광주지의 거리)판매 돌파
                                       ⑧ 바르다김선생, 150호점 돌파                    ⑪ 죠스떡볶이, 매장 근무 알바생 본사 정식원 채용               ⑭ 나상균 대표, 서울경제신문 선정 한국창업경영인 대상 수상

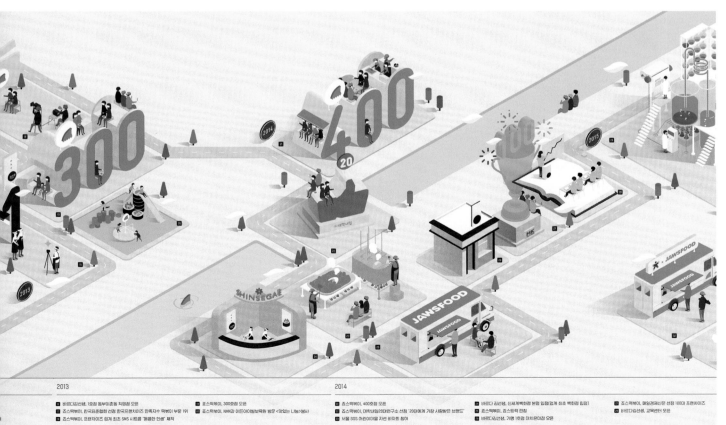

2013                                          2014

⑮ 바르다김선생, 1호점 동부이촌동 직영점 오픈        ⑰ 죠스떡볶이, 300호점 오픈              ⑲ 죠스떡볶이, 400호점 오픈                       ㉒ 바르다 김선생, 신세계백화점 분점 입점(업계 최초 백화점 입점)        ㉕ 죠스떡볶이, 매일경제신문 선정 100대 프랜차이즈
⑯ 죠스떡볶이, 한국표준협회 선정 한국프랜차이즈 만족지수 떡볶이 부문 1위   ⑱ 죠스떡볶이, NHN과 이든아이빌보육원 방문 <맛있는 나눔>봉사   ⑳ 죠스떡볶이, 대학내일20대연구소 선정 '20대에게 가장 사랑받은 브랜드'     ㉓ 죠스떡볶이, 죠스트럭 런칭                        ㉖ 바르다김선생, 교육센터 오픈
   죠스떡볶이, 프랜차이즈 업계 최초 SNS 시트콤 <매콤한 인생> 제작                              ㉑ 서울 SOS 어린이마을 자선 바자회 참여             ㉔ 바르다김선생, 가맹 1호점 대치은마점 오픈

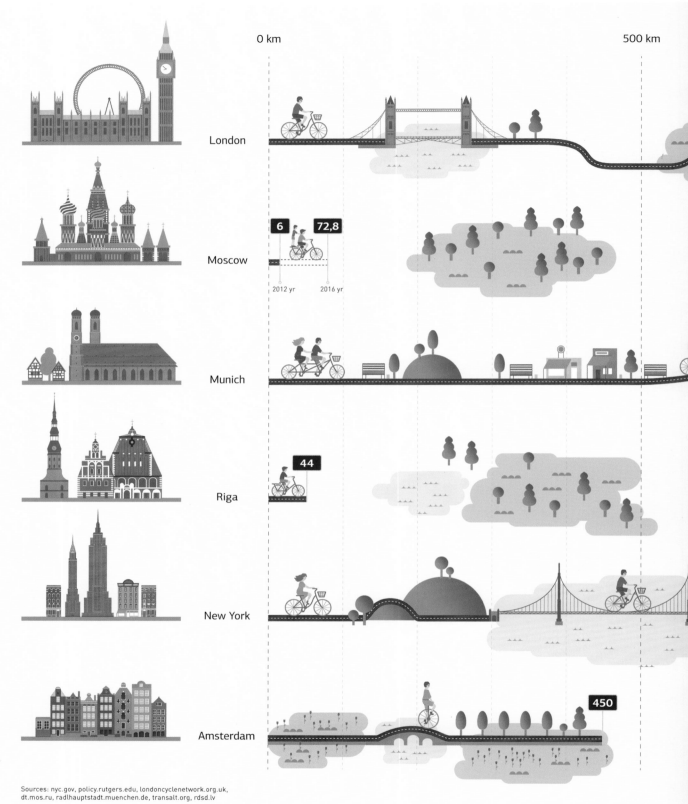

London

Moscow

6    72,8

2012 yr    2016 yr

Munich

Riga

44

New York

Amsterdam

450

0 km

500 km

Sources: nyc.gov, policy.rutgers.edu, londoncyclenetwork.org.uk,
dt.mos.ru, radlhauptstadt.muenchen.de, transalt.org, rdsd.lv

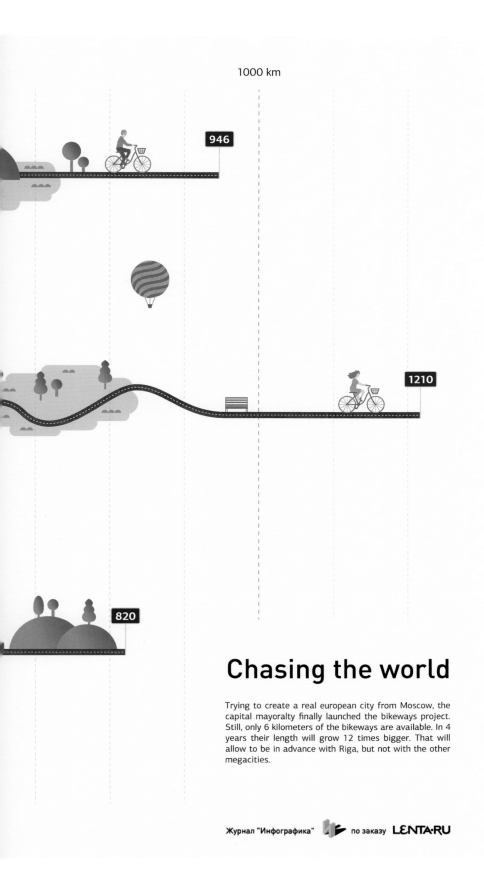

1000 km

946

1210

820

# Chasing the world

Trying to create a real european city from Moscow, the capital mayoralty finally launched the bikeways project. Still, only 6 kilometers of the bikeways are available. In 4 years their length will grow 12 times bigger. That will allow to be in advance with Riga, but not with the other megacities.

Журнал "Инфографика"   по заказу LENTA·RU

## Bikeways in Moscow and the World's Megacities

. . . . . . . . . . . . . . . . . . . . . . . . . . . . . . . . . . . . . . . . . . . .

Agency: **INFOGRAFIKA Agency**
Design: **Irina Oloeva**
Art direction: **Artem Koleganov**
Information: **Nikolai Romanov**
Client: **Lenta.ru**

This infographic was created for infographicsmag.ru and Lenta.ru. It is about the bikeway in Moscow and that of the world's megacities. The capital mayoralty is going to increase the total length of tracks for cyclists to almost a total of 73 kilometers in the coming years, 12 times bigger than the current bikeway of only 6 kilometers. The infographic compared the length of bikeway in Moscow and that of some major cities of the world and concluded that this was still only a decorative initiative.

# Amorino Gelato

Agency: **ONO Creates**
Design: **Med Ness, Jing Ng**

The Amorino Gelato team from the United States wanted to create
a series of three infographic posters to explain the brand's history,
offerings, and to educate their customers on the difference between
gelato and ice cream.

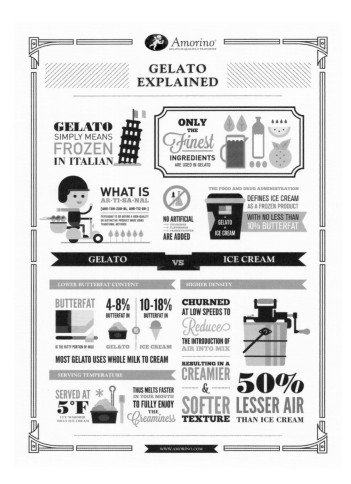

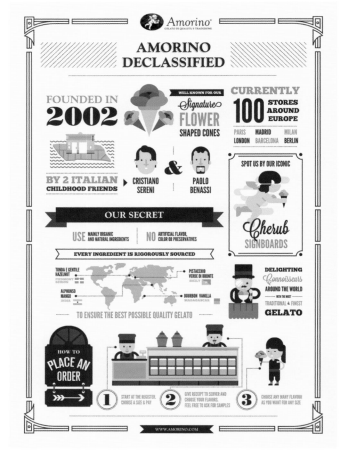

# OUR OFFERINGS

## OUR GELATO FLAVOURS

### FOUR CHOCOLATE FLAVOURS

**CIOCCOLATO AMORINO**
The perfect combination of pure cocoa and whole milk

**L'INIMITABLE**
The traditional chocolate & hazelnut spread

**CIOCCOLATO ECUADOR**
70% cocoa dark chocolate from Ecuadorian cocoa beans

**SORBETTO AL CIOCCOLATO BIO**
The lactose-free organic chocolate sorbet

### AND MANY MORE!

- STRACCIATELLA
- COFFEE
- PISTACHIO
- AMARENA
- SPECULOOS
- TIRAMISU
- CARAMELLO AL BURRO SALATO
- COCCO PURO SRI LANKA
- YOGURT CON YOGURT 0%
- NOCCIOLA TONDA E GENTILE

### 2 AMORINO ORIGINAL VANILLA FLAVORS

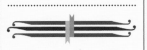

**VANIGLIA BOURBON** *from* **MADAGASCAR**
REVEALING A FLORAL BUT SLIGHTLY WOODY TASTE

**VANIGLIA** *from* **TAHITI**
PROVIDING A MORE PRONOUNCED TASTE WITH FLOWERY NOTES

## OUR SORBET FLAVOURS

**LAMPONE**
RASPBERRY

**MANGO**
MANGO

**FRUTTO DELLA PASSIONE**
PASSION FRUIT

**FRAGOLA**
STRAWBERRY

**LIMONE**
LEMON

**BANANA**
BANANA

**WE PROVIDE TO GO & DELIVERY SERVICE FOR OUR Pints**
18 OZ | 36 OZ

## OUR OTHER PRODUCTS

### BEVERAGES

#### FRAPPÈS

ESPRESSO     MILKSHAKE

#### AFFOGATO

#### GRANITAS

**LIMONE** LEMON
**FRAGOLA** STRAWBERRY
**MANDARINO** MANDARIN ORANGE

#### HOT BEVERAGES

| | |
|---|---|
| ESPRESSO | LATTE MACCHIATO |
| COFFEE | CAPPUCCINO |
| CAFFÈ | AMERICANO |
| TEA | HOT CHOCOLATE |

### SNACKS

#### MACARONS AL GELATO

Our gelato sandwiched between two delicate almond shells

- CAFFÈ
- MANGO
- VANIGLIA
- LAMPONE
- CIOCCOLATO
- PISTACCHIO
- INIMITABILE
- CARAMELLO

#### GELATO CAKES

#### WAFFLES

#### FOCCACINES

#### CHOCOLATE COLLECTIONS

#### CREPES

#### GOURMET PRODUCTS

# PastaFacts Poster

Agency: **ONO Creates**
Design: **Med Ness, Jing Ng**

Everybody loves pasta and so does ONO Creates! This topic came naturally to the designers when they wanted to create fun infographic posters for sale.

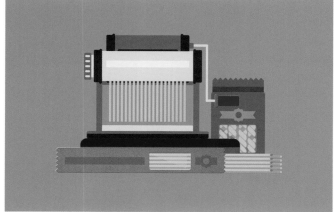

# 5 French Mother Sauces

Agency: **ONO Creates**
Design: **Med Ness, Jing Ng**

This infographic was commissioned by *Michelin Guide Singapore* to showcase the five French Mother Sauces. Apart from breaking down each sauce to the base and flavorings, ONO Creates also included classic pairings and common secondary sauces derived from the five sauces.

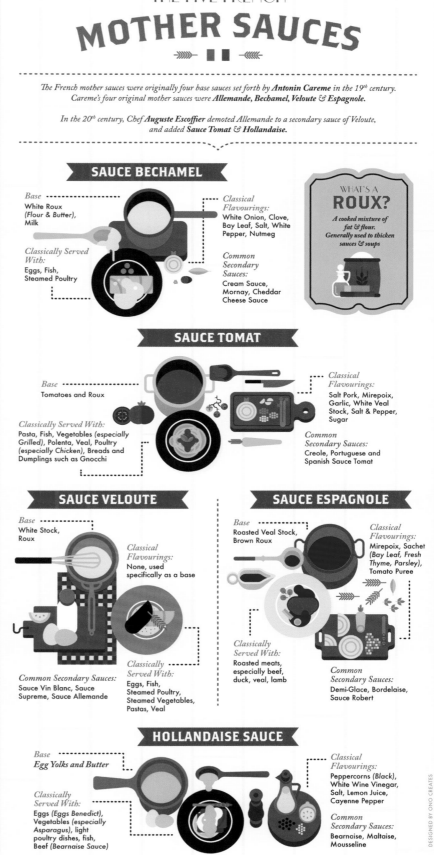

## THE FIVE FRENCH MOTHER SAUCES

*The French mother sauces were originally four base sauces set forth by **Antonin Careme** in the 19th century. Careme's four original mother sauces were **Allemande, Bechamel, Veloute & Espagnole**.*

*In the 20th century, Chef **Auguste Escoffier** demoted Allemande to a secondary sauce of Veloute, and added **Sauce Tomat & Hollandaise**.*

### SAUCE BECHAMEL

**Base**
White Roux (Flour & Butter), Milk

*Classically Served With:*
Eggs, Fish, Steamed Poultry

*Classical Flavourings:*
White Onion, Clove, Bay Leaf, Salt, White Pepper, Nutmeg

*Common Secondary Sauces:*
Cream Sauce, Mornay, Cheddar Cheese Sauce

**WHAT'S A ROUX?**
*A cooked mixture of fat & flour. Generally used to thicken sauces & soups*

### SAUCE TOMAT

**Base**
Tomatoes and Roux

*Classically Served With:*
Pasta, Fish, Vegetables (especially Grilled), Polenta, Veal, Poultry (especially Chicken), Breads and Dumplings such as Gnocchi

*Classical Flavourings:*
Salt Pork, Mirepoix, Garlic, White Veal Stock, Salt & Pepper, Sugar

*Common Secondary Sauces:*
Creole, Portuguese and Spanish Sauce Tomat

### SAUCE VELOUTE

**Base**
White Stock, Roux

*Classical Flavourings:*
None, used specifically as a base

*Common Secondary Sauces:*
Sauce Vin Blanc, Sauce Supreme, Sauce Allemande

*Classically Served With:*
Eggs, Fish, Steamed Poultry, Steamed Vegetables, Pastas, Veal

### SAUCE ESPAGNOLE

**Base**
Roasted Veal Stock, Brown Roux

*Classical Flavourings:*
Mirepoix, Sachet (Bay Leaf, Fresh Thyme, Parsley), Tomato Puree

*Classically Served With:*
Roasted meats, especially beef, duck, veal, lamb

*Common Secondary Sauces:*
Demi-Glace, Bordelaise, Sauce Robert

### HOLLANDAISE SAUCE

**Base**
*Egg Yolks and Butter*

*Classically Served With:*
Eggs (Eggs Benedict), Vegetables (especially Asparagus), light poultry dishes, fish, Beef (Bearnaise Sauce)

*Classical Flavourings:*
Peppercorns (Black), White Wine Vinegar, Salt, Lemon Juice, Cayenne Pepper

*Common Secondary Sauces:*
Bearnaise, Maltaise, Mousseline

DESIGNED BY ONO CREATES

# EatMe Cooperation Guide

Agency: **Re-lab**
Illustration: **Chia-Wei Liu**
Art Direction: **Chia-Wei Liu**
Project Management: **An Hsiao**
Client: **EatMe Catering Consulting Co. Ltd.**

EatMe is a consulting company that allies with various restaurants to promote their food and sales strategies. All cooperation starts with mutual understanding and reliance on each other's services. Hoping to decrease the time spent on explaining their strengths, the EatMe Cooperation Guide helps shorten the introductory details of their services. With the isometric design of the restaurant displaying the interior and human interactions, the audience will get the picture of the services that EatMe provides and how the procedures work. Everything in the Guide is expressed vividly in the layout.

## 合作流程

**1. 優惠簽約合作**

現在就馬上與食我合作，提供優惠給全國數百萬的外食族吧

**2. 選擇套裝方案**

依照您的需求，選擇最適當的行銷套裝！

**3. 網路發佈訊息**

優惠上線，源源不絕的客人就在你面前！還等什麼呢？

## 如何帶來營業額

**1. APP搜尋**

1. 行動查詢
2. 優惠列表
3. 免費使用

**2. 用餐優惠**

1. 到店用餐
2. 出示APP
3. 獲得優惠

**3. 結帳積點**

1. 櫃檯結帳
2. 結算點數
3. 積點密碼

**4. 紅利兌換**

1. 累積點數
2. 尋找贈品
3. 兌換商品

## 客群來源

**都市粉領族**

姊妹們相約享受生活。

**年輕上班族**

下班後同事聚餐小酌。

**熱血大學生**

與同學一起體驗美食。

## 現有會員與成長趨勢

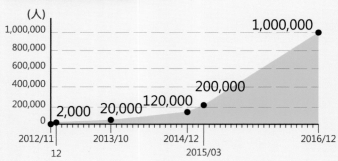

(人)

1,000,000
800,000
600,000
400,000
200,000
0

1,000,000

200,000

120,000

2,000   20,000

2012/11    2013/10    2014/12    2016/12

12    2015/03

# 食我產品服務

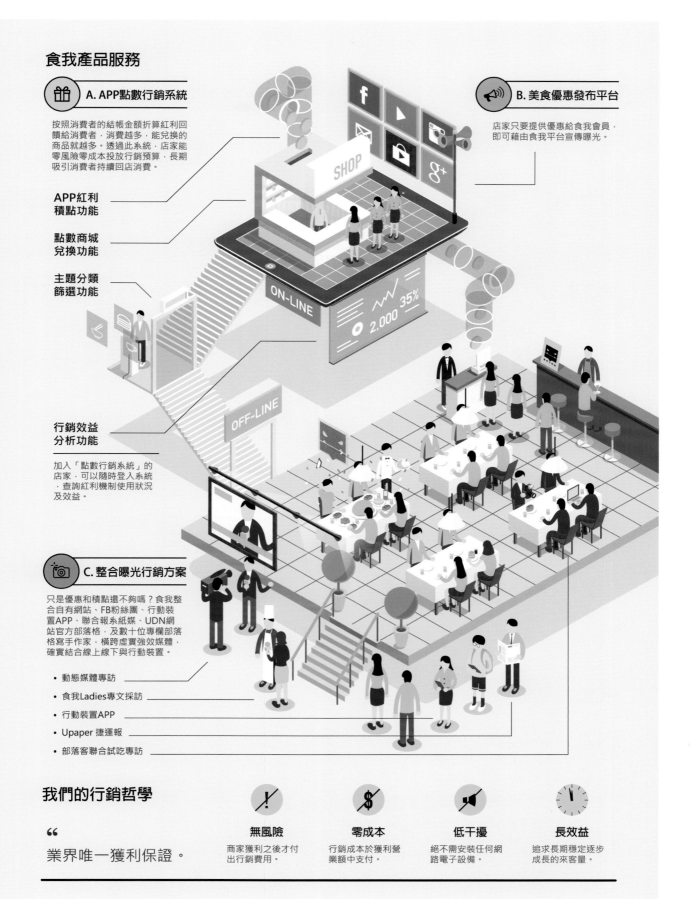

## A. APP點數行銷系統

按照消費者的結帳金額折算紅利回饋給消費者，消費越多，能兌換的商品就越多。透過此系統，店家能零風險零成本投放行銷預算，長期吸引消費者持續回店消費。

**APP紅利積點功能**

**點數商城兌換功能**

**主題分類篩選功能**

**行銷效益分析功能**

加入「點數行銷系統」的店家，可以隨時登入系統，查詢紅利機制使用狀況及效益。

## B. 美食優惠發布平台

店家只要提供優惠給食我會員，即可藉由食我平台宣傳曝光。

## C. 整合曝光行銷方案

只是優惠和積點還不夠嗎？食我整合自有網站、FB粉絲團、行動裝置APP、聯合報系紙媒、UDN網站官方部落格，及數十位專欄部落格寫手作家，橫跨虛實強效媒體，確實結合線上線下與行動裝置。

- 動態媒體專訪
- 食我Ladies專文採訪
- 行動裝置APP
- Upaper 捷運報
- 部落客聯合試吃專訪

## 我們的行銷哲學

> 業界唯一獲利保證。

**無風險**
商家獲利之後才付出行銷費用。

**零成本**
行銷成本於獲利營業額中支付。

**低干擾**
絕不需安裝任何網路電子設備。

**長效益**
追求長期穩定逐步成長的來客量。

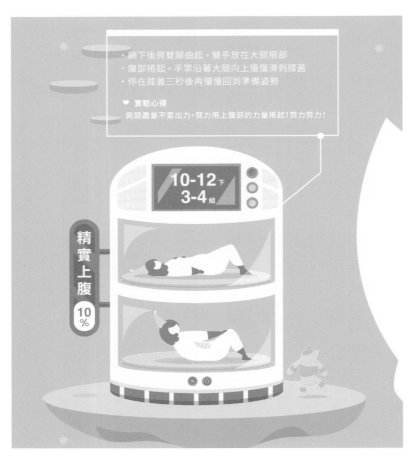

· 躺下後將雙腳曲起，雙手放在大腿根部
· 腹部捲起，手掌沿著大腿向上慢慢滑到膝蓋
· 停在膝蓋三秒後再慢慢回到準備姿勢

♥ 實驗心得
肩頸盡量不要出力，努力用上腹部的力量捲起！努力努力！

10-12 下
3-4 組

精實上腹
10%

· 在瑜珈墊上將手掌平放於肩膀下方，膝蓋著地雙腳提起略交疊
· 身體下壓至上臂與背部同高
· 接著用胸肌的力量上抬身體，回到原本的預備位置

♥ 實驗心得
下壓時記得收緊腹部，並讓臀部跟著身體一起往下，才不會對腰椎造成壓迫！

10-12 下
2-3 組
待上手後可增加
次數與組數

豐挺美胸
15%

# The Elfit Lab

· · · · · · · · · · · · · · · · · · · · · · · · · · · · · · · · · · · · · · · · · · · · · · · · ·

Agency: **Re-lab**
Illustration: **Coco Chen**
Art Direction: **Yu-Hsuan Liu**

People busy at work always find excuses to postpone their exercise schedules, so we decide to terminate their bad habits. Elfit is an enthusiastic expert in fitness, and her main purpose is to lead people to stay fit and healthy with least troubles. The Elfit Lab introduces a serial workout schedule, which is easy to follow, not too time-consuming, and does not require extra equipment. Elfit helps people maintain training habits, stay fit and beautiful with ease!

# The Anatomy of Graphics: Book

Agency: **maroomo**
Illustration: **Donchern Cin**
Art Direction: **Donchern Cin**

Paper is derived from trees so there is life in the paper. That is why one should realize that a small mistake can hurt several trees when making a book. A book designer requires to understand the structure of the book and comprehend and use accurate terminology. The aim of the poster is to introduce a popular type of binding—the origin of most modern books. A variety of terms are explained in the poster.

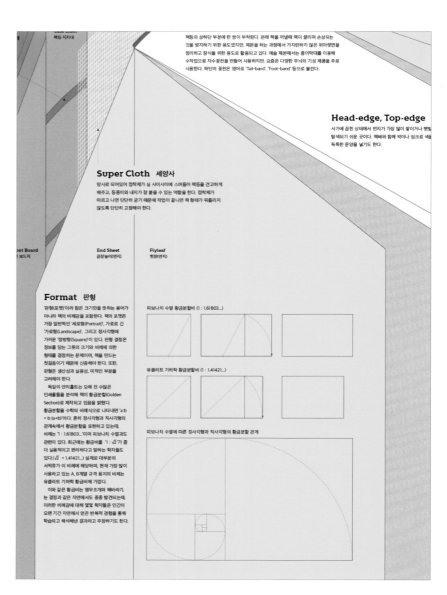

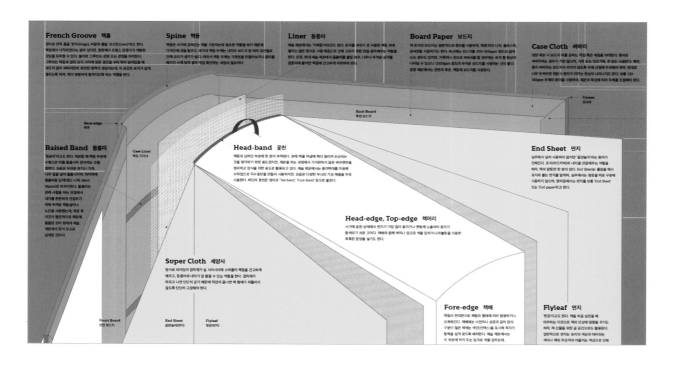

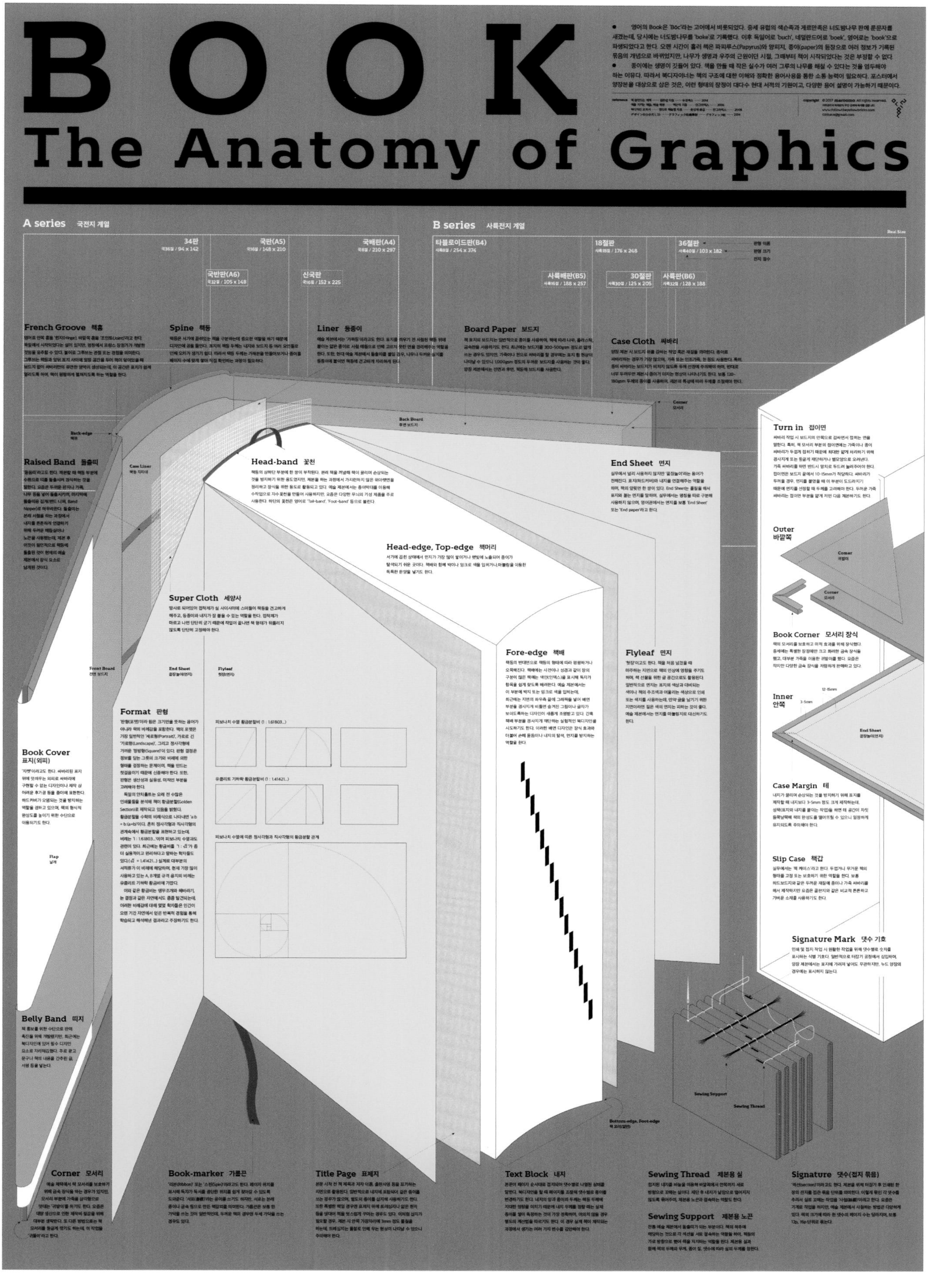

# B O O K
## The Anatomy of Graphics

**A series** 국전지 계열

| 34판 | 국판(A5) | 국배판(A4) |
| --- | --- | --- |
| 국36광 / 94 x 142 | 국4광 / 148 x 210 | 국배 / 210 x 297 |

| 국반판(A6) | 신국판 |
| --- | --- |
| 국22광 / 105 x 148 | 국16광 / 152 x 225 |

**B series** 사륙전지 계열

| 타블로이드판(B4) | 18절판 | 36절판 |
| --- | --- | --- |
| 사륙8광 / 254 x 374 | 사륙8광 / 176 x 248 | 사륙8광 / 103 x 182 |

| 사륙배판(B5) | 30절판 | 사륙판(B6) |
| --- | --- | --- |
| 사륙16광 / 188 x 257 | 사륙30광 / 125 x 205 | 사륙32광 / 128 x 188 |

Real Size

### French Groove 책홈
### Spine 책등
### Liner 등종이
### Board Paper 보드지
### Case Cloth 싸바리

### Raised Band 돌출띠
### Head-band 꽃천
### End Sheet 면지
### Turn in 접이면
### Outer 바깥쪽
### Head-edge, Top-edge 책머리
### Super Cloth 세양사
### Book Corner 모서리 장식
### Fore-edge 책배
### Flyleaf 면지
### Inner 안쪽
### Format 판형
### Case Margin 테
### Book Cover 표지(외피)
### Slip Case 책갑
### Signature Mark 댓수 기호
### Belly Band 띠지
### Corner 모서리
### Book-marker 가름끈
### Title Page 표제지
### Text Block 내지
### Sewing Thread 제본용 실
### Sewing Support 제본용 노끈
### Signature 댓수(접지 묶음)

Back Board 뒷면 보드지
Corner 모서리
Back-edge 책홈
Case Liner 책등 지지대
Front Board 앞면 보드지
End Sheet 공원늬여맥지
Flyleaf 행경(다치)
Sewing Support
Sewing Thread
Bottom-edge, Foot-edge 책 모서리밑단

# Inside Information: Apple Macintosh

Design: **Malik Thomas-Smeda**
Art Direction: **Dorothy Creative Ltd.**
Concept: **Dorothy Creative Ltd.**

"Inside Information: Apple Macintosh" reveals an imaginary world filled with 29 references to Apple (and popular culture). Instead of circuit boards and chips, there are floors filled with people, robots, and animals—all doing things that relate to the history and legacy of Apple and the Mac. From a Steve Jobs statue on the top floor titled "El Capitan" all the way to a room filled with big cat taxidermy, this project gives a nod to the early OS X software releases.

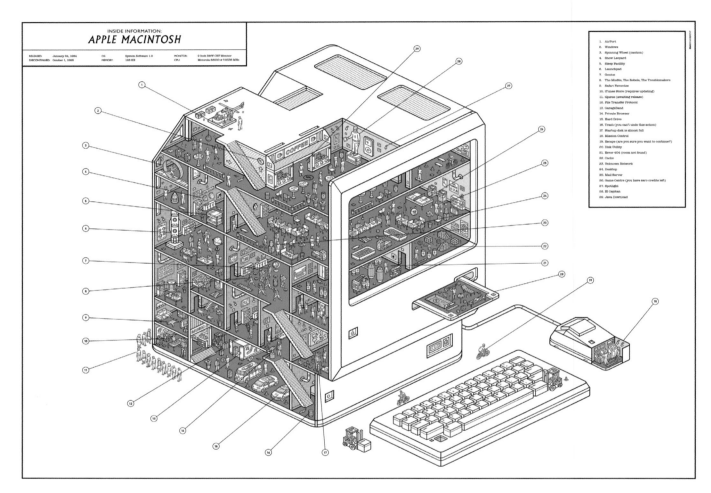

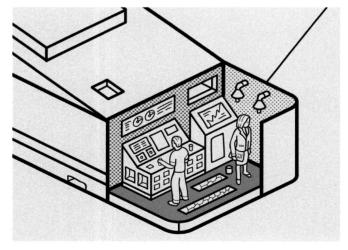

# Luxembourg 2016

Agency: **HUMAN MADE**
Design: **Kamil Iwaszczyszyn**
Art Direction: **Kamil Iwaszczyszyn**
Layout: **Jan Hilken**
Copywriter: **Service Information et Presse Luxembourg**
Client: **Service Information et presse, STATEC**

"Luxembourg 2016" is a set of 14 infographics on the Grand Duchy of Luxembourg developed for the Information and Press Service of the Luxembourg government, in collaboration with the National Institute of Statistics and Economic Studies (STATEC). The purpose of these infographics is to present and promote the country in a visual and funny way with an emphasis on the following topics: geography, multicultural population, history of the Grand Duchy, linguistic situation, national symbols, culture and traditions, politics and institutions, economy, labor market, mobility, quality of life, and Luxembourg's image in the world.

# LUXEMBOURG 2016

AT A GLANCE

- 49°37'N  6°8'E
- Luxembourg, the capital
- National flag
- 563.000 inhabitants
- Time zone
- 1839
- GMT/UTC +1
- +352
- www.lu
- 220 V – 240 V / 50 Hz
- Constitutional monarchy
- Founding member of the EU
- Luxembourg, one of the three 'capitals' of the EU
- Year of its independence
- HRH Grand Duke Henri
- Xavier Bettel, Prime Minister, Minister of State
- Decimal system: 1 kg = 1,000 g
- Metric system: 1 m = 100 cm
- Currency: 1 EUR = 100 cents
- Deutschland
- France
- Belgique
- Borders
  - 148 km
  - 135 km
  - 73 km

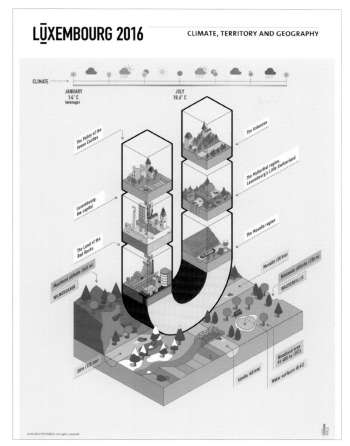

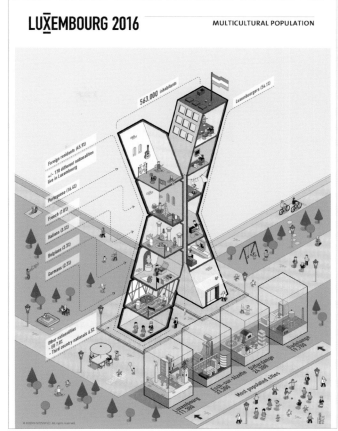

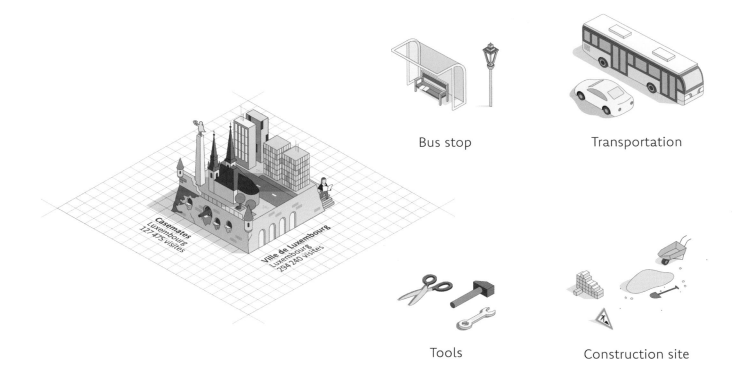

Bus stop

Transportation

Tools

Construction site

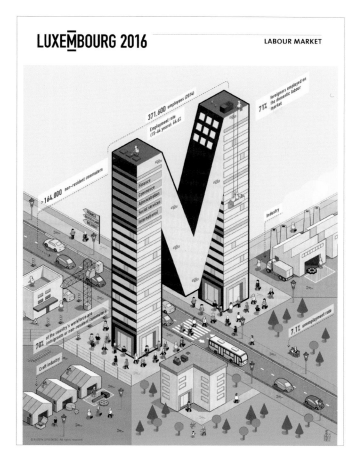

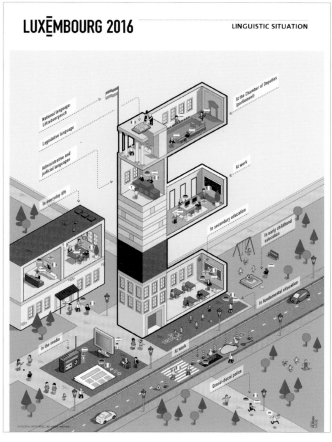

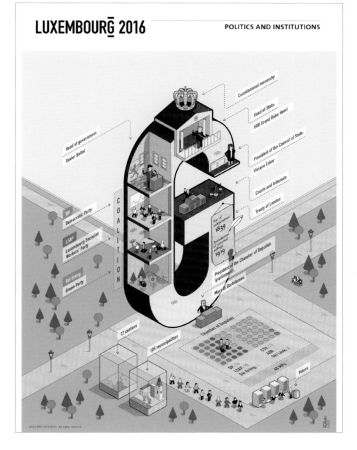

## LU✕EMBOURG
LET'S MAKE IT HAPPEN

CLIMATE, TERRITORY
AND GEOGRAPHY

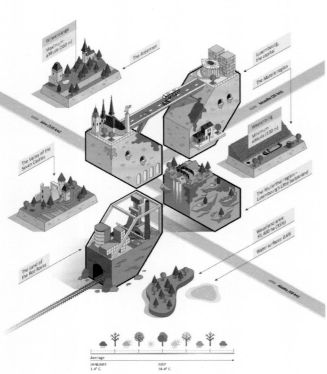

# Luxembourg Infographics 2017

Agency: **HUMAN MADE**
Design: **Kamil Iwaszczyszyn**
Art Direction: **Kamil Iwaszczyszyn**
Layout: **Jan Hilken**
Copywriter: **Service Information et Presse Luxembourg**
Client: **Service Information et presse, STATEC**

"Luxembourg 2017" is a set of 14 infographics on the Grand Duchy of Luxembourg developed for the Information and Press Service of the Luxembourg government, in collaboration with the National Institute of Statistics and Economic Studies (STATEC). The purpose of these infographics is to present and promote the country in a visual and funny way with an emphasis on the following topics: geography, multicultural population, history of the Grand Duchy, linguistic situation, national symbols, culture and traditions, politics and institutions, economy, labor market, mobility, quality of life, and Luxembourg's image in the world. This is an updated version for the year of 2017.

## LU✕EMBOURG
LET'S MAKE IT HAPPEN

LABOUR MARKET

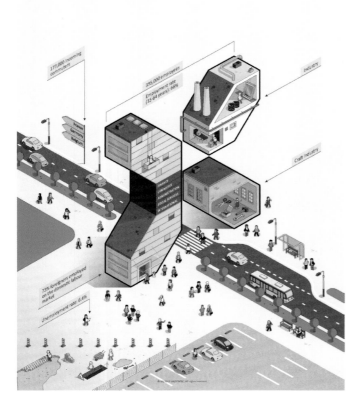

## LU✕EMBOURG
LET'S MAKE IT HAPPEN

ECONOMY AND
KEY ECONOMIC SECTORS

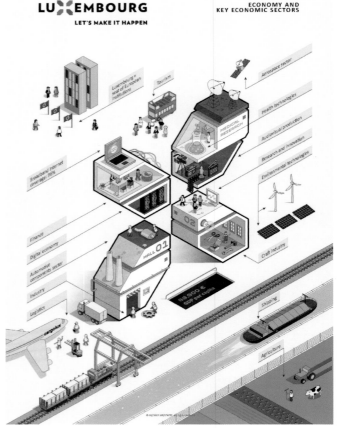

LET'S MAKE IT HAPPEN

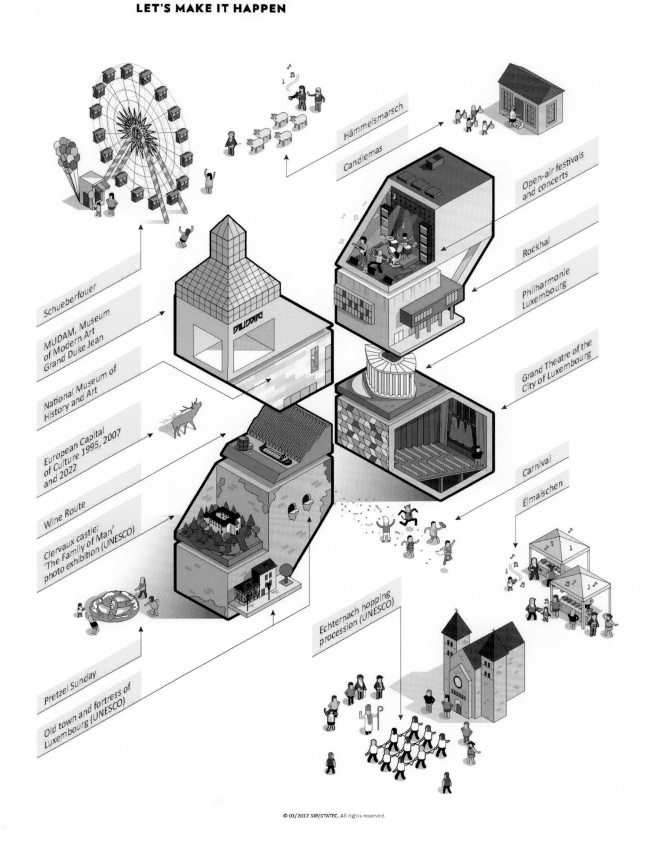

# Sowing Schedule

Design: **el abrelatas**
Client: *Mr. Natural*

This Sowing Schedule is the result of a huge list of garden products. The poster collects valuable data such as periods of cultivation, harvesting and treatments with other plants. The semi-circle composition and the format allow the viewer to easily find the information.

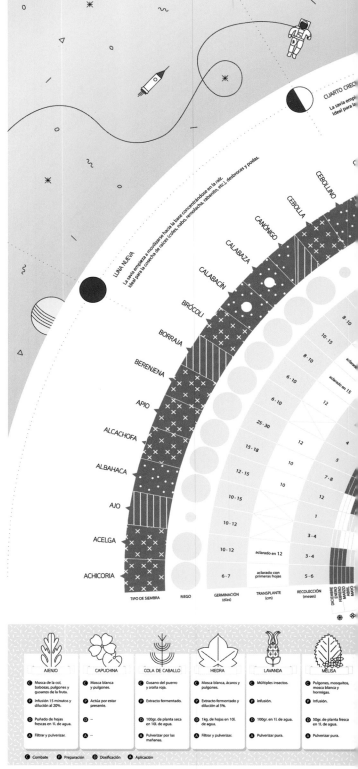

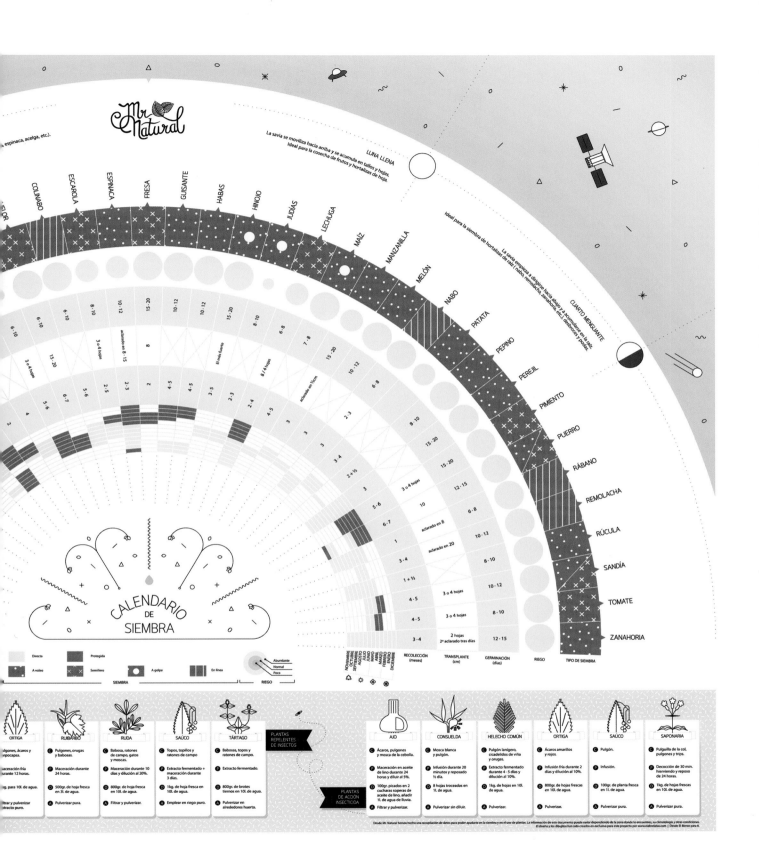

# LOS QUE TODO LO VEN

**TURISMO CIENTÍFICO**
La mejor selección de los observatorios y radiobservatorios más destacados distribuidos a lo largo y ancho del planeta Tierra.

**LEYENDA**
- ● Observatorio
- ○ Radiobservatorio
- ⊙ Localización
- ⚓ Altitud
- ✳ Telescopios
- ☀ Telescopios solares
- Ⓐ Radiotelescopios

---

**① ROQUE DE LOS MUCHACHOS**
- ⊙ La Palma · España  ⚓ 2396 m.
- ✳ 1 · 10,4 m. ø  ☀ Varios
- Visitable previa reserva del 15 de junio al 15 de septiembre.

**④ MONTE PALOMAR**
- ⊙ California · EEUU  ⚓ 1712 m.
- ✳ Varios
- Visitable todos los días del año.

**⑦ PIC DU MIDI**
- ⊙ Pirineos · Francia  ⚓ 2877 m.
- ✳ 4  ☀ 2
- Visitable previa reserva.

**⑩ TEIDE**
- ⊙ Tenerife · España  ⚓
- ✳ 8  ☀ 4
- Visitable previa reserva. 3 y 4 de julio de puertas abiertas.

**② VLT (VERY LARGE TELESCOPE)**
- ⊙ Desierto Atacama · Chile  ⚓ 2635 m.
- ✳ 4 · 8,4 m. ø
- Visitable los sábados previo registro.

**⑤ MONTE WILSON**
- ⊙ California · EEUU  ⚓ 1742 m.
- ✳ Varios  ☀ 2
- Visitable los sábados y domingos.

**⑧ LA SILLA**
- ⊙ Desierto Atacama · Chile  ⚓ 2400 m.
- ✳ 9
- Visitable los sábados excepto julio y agosto.

**⑪ SIDING SPRING**
- ⊙ Nueva Gales · Australia  ⚓
- ✳ 2 / 1 · 3,9 m. ø y 1 · 1,2 m. ø
- Visitable para el gran público.

**③ MAUNA KEA**
- ⊙ Volcán Mauna Kea · Hawái  ⚓ 4200 m.
- ✳ 9 / 2 · 10 m. ø y 2 · 8 m. ø  Ⓐ 4
- Visitable. Acceso en vehículo 4x4.

**⑥ MONTE GRAHAM**
- ⊙ Arizona · EEUU  ⚓ 3267 m.
- ✳ 2 · 8,4 m. ø
- Visitable desde la mitad de mayo a la mitad de noviembre.

**⑨ ESTACIÓN AMUNDSEN-SCOTT**
- ⊙ Polo Sur geográfico  ⚓ 2800 m.
- ✳ Varios  Ⓐ Varios
- No visitable.

**⑫ CALAR ALTO**
- ⊙ Almería · España  ⚓
- ✳ 5 / 1 · reflector 3,5 m. ø
- Visitable previa reserva.

Infografía

# World Observatories

Design: **el abrelatas**
Client: *Principia Magazine*

The infographic was born from the article "Observando el Universo" written by Nahúm Méndez. It was about an analysis and selection of observatories and radio-observatories top of the world.

Altitude, location, number of telescopes, and accessibility are some essential data included in this infographic published on a double-page in *Principia Magazine*.

RECIBO

Puerto Rico     ⬍ 323 m.

1 · 305 m. ø

itable.

④ IRAM

◉ Sierra Nevada · España     ⬍ 2850 m.

Ⓐ 1 · 30 m. ø

Visitable de mayo a septiembre.

.MA

Desierto Atacama · Chile     ⬍ 5000 m.

66 / 54 · 12 m. ø y 12 · 7 m. ø

itable los sábados y domingos.

⑤ FAST

◉ Piantang · China     ⬍ 1170 m.

Ⓐ 1 · 550 m. ø

.A (VERY LARGE ARRAY)

Nuevo México / EEUU     ⬍ 2124 m.

27 · 25 m. ø

itable. Visitas guiadas primer sábado
mes.

⑥ RATAN-600

◉ Zelenchukskaya · Rusia     ⬍ 938 m.

Ⓐ 1 · 576 m. ø con antena móvil.

Visitable previa reserva.

partir del artículo *"Observando el Universo"* de Nahúm Méndez para *Principia Magazine*.

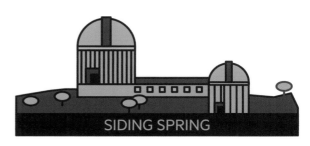

SIDING SPRING

CALAR ALTO

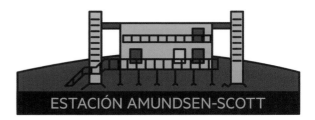

ESTACIÓN AMUNDSEN-SCOTT

# COLISIONES DIVINAS

MAGNETOSFERA

Las auroras polares son un fenómeno natural consistente en la emisión de luz causada por la excitación de algunos átomos que componen la atmósfera cuando contra ellos chocan partículas cargadas, como protones y electrones, que provienen de la corriente continua de una estrella. Solo se pueden apreciar cuando, en determinados momentos, esa corriente continua puede alcanzar una velocidad y densidad suficientes.

AURORA BOREAL
AURORA AUSTRAL

REQUISITOS
PARA CREA
UNA AUROR

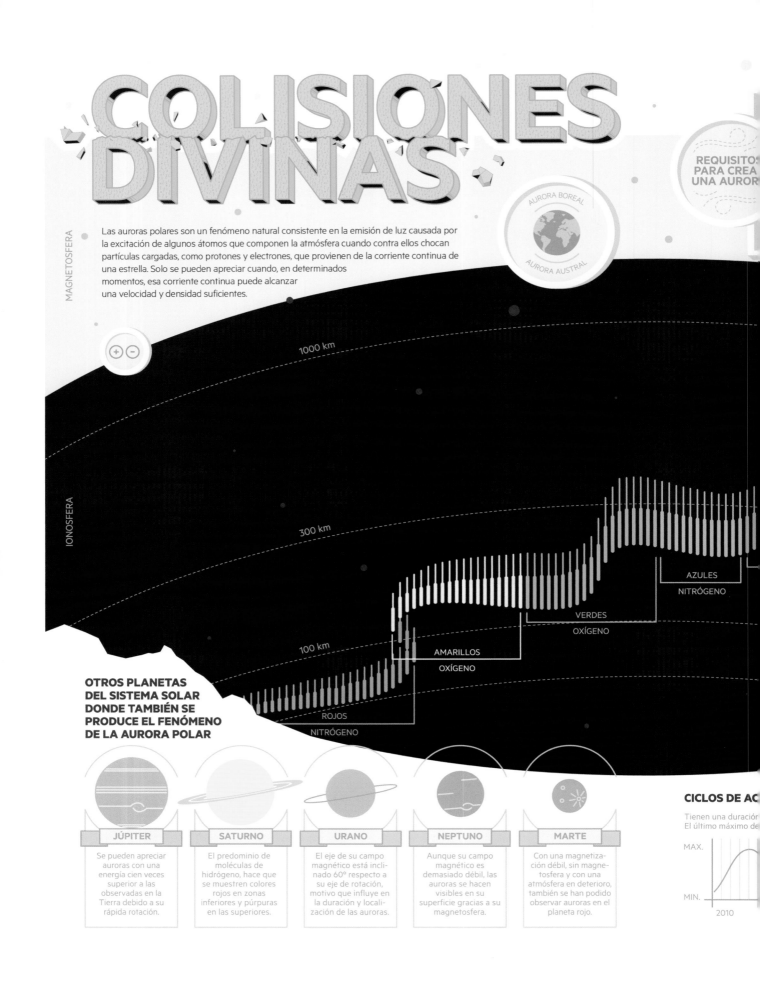

IONOSFERA

1000 km

300 km

100 km

AZULES
NITRÓGENO

VERDES
OXÍGENO

AMARILLOS
OXÍGENO

ROJOS
NITRÓGENO

## OTROS PLANETAS DEL SISTEMA SOLAR DONDE TAMBIÉN SE PRODUCE EL FENÓMENO DE LA AURORA POLAR

### JÚPITER
Se pueden apreciar auroras con una energía cien veces superior a las observadas en la Tierra debido a su rápida rotación.

### SATURNO
El predominio de moléculas de hidrógeno, hace que se muestren colores rojos en zonas inferiores y púrpuras en las superiores.

### URANO
El eje de su campo magnético está inclinado 60° respecto a su eje de rotación, motivo que influye en la duración y localización de las auroras.

### NEPTUNO
Aunque su campo magnético es demasiado débil, las auroras se hacen visibles en su superficie gracias a su magnetosfera.

### MARTE
Con una magnetización débil, sin magnetosfera y con una atmósfera en deterioro, también se han podido observar auroras en el planeta rojo.

## CICLOS DE AC
Tienen una duración
El último máximo de

MAX.

MIN.

2010

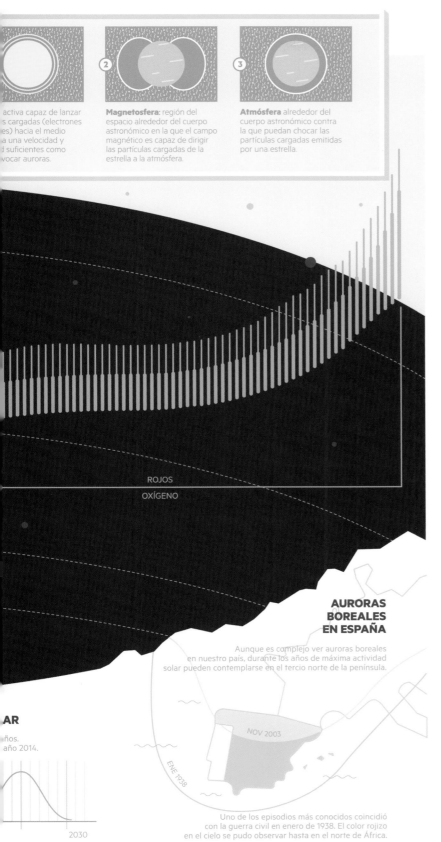

② **Magnetosfera**: región del espacio alrededor del cuerpo astronómico en la que el campo magnético es capaz de dirigir las partículas cargadas de la estrella a la atmósfera.

③ **Atmósfera** alrededor del cuerpo astronómico contra la que puedan chocar las partículas cargadas emitidas por una estrella.

...activa capaz de lanzar s cargadas (electrones es) hacia el medio a una velocidad y d suficientes como vocar auroras.

ROJOS
OXÍGENO

**AURORAS BOREALES EN ESPAÑA**

Aunque es complejo ver auroras boreales en nuestro país, durante los años de máxima actividad solar pueden contemplarse en el tercio norte de la península.

AR

ños.
año 2014.

2030

NOV 2003

ENE 1938

Uno de los episodios más conocidos coincidió con la guerra civil en enero de 1938. El color rojizo en el cielo se pudo observar hasta en el norte de África.

Infografía creada por el abrelatas a partir del artículo *La importancia de llamarse aurora* de Nahum Méndez para Principia Magazine.

# Colisiones Divinas

Design: **el abrelatas**
Client: *Principia Magazine*

"Colisiones divinas," translated as "Divine Collisions" in English, is an infographic about auroras in the universe. Why do they appear? Where do they appear? And how can we see from the Earth?

All information is sum up in a double-page published in the 4th issue of *Principia Magazine*.

# Half a Century: ZH

..................................

Design: **Leo Natsume**
UX: **Henrique Monteiro**
UI: **Leo Natsume**
Web Development: **Guilherme Maron**
Client: **Zero Hora**

"Half a Century" illustrates arts, music, performances, literature, and a lot of cultures in *2° Caderno Zero Hora*—a big newspaper from Brazil. This project has compiled the most important facts of the journalistic and social information of *Zero Hora* over the past five decades. For this, the designers have developed an interactive, illustrated, and dynamic website that adds a content dashboard style, and that is mostly navigable by a timeline. Through slides, they used the concept of change and renewal. With a clean navigation, they had the goal of making the user to get what he/she would like to see in a clear and easily accessible way.

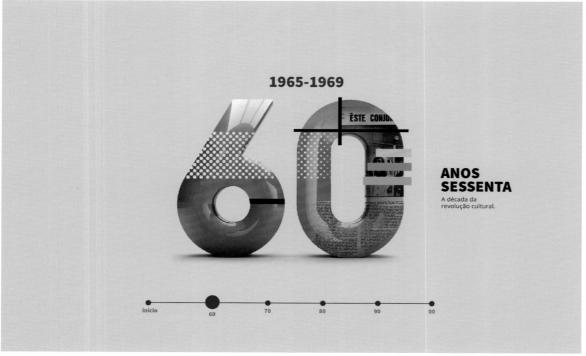

**1970-1979**

**1980-1989**

**1980-1989**

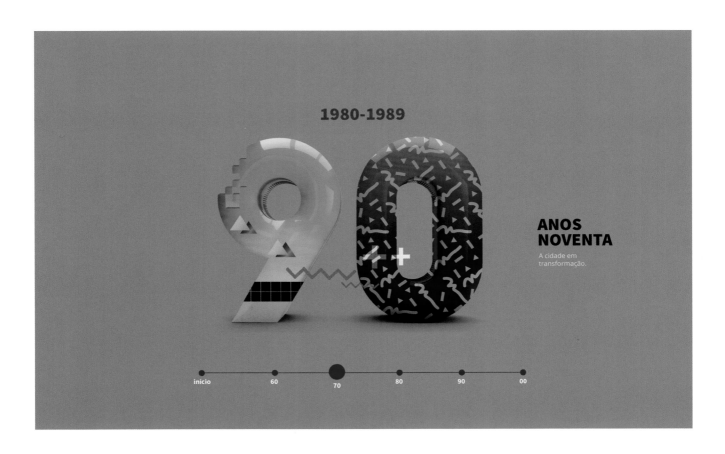

ANOS
NOVENTA

A cidade em
transformação.

# Multiple Sclerosis: Research on Disability

The infographic and illustration show the potential of technology to help people suffered from multiple sclerosis by visualizing some of the most common problems encountered by the patients, like incontinence, temperature leap, or just a walk in the streets.

Agency: **Studio Mistaker**
Art Direction: **Nino Brisindi**
Client: *La Repubblica*

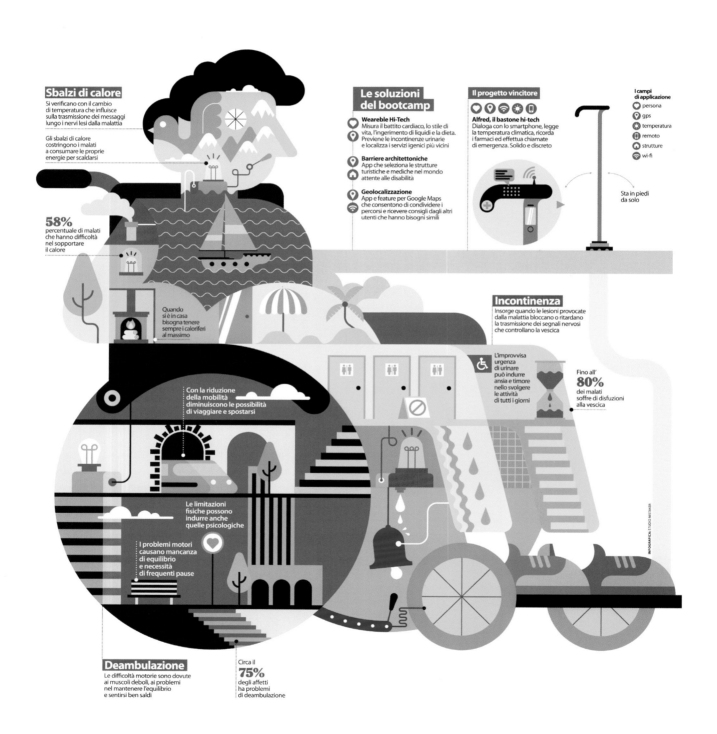

## Sbalzi di calore
Si verificano con il cambio di temperatura che influisce sulla trasmissione dei messaggi lungo i nervi lesi dalla malattia

Gli sbalzi di calore costringono i malati a consumare le proprie energie per scaldarsi

**58%**
percentuale di malati che hanno difficoltà nel sopportare il calore

Quando si è in casa bisogna tenere sempre i caloriferi al massimo

## Le soluzioni del bootcamp

**Weareble Hi-Tech**
Misura il battito cardiaco, lo stile di vita, l'ingerimento di liquidi e la dieta. Previene le incontinenze urinarie e localizza i servizi igenici più vicini

**Barriere architettoniche**
App che seleziona le strutture turistiche e mediche nel mondo attente alle disabilità

**Geolocalizzazione**
App e feature per Google Maps che consentono di condividere i percorsi e ricevere consigli dagli altri utenti che hanno bisogni simili

## Il progetto vincitore

**Alfred, il bastone hi-tech**
Dialoga con lo smartphone, legge la temperatura climatica, ricorda i farmaci ed effettua chiamate di emergenza. Solido e discreto

## I campi di applicazione
- persona
- gps
- temperatura
- remoto
- strutture
- wi-fi

Sta in piedi da solo

## Incontinenza
Insorge quando le lesioni provocate dalla malattia bloccano o ritardano la trasmissione dei segnali nervosi che controllano la vescica

L'improvvisa urgenza di urinare può indurre ansia e timore nello svolgere le attività di tutti i giorni

Fino all'
**80%**
dei malati soffre di disfuzioni alla vescica

Con la riduzione della mobilità diminuiscono le possibilità di viaggiare e spostarsi

Le limitazioni fisiche possono indurre anche quelle psicologiche

I problemi motori causano mancanza di equilibrio e necessità di frequenti pause

## Deambulazione
Le difficoltà motorie sono dovute ai muscoli deboli, ai problemi nel mantenere l'equilibrio e sentirsi ben saldi

Circa il
**75%**
degli affetti ha problemi di deambulazione

INFOGRAFICA/STUDIO MISTAKER

# SNCF: FAB DESIGN

This is an infographic highlighting the 2016 report of Fab Design, the digital agency of the SNCF group, France's national state-owned railway company. Each data has been illustrated to represent a building under construction. This building will be developed in the future.

Design: **Creamcrackers**
Client: **SNCF**

## CONSEIL & EXPERTISE

### ACCOMPAGNEMENT DES PROJETS
Audit ergonomique, parcours client, maquettage, optimisation d'interfaces, tests utilisateurs, etc.

### FORMATIONS ET CONFÉRENCES
Partage et diffusion de l'expertise et des tendances UX/Design

## PROJETS

### SNCF.MOBI
Version mobile du site sncf.com

### SNCF.COM
Refonte complète du site pour l'été 2017

### DIGITAL.SNCF.COM
Nouveau site, point d'entrée unique et boite à outils du digital

## OUTILS

### FEEDBACK ONLINE
Solution de récolte de commentaires en ligne

### STYLEGUIDE
Kit de développement sur la charte graphique

### SDK SNCF.ID
Kit de développement pour faciliter l'authentification des agents

### STORE.SNCF
Plateforme des 300 applications et sites mobiles du groupe SNCF

### GUIDELINES
Bonnes pratiques et méthodologies pour améliorer et réaliser des outils digitaux

# Emotions & Trauma

Design: **Krystyna Oniszczuk-Dylik**
Client: **Faculty of Psychology,
University of Warsaw, Poland**

The purpose of this project was to showcase the psychological academic text by the images. The concept was to illustrate the emotions and trauma through the elements—the impulses that make people feel a certain kind of feeling. These are the difficult and painful topics for both patients and students to talk about, so it was important to interpret them in a light-hearted way.

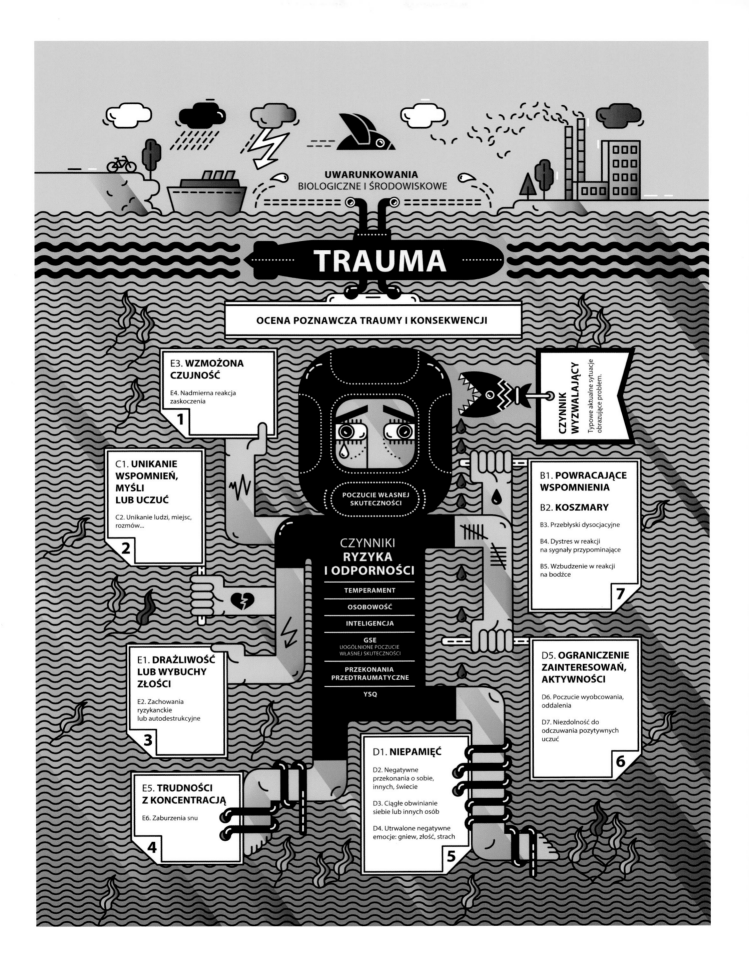

UWARUNKOWANIA
BIOLOGICZNE I ŚRODOWISKOWE

# TRAUMA

## OCENA POZNAWCZA TRAUMY I KONSEKWENCJI

**E3. WZMOŻONA CZUJNOŚĆ**

E4. Nadmierna reakcja zaskoczenia

**1**

**C1. UNIKANIE WSPOMNIEŃ, MYŚLI LUB UCZUĆ**

C2. Unikanie ludzi, miejsc, rozmów...

**2**

**E1. DRAŻLIWOŚĆ LUB WYBUCHY ZŁOŚCI**

E2. Zachowania ryzykanckie lub autodestrukcyjne

**3**

**E5. TRUDNOŚCI Z KONCENTRACJĄ**

E6. Zaburzenia snu

**4**

POCZUCIE WŁASNEJ SKUTECZNOŚCI

CZYNNIKI **RYZYKA I ODPORNOŚCI**

TEMPERAMENT

OSOBOWOŚĆ

INTELIGENCJA

GSE
UOGÓLNIONE POCZUCIE WŁASNEJ SKUTECZNOŚCI

PRZEKONANIA PRZEDTRAUMATYCZNE

YSQ

**D1. NIEPAMIĘĆ**

D2. Negatywne przekonania o sobie, innych, świecie

D3. Ciągłe obwinianie siebie lub innych osób

D4. Utrwalone negatywne emocje: gniew, złość, strach

**5**

CZYNNIK WYZWALAJĄCY
Typowe aktualne sytuacje obrazujące problem.

**B1. POWRACAJĄCE WSPOMNIENIA**

**B2. KOSZMARY**

B3. Przebłyski dysocjacyjne

B4. Dystres w reakcji na sygnały przypominające

B5. Wzbudzenie w reakcji na bodźce

**7**

**D5. OGRANICZENIE ZAINTERESOWAŃ, AKTYWNOŚCI**

D6. Poczucie wyobcowania, oddalenia

D7. Niezdolność do odczuwania pozytywnych uczuć

**6**

# GOGREEN Book Various Diagrams

Design: **Peter Grundy**
Client: **DHL**

DHL asked Peter Grundy to create an information booklet to explain their green credentials under the umbrella of GOGreen.

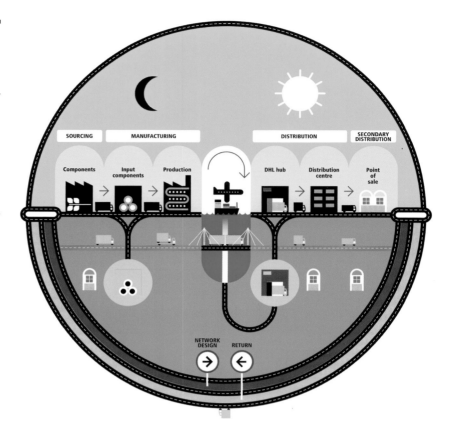

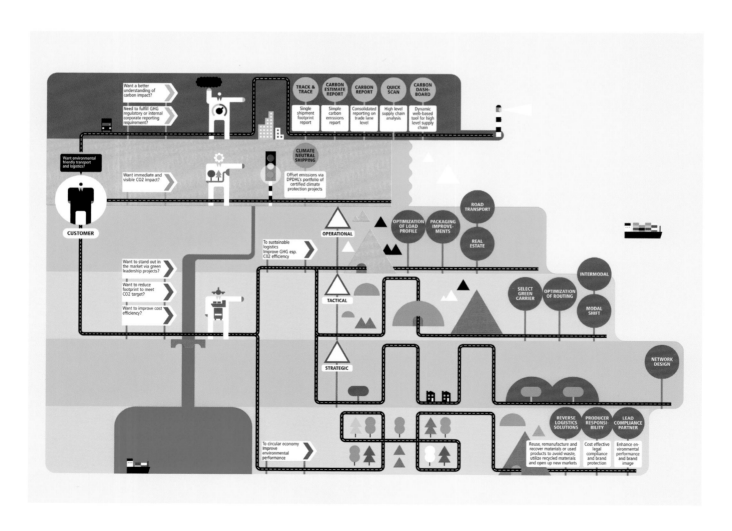

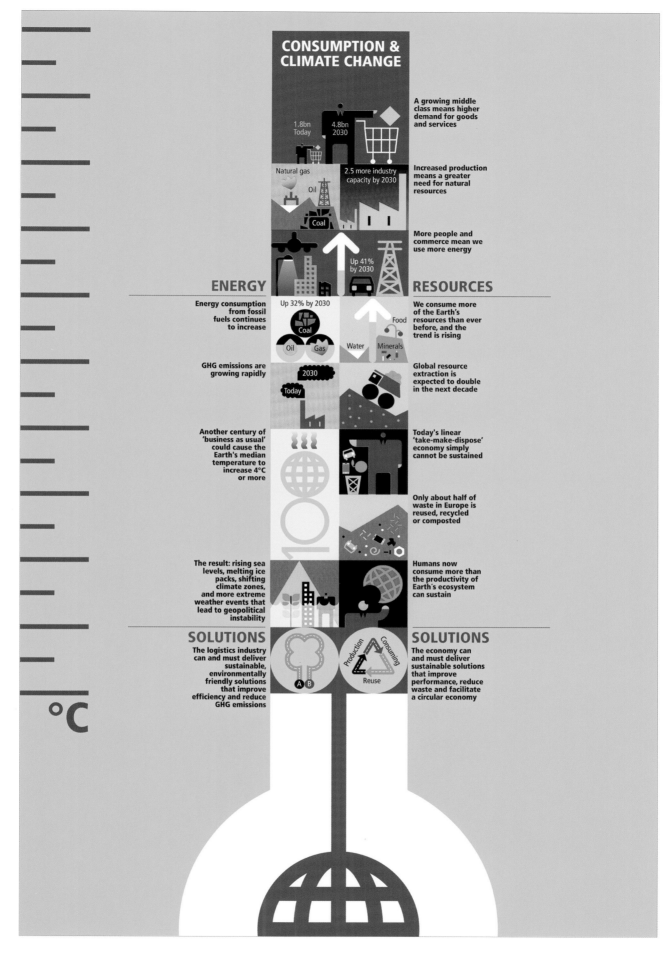

# CONSUMPTION & CLIMATE CHANGE

1.8bn Today

4.8bn 2030

A growing middle class means higher demand for goods and services

Natural gas

Oil

Coal

2.5 more industry capacity by 2030

Increased production means a greater need for natural resources

Up 41% by 2030

More people and commerce mean we use more energy

## ENERGY

## RESOURCES

Energy consumption from fossil fuels continues to increase

Up 32% by 2030

Coal

Oil

Gas

Food

Water

Minerals

We consume more of the Earth's resources than ever before, and the trend is rising

GHG emissions are growing rapidly

2030

Today

Global resource extraction is expected to double in the next decade

Another century of 'business as usual' could cause the Earth's median temperature to increase 4°C or more

Today's linear 'take-make-dispose' economy simply cannot be sustained

Only about half of waste in Europe is reused, recycled or composted

The result: rising sea levels, melting ice packs, shifting climate zones, and more extreme weather events that lead to geopolitical instability

Humans now consume more than the productivity of Earth's ecosystem can sustain

## SOLUTIONS

The logistics industry can and must deliver sustainable, environmentally friendly solutions that improve efficiency and reduce GHG emissions

A  B

Production

Consuming

Reuse

## SOLUTIONS

The economy can and must deliver sustainable solutions that improve performance, reduce waste and facilitate a circular economy

°C

# CLIMATE NEUTRAL

**1st**

Carbon neutral product in parcel and express sector in 2006

Total offset for of all high quality and verified climate neutral services

| 2006 | 2014 |
|---|---|
| 1,014 tCO2 offset | 200,000 tCO2 offset |

# GREEN ROAD TRANSPORT

Green road transport technologies for all purposes

**Burn less**
- Aerodynamics
- Engine modifications
- Hybrids

**Burn clean**
- Alternative fuels
- Electric vehicles (powered by green electricity)

DPDHL's total global green fleet

2008 / **544 vehicles**      2014 / **12,500 vehicles**

# TEARDROP TRAILER

More than 1500 teardrop trailer in operation

1st to market in UK         1st to market in mainland Europe

2〓09  2●14

# ELECTRIC FLEET

1st in industry to develop and produce own fully electric mail and parcel vehicles with a fleet of 45 in 2014

- The largest global logistics fleet of fully electric vehicles

- Over 400 fully electric vehicles in operation in 2014

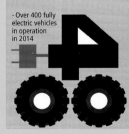

# REAL ESTATE

Green real estate technologies for all purposes

**Burn less**
Energy-efficient lighting, heating and air conditioning

**Burn clean**
Green electricity globally: more than 60%

**60%**

The first zero-to-landfill warehouse

# CARBON ACCOUNTING AND CONTROLLING

Industry leading Carbon Accounting and Controlling system

Covers entire group with multiple parameters
- 28 mt CO2
- 220 countries and territories
- All transport and logistics activities

Road        Air    Business travel

Rail    Real estate        Ocean

# CLIMATE PROTECTION PROJECT

1st in industry to launch own climate protection project to generate carbon credits

Energy efficient wood stoves in Lesotho to generate carbon credits for Climate Neutral shipping service

# INITIATIVES AND ADVISORY ROLES

Co-initiator of Green Freight Europe and Green Freight Asia

CEO is a representative in UN High Level Advisory Group on Sustainable Transport

1st logistics company to put a Biofuels Guideline in place

# AVIATION

Carbon efficiency of own aviation increased by 45% in 2013, compared to 2007

**45%**

# CARBON REPORT SOLUTIONS

Carbon Report solutions for all customer needs

Globally available for all transport and logistics services

**Carbon Report solutions**
- Track and Trace
- Carbon Estimate Report
- Carbon Dashboard

# 1 GOGREEN LOGISTICS

Deutsche Post DHL Carbon Efficiency Index (Index points)

2007 / **100**
2014 / **78**
2020 / **70**

**TARGET**

NEW MARKETS ACCESSED

NEW PRODUCTS & BRAND STRENGTHENED

COST, ENERGY, WATER & TIME SAVED

WASTE MINIMIZED

REDUCED CARBON FOOTPRINT

PROCESS OPTIMIZED

TIME

SUSTAINABLE CHANGE

This is a series of infographics in A1 size explaining various aspects of the craft beer industry, from the different types of beer to the brewing process. The project is made for a pop-up beer festival in Romania organized by the local company called Beerologique.

Tipuri de bere

**Red Ale**
ABV = 3.5 - 5.5%
Culoare = Roșu aprins    Gust dulceag, de caramel

**Stout**
ABV = 4 - 7%
Culoare = Negru    Corpolenta și cremoasă
Aroma complexa, de cafea
prăjita și ciocolată neagra

**Pilsner**
ABV = 4 - 5.5%
Culoare = Galben pal    Spumoasă
Gust curat, neutru

**IPA**
ABV = 5 - 7.5%
Culoare = Portocaliu    Gust pronunțat de hamei
Amăruie și aromata

**Wheat Beer**
ABV = 4 - 7%
Culoare = Galben    Nefiltrată
Gust de banane și cuișoară

Enjoyed by
**DAISLER®**
PRINT HOUSE

# Micro
## Vs
# Macro

Gustați diferența dintre cele doua azi!

Malț
+ Hamei
+ Drojdie
+ Apă
+ Timp
+ Pasiune
=
O bere pe cinste!

Orz Brut
+ Orez
+ Porumb
+ Zahăr
+ Enzime
+ Extract de Hamei
+ Drojdie
+ Apă
- Timp și fără Pasiune
=
O bere generică, fără suflet...

Enjoyed by
**DAISLER**
PRINT HOUSE

Brasaj 66°C
Malț Măcinat
+
Apă Caldă
=
Must de Bere

Fierbător
100°C
Must de Bere          Must de Bere
+                     +
hamei adăugat la      hamei adăugat la
început x 1 ora        sfârșit x 0 minute
=                     =
gust amărui           aromă

Fermentație
20°C
Must de Bere
+
Drojdie x 4 Zile
=
o bere care nu-i chiar gata incă

Condiț-ionat
12°C
Bere
+
CO2 x 3
Săptămâni sau mai multe
=
o bere ajunsa la desăvârșire!

# Bere!

Noroc!

**Cum se produce berea**

Enjoyed by
**DAISLER**
PRINT HOUSE

## Malț
Oferă zaharuri care sunt transformate în alcool

• Malț de bază = gust de bisuite, paine
• Malț caramelizat = gust dulce, de caramele
• Malț prăjit = gust de nucă, ciocolată neagra, cafea

## Hamei
Asigură gustul amărui și aromă

• Floral      • Fructe de pădure
• Fructat     • Pământiu
• Citric      • Herbal
• Picant      • Ierbos

## Apa
95% din bere este apă

## Drojdie
Transforma zaharurile in alcool și creeasă dioxid de carbon (co2)

• Banană      • Esteri
• Cuișoară    • Acru
• Măr Verde   • Alcool
• Fructat

**Ce este într-o bere?**

Enjoyed by
**DAISLER**
PRINT HOUSE

# Beer

Agency: **203 × Infographics Lab**

The beer is known as the world's oldest alcoholic beverage, brewed back in 6,000 BC. Today the beer is loved by people all over the world. There started a boom of imported beer in Korea in 2015. It was a good subject for an infographic to portray the season and market of the imported beer. The good season to drink beer is not strictly defined. If the consumer thinks about "coolness," perhaps it is the best to have a cool beer in Summer. 203 × Infographics Lab tried to introduce all kinds of beer which are divided largely into ale, lager, and a unique beer in front of Hongik University.

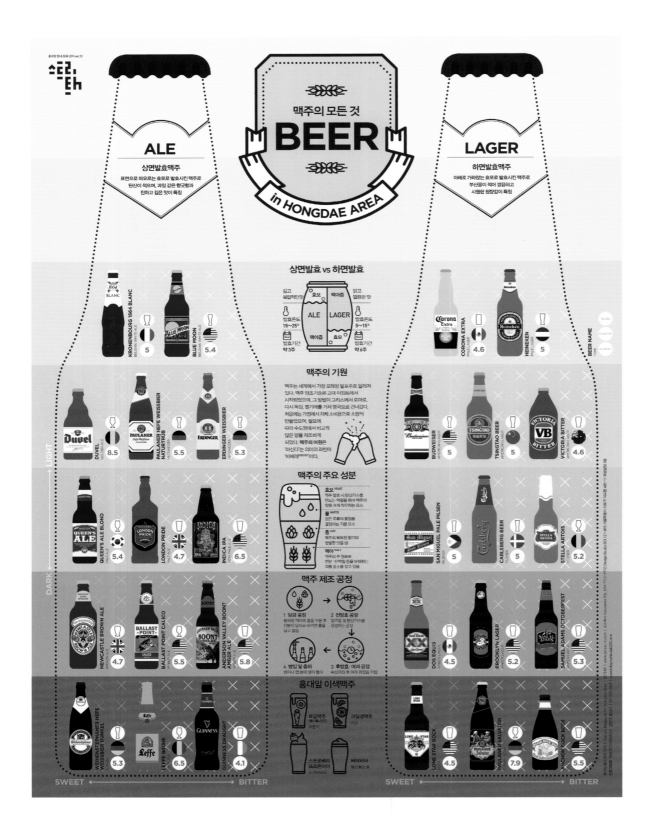

# Burger

Agency: **203 × Infographics Lab**

Hamburger has gradually become synonymous with fast food and junk food. It was once an icon representing the American culture. It made it easy to put a meal on the table and it spread like a fashion, but this fashion was against the wind because it was referred to being unhealthy. But when it comes to homemade burgers, there is a new trend again. In addition, compared to the franchise burger shops, nowadays more homemade burger shops start to sell unusual burgers in front of Hongik University.

# Bicycle

Agency: **203 × Infographics Lab**

The bicycle is considered as one of the most effective and great vehicles that were invented more than 200 years ago. Its human-powered moving system makes this invention more valuable. With endless improvement and the boom of fitness and leisure industry, the bicycle is on its golden age in Korea. Over the last 15 years, many bicycle roads have been made across the country. Without distinction of sex or age, many people are enjoying this vehicle. This infographic helps many riders to understand their favorite "horse."

# Letter Press

..............................

Agency: **203 × Infographics Lab**

Letterpress printing is a technique of relief printing using a printing press—many copies are produced in this way by repeating the direct impression of an inked, raised surface against sheets or a continuous roll of paper. It is an analog printing method which is out of date. But today it has revived as a classical printing technique. Young people who get used to digital life do not know clearly about this old printing technique. 203 × Infographics Lab hope that this infographic will be useful for them to understand the history of printing and letterpress.

## 24 Hours of Le Mans Winners Since 1923

..........................................

Agency: **Big Group**

The legendary 24 Hours of Le Mans race is one of the most coveted motorsports prizes. It has been going since 1923 and sees the world's leading car manufacturers and drivers compete to prove that they are not only the fastest but also the most reliable and enduring by racing non-stop for 24 hours. Teams of three drivers will cover over 5000 kilometers and run up nearly 400 laps of the course during the day.

Big Group has more than a few motorsport fans as well as a talented pool of researchers, illustrators, and designers, all of which meant that they could not help but produce a graphic showing the 84 cars that have won Le Mans.

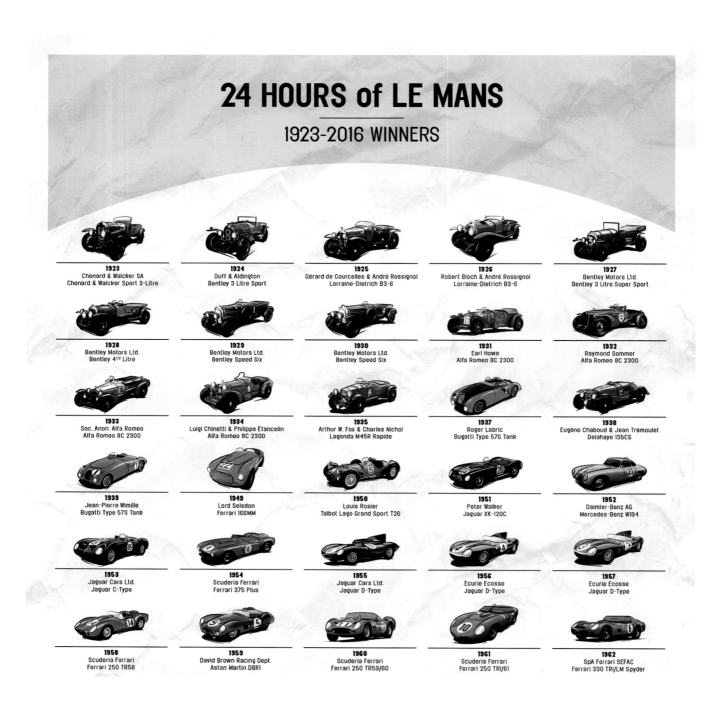

**1963**
SpA Ferrari SEFAC
Ferrari 250P

**1964**
SpA Ferrari SEFAC
Ferrari 275P

**1965**
North American Racing Team
Ferrari 250LM

**1966**
Shelby-American Inc.
Ford GT40 Mk. II

**1967**
Shelby-American Inc.
Ford GT40 Mk. IV

**1968**
J.W. Automotive Engineering
Ford GT40 Mk. I

**1969**
J.W. Automotive Engineering
Ford GT40 Mk. I

**1970**
Porsche KG Salzburg
Porsche 917K

**1971**
Martini Racing Team
Porsche 917K

**1972**
Equipe Matra-Simca Shell
Matra MS670

**1973**
Equipe Matra-Simca Shell
Matra MS670B

**1974**
Equipe Gitanes
Matra MS670C

**1975**
Gulf Research Racing Co.
Mirage GR8-Ford Cosworth

**1976**
Martini Racing Porsche System
Porsche 936

**1977**
Martini Racing Porsche System
Porsche 936/77

**1978**
Alpine Renault
Renault Alpine A442B

**1979**
Porsche Kremer Racing
Porsche 935 K3

**1980**
Jean Rondeau
Rondeau M379B-Ford Cosworth

**1981**
Porsche System
Porsche 936

**1982**
Rothmans Porsche System
Porsche 956

**1983**
Rothmans Porsche
Porsche 956

**1984**
Joest Racing
Porsche 956

**1985**
Joest Racing
Porsche 956

**1986**
Rothmans Porsche AG
Porsche 962C

**1987**
Rothmans Porsche AG
Porsche 962C

**1988**
Silk Cut Jaguar
Jaguar XJR-9LM

**1989**
Team Sauber Mercedes
Sauber C9-Mercedes-Benz

**1990**
Silk Cut Jaguar
Jaguar XJR-12

**1991**
Mazdaspeed Co. Ltd.
Mazda 787B

**1992**
Peugeot Talbot Sport
Peugeot 905 Evo 1B

**1993**
Peugeot Talbot Sport
Peugeot 905 Evo 1B

**1994**
Le Mans Porsche Team
Dauer 962 Le Mans

**1995**
Kokusai Kaihatsu Racing
McLaren F1 GTR

**1996**
Joest Racing
TWR Porsche WSC-95

**1997**
Joest Racing
TWR Porsche WSC-95

**1998**
Porsche AG
Porsche 911 GT1-98

**1999**
Team BMW Motorsport
BMW V12 LMR

**2000**
Audi Sport Team Joest
Audi R8

**2001**
Audi Sport Team Joest
Audi R8

**2002**
Audi Sport Team Joest
Audi R8

**2003**
Team Bentley
Bentley Speed 8

**2004**
Audi Sport Japan Team Goh
Audi R8

**2005**
ADT Champion Racing
Audi R8

**2006**
Audi Sport Team Joest
Audi R10 TDI

**2007**
Audi Sport North America
Audi R10 TDI

**2008**
Audi Sport North America
Audi R10 TDI

**2009**
Peugeot Sport Total
Peugeot 908 HDi FAP

**2010**
Audi Sport North America
Audi R15 TDI plus

**2011**
Audi Sport Team Joest
Audi R18 TDI

**2012**
Audi Sport Team Joest
Audi R18 e-tron quattro

**2013**
Audi Sport Team Joest
Audi R18 e-tron quattro

**2014**
Audi Sport Team Joest
Audi R18 e-tron quattro

**2015**
Porsche Team
Porsche 919 Hybrid

**2016**
Porsche Team
Porsche 919 Hybrid

BIG
GROUP

# History of the Automobile

The visualization shows the history of automobile for decades from steam propelled vehicles in the 19th century to the sports cars of the 21st century.

Design: **Raquel Jove**

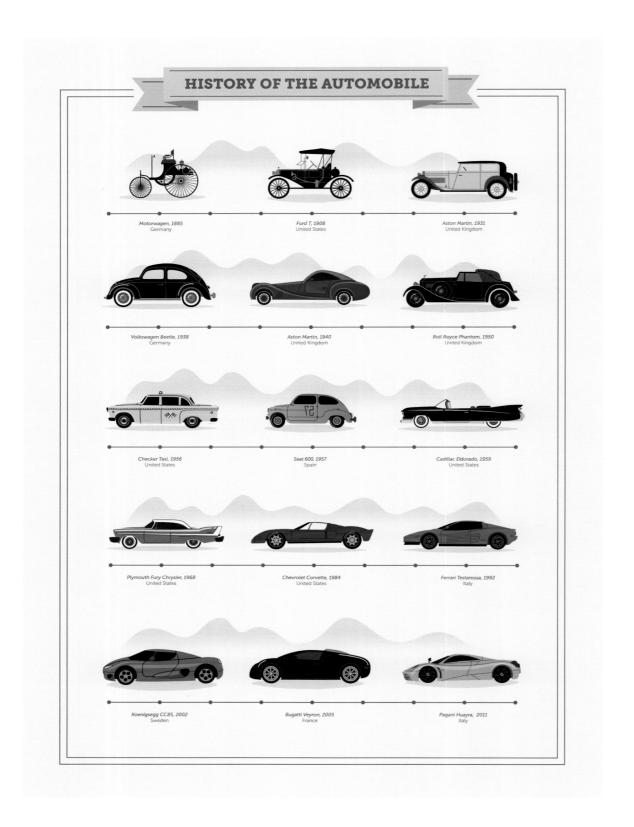

# The Oscar Dresses Infographic 2016

Agency: **Big Group**

As the dust settles on another Academy Awards and Hollywood's elites emerge bleary-eyed from their after parties, Big Group present to the viewers the latest incarnation of the Oscar Dresses Infographic.

This year's update has two brand new dress illustrations to savor. Congratulations to Brie Larson and a big apology to Julianne Moore for taking so long!

# OSCAR DRESSES
## EVERY DRESS WORN BY BEST ACTRESS ACADEMY AWARD WINNERS

| 1929 | 1930 | 1930 | 1931 | 1932 | 1935 | 1936 | 1937 |
|---|---|---|---|---|---|---|---|
| JANET GAYNOR 'Off The Rack' | MARY PICKFORD Unknown | NORMA SHEARER Unknown | MARIE DRESSLER Unknown | HELEN HAYES Unknown | CLAUDETTE COLBERT Travis Banton | BETTE DAVIS Orry-Kelly | LUISE RAINER Unknown |

| 1938 | 1939 | 1940 | 1941 | 1942 | 1943 | 1944 | 1945 |
|---|---|---|---|---|---|---|---|
| LUISE RAINER Unknown | BETTE DAVIS Unknown | VIVIEN LEIGH Irene Gibbons | GINGER ROGERS Irene Gibbons | JOAN FONTAINE I. Magnin & Co. | GREER GARSON Unknown | JENNIFER JONES Anita Colby | INGRID BERGMAN Howard Greer |

| 1947 | 1948 | 1949 | 1950 | 1953 | 1954 | 1955 | 1958 |
|---|---|---|---|---|---|---|---|
| OLIVIA DE HAVILLAND Ann Lowe for Sonia Gowns | LORETTA YOUNG Adrian | JANE WYMAN Unknown | OLIVIA DE HAVILLAND Orry-Kelly | SHIRLEY BOOTH Unknown | AUDREY HEPBURN Edith Head / Givenchy | GRACE KELLY Edith Head | JOANNE WOODWARD Made her own |

| 1959 | 1960 | 1961 | 1965 | 1966 | 1969 | 1972 | 1973 |
|---|---|---|---|---|---|---|---|
| SUSAN HAYWARD Unknown | SIMONE SIGNORET Jean Dèsses | ELIZABETH TAYLOR Christian Dior | JULIE ANDREWS Unknown | JULIE CHRISTIE Made her own | BARBRA STREISAND Arnold Scaasi | JANE FONDA Yves Saint Laurent | LIZA MINNELLI Halston |

| 1976 | 1977 | 1978 | 1979 | 1980 | 1981 | 1983 | 1984 |
|---|---|---|---|---|---|---|---|
| LOUISE FLETCHER Alfred Fiandaca | FAYE DUNAWAY Geoffrey Beene | DIANE KEATON Ruth Morley | JANE FONDA James Reva | SALLY FIELD Bob Mackie | SISSY SPACEK 'Off the Rack' | MERYL STREEP Christian Leigh | SHIRLEY MACLAINE Fabrice |

| 1985 | 1986 | 1987 | 1988 | 1989 | 1990 | 1991 | 1992 |
|---|---|---|---|---|---|---|---|
| SALLY FIELD Holly Harp | GERALDINE PAGE Gail Cooper-Hecht | MARLEE MATLIN Theoni V. Aldredge | CHER Bob Mackie | JODIE FOSTER 'Off The Rack' | JESSICA TANDY Giorgio Armani | KATHY BATES Donna Karan | JODIE FOSTER Armani |

| 1993 | 1994 | 1995 | 1996 | 1997 | 1998 | 1999 | 2000 |
|---|---|---|---|---|---|---|---|
| EMMA THOMPSON Caroline Charles | HOLLY HUNTER Vera Wang | JESSICA LANGE Calvin Klein | SUSAN SARANDON Dolce & Gabbana | FRANCES MCDORMAND Richard Tyler | HELEN HUNT Tom Ford for Gucci | GWYNETH PALTROW Ralph Lauren | HILARY SWANK Randolph Duke |

| 2001 | 2002 | 2003 | 2004 | 2005 | 2006 | 2007 | 2008 |
|---|---|---|---|---|---|---|---|
| JULIA ROBERTS Valentino | HALLE BERRY Elie Saab | NICOLE KIDMAN Jean Paul Gaultier | CHARLIZE THERON Gucci | HILARY SWANK Guy Laroche | REESE WITHERSPOON Christian Dior | HELEN MIRREN Christian Lacroix | MARION COTILLARD Jean Paul Gaultier |

| 2009 | 2010 | 2011 | 2012 | 2013 | 2014 | 2015 | 2016 |
|---|---|---|---|---|---|---|---|
| KATE WINSLET Yves Saint Laurent | SANDRA BULLOCK Marchesa | NATALIE PORTMAN Rodarte | MERYL STREEP Lanvin | JENNIFER LAWRENCE Christian Dior | CATE BLANCHETT Armani Privé | JULIANNE MOORE Chanel | BRIE LARSON Gucci |

### ACTRESSES WHO DIDN'T ATTEND TO ACCEPT THEIR AWARDS:

| | | | | |
|---|---|---|---|---|
| 1934 – KATHARINE HEPBURN | 1952 – VIVIEN LEIGH | 1962 – SOPHIA LOREN | 1967 – ELIZABETH TAYLOR | 1970 – MAGGIE SMITH | 1975 – ELLEN BURSTYN |
| 1946 – JOAN CRAWFORD | 1956 – ANNA MAGNANI | 1963 – ANNE BANCROFT | 1968 – KATHARINE HEPBURN | 1971 – GLENDA JACKSON | 1982 – KATHARINE HEPBURN |
| 1951 – JUDY HOLLIDAY | 1957 – INGRID BERGMAN | 1964 – PATRICIA NEAL | 1969 – KATHARINE HEPBURN | 1974 – GLENDA JACKSON | |

# Infographic Design of Plants

Design: **Biqi Zhang**
Art Direction: **Hao Chen**

People rarely observe the beauty of nature, so Biqi Zhang used three pieces of infographics to show the plants that are common in our life: Pteridophytes, Gymnosperms, and Angiosperms.

In the diagram, the expressive illustration is used to convey the morphological characteristics, growth, and development of these plants.

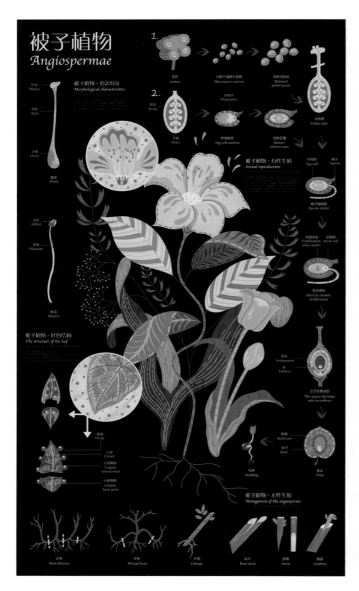

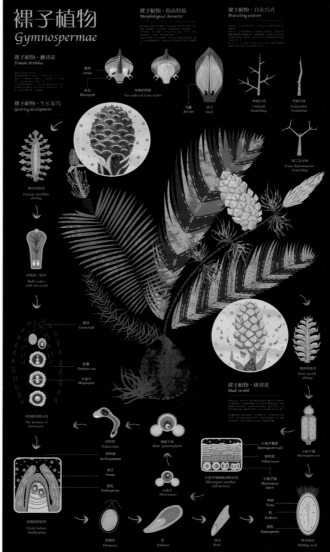

# Hankook Coffee

Agency: **DAEKI & JUN Studio**
Design: **Daeki Shim, Hyojun Shim, Seoeun Kim**
Art Direction: **Daeki Shim, Hyojun Shim**
Client: **Hankook Coffee**

Hankook Coffee is a company selling coffee in Korean market by importing the best specialty coffee (specialty coffee, the highest-quality green coffee beans) which has been rated as one of the top seven percent of A-grade coffee beans in the world since 1992. To represent the top seven percent of A-grade, the designers visualized the coffee in a diagram using the form of coffee drops. The whole series includes a poster (420mm × 594mm) and postcards (90mm × 130mm).

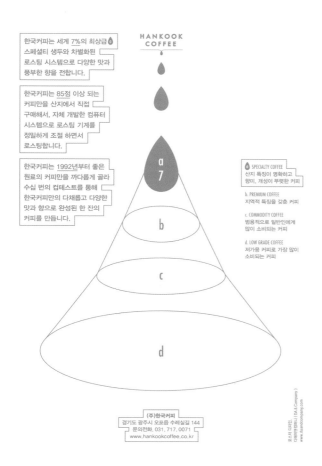

한국커피는 세계 7%의 최상급
스페셜티 생두와 차별화된
로스팅 시스템으로 다양한 맛과
풍부한 향을 전합니다.

한국커피는 85점 이상 되는
커피만을 산지에서 직접
구매해서, 자체 개발한 컴퓨터
시스템으로 로스팅 기계를
정밀하게 조절 하면서
로스팅합니다.

한국커피는 1992년부터 좋은
원료의 커피만을 까다롭게 골라
수십 번의 컵테스트를 통해
한국커피만의 다채롭고 다양한
맛과 향으로 완성한 한 잔의
커피를 만듭니다.

HANKOOK COFFEE

a
7

b

c

d

**SPECIALTY COFFEE**
산지 특징이 명확하고
향미, 개성이 뚜렷한 커피

b. PREMIUM COFFEE
지역적 특징을 갖춘 커피

c. COMMODITY COFFEE
범용적으로 일반인에게
많이 소비되는 커피

d. LOW GRADE COFFEE
저가용 커피로 가장 많이
소비되는 커피

(주)한국커피
경기도 광주시 오포읍 수레실길 144
문의전화. 031. 717. 0071
www.hankookcoffee.co.kr

# ESPRESSO N♦.1

콜롬비아 산어거스틴. 온두라스 라 파즈. 브라질 카모 디 미나스
**고소한 견과류 풍미, 부드러운 사탕수수의 단맛과 투명하고 고급스러운 산미**

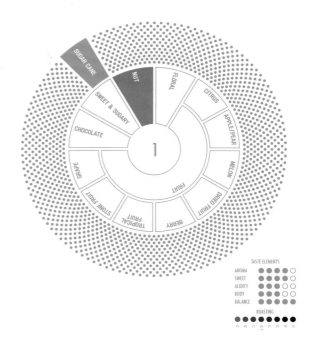

# ESPRESSO N♦.2

온두라스 라 파즈. 콜롬비아 산어거스틴
**진한 초콜렛, 건포도의 단맛과 카라멜 향이 어우러진 진한 바디감**

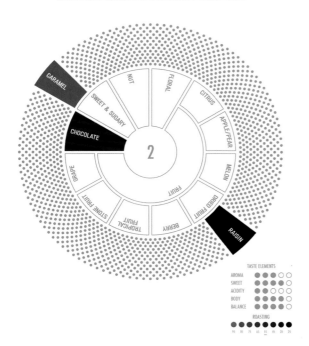

# ESPRESSO N♦.3

에티오피아 내추럴 G1 70%. 온두라스 라 파즈 30%
**잘 익은 체리, 딸기의 단맛과 진한 카카오 느낌을 가지고 있는 특별한 블렌딩**

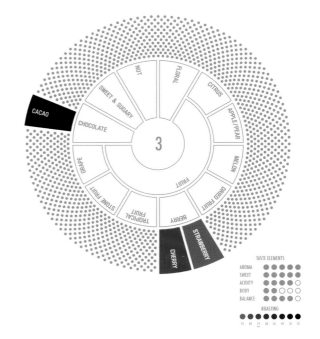

# Restaurant Decorative Paintings

Agency: **Syouwa Design**
Design: **Yuanyuan Zhang**

This is a series of hand-drawn charts including cuts of pig, cow, and lamb, types of deep-sea fish and shrimp, and coffee/wine tasting map. The below infographics show the different parts of pork, beef, and lamp as well as their taste and texture. Each infographic is created with precision painting and pleasant composition between text and image, backed with the information sourced strictly from Wikipedia.

The content is available in both Chinese and English, offering the infographics an informative, communicative, and decorative function. It can be used for restaurant decorations as well as an indispensable decorative picture of arty fine dining.

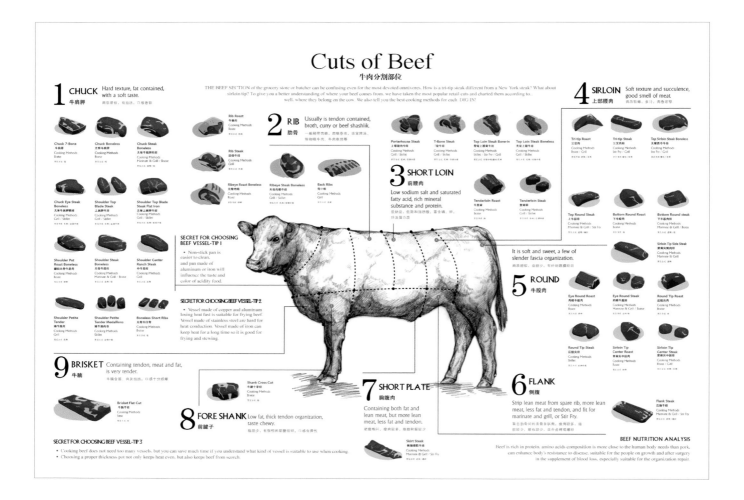

# Cuts of Lamb
羊肉分割部位

As one of the most frequent cooking ingredients all over the world, the lamb generally referring to a young sheep under 12 months of age can be prepared in a variety of forms by chefs from all corners of the earth, be it braising, stewing, grilling and sauteing. However, few people could figure out the specific and appropriate cooking styles for different cuts of a lamb. It is also perplexed to pick out a lamb which is fresh, tender and juicy when you are shopping in the lamb section of the grocery store. To give you a comprehensive understanding of lamb, we have presented you with follwing details which will be superbly instructive.

## 1 NECK 羊颈肉
With chewable bone and less meat, the lamb neck is very fresh after being stewed or steamed.
骨多肉少，耐嚼，炖之后，清蒸都十分鲜美

**Scrag End** 颈肉
Cooking Methods
Stewed / Steamed

**Neck of Lamb Fillet** 羊颈部分
Cooking Methods
Stewed / Steamed / Grilled

## 2 BEST END OF NECK 羊脯排
The streaky lamb meat attached to the bones is very soft and tender.
多骨，肉质肥瘦结合，连皮松软

**Valentine Steak** 瓦伦丁牛排
Cooking Methods
Roasted / Braised

**Lamb Cutlet** 羊肉排
Cooking Methods
Stewed / Braised with Sauce / Roasted / Boned

### FIND THE BEST LAMBS IN THE WORLD-TIP1
• Benefiting from natural pasture, abundant sunshine and mild climate, the Australian lamb is prominently fatty, juicy and internationally popularized, for which reason. Australia is also renowned as "a country riding on lamb back".

**Guard of Honour**
Cooking Methods
Grilled / Roasted

**Crown of Lamb** 皇冠羊排
Cooking Methods
Grilled / Boiled / Baked

**Trimmed Rack** 修剪架
Cooking Methods
Grilled / Boiled / Baked

## 3 LOIN 腰脊肉
Lamb with fine and long fibers, the easily digested lamb loin contains high protein, low fat and rich phospholipid.
纤维细长，易消化，高蛋白，低脂肪，含磷脂多

**Loin Chop** 羊腰肉
Cooking Methods
Broiled / Pan-Fried / Sauteed / Kebabs

**Noisette** 羊脊骨肉
Cooking Methods
Sauteed / Pan-Fried / Simmered / Kebabs

**Barnsley Chop** 巴恩斯利羊排
Cooking Methods
Simmered / Stewed / Boiled

**Cannon** 羊脊肉
Cooking Methods
Stewed / Steamed / Kebabs

## 4 CHUMP 羊臀肉
The meat is lean, fine and chewable with less fat.
肉质瘦而有嚼劲，脂肪多，细腻含量少

**Boneless Chump Joint**
Cooking Methods
Char-Coal Grilled / Roasted / Braised

**Chump Steak** 羊臀排
Cooking Methods
Char-Coal Grilled / Roasted / Baked

**Half Leg(Knuckle)** 去骨羊腿肉
Cooking Methods
Broiled / Boiled with Salt / Stewed / Kebabs

**Boneless Joint** 去骨羊腿肉
Cooking Methods
Char-coal Grilled / Stewed / Kebabs

**Whole Leg** 全腿
Cooking Methods
Pan-Fried / Broiled with Sauce / Grilled / Baked

## 5 LEG 羊腿
The meat is lean, tender and savory.
肉质瘦而有嚼劲，口感香软

**Shank** 羊腱子肉
Cooking Methods
Marinate / Stewed / Kebabs

**Topside Leg Steaks** 上部腿肉
Cooking Methods
Pan-Fried / Broiled / Kebabs

**Bone-In Leg Steak** 带骨羊腿肉
Cooking Methods
Sauteed / Broiled / Baked

**Kebabs** 羊肉串
Cooking Methods
Char-coal Grilled

**Stir Fry Strips** 羊肉条
Cooking Methods
Sauteed / Pan-Fried / Sauteed / Kebabs

**Rolled Mini Joint** 小腿肉卷
Cooking Methods
Sauteed / Pan-Fried / Boiled / Kebabs

## 7 SHOULDER 羊肩肉
Without bone, the streaky lamb shoulder is very tender and savory.
肉质滑嫩，有肥肉，口感各软

### FIND THE BEST LAMBS IN THE WORLD-TIP2
• In China, you can have an opportunity to try the most superb lamb in several regions, such as Inner Mongolia, Loess Plateau and Xinjiang province. The distinctive flavors have enticed many people from worldwide.

**Half Shoulder(Knuckle)** 高肖内
Cooking Methods
Stewed / Sauteed

**Half Shoulder(Blade)** 肩肉
Cooking Methods
Grilled / Stewed / Steamed

**Whistle Shoulder** 肩肉
Cooking Methods
Sauteed / Grilled / Broiled

**Mince** 绞肉末
Cooking Methods
Simmer / Braised with Sauce / Dry-Braised

**Boned Rolled Shoulder** 去骨羊肩肉
Cooking Methods
Boiled / Sauteed / Roasted

**Cubes** 羊肉粒
Cooking Methods
Stir-Fried / Pan-Fried / Broiled

**Shoulder Steaks** 肩排
Cooking Methods
Pan-Fried / Roasted

## 6 BREAST 羊胸
Lamb breast is soft, tender and fat with abundant nutritions.
肉质带油脂软嫩，肥而不腻，富含多种营养元素

**Boned Rolled Breast** 去骨羊胸肉
Cooking Methods
Sauteed / Pan-Fried / Boiled / Kebabs

### THREE STEPS FOR CHOOSING HIGH QUALITY LAMB
First, smell: a high quality lamb is endowed with strong mutton smell while the lamb added with additive is much less stronger.
Second, color: natural and fresh lamb is brightly red while the lamb with additive turns dark red.
Third, meat: the lamb meat with clenbuterol is lean or with few fat while the fat part always turns dark yellow.

### A FEW TIPS FOR REMOVING MUTTON SMELL
First, you can add some hawthorns, radish or green beans into the lamb soup. Second, you can soak the lamb in the cooled black tea before cooking.
Third, also the most effective one is to cut the lamb into chunks, then boil them with rice vinegar and water.

---

# Cuts of Pork
猪肉分割部位

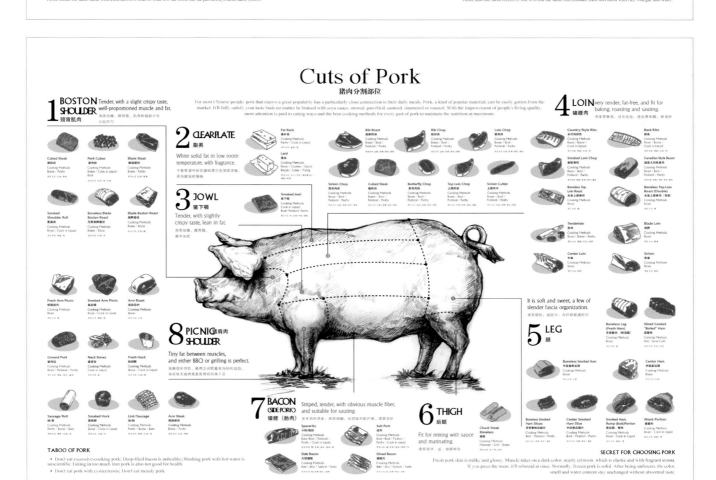

For most Chinese people, pork that enjoys a great popularity has a particularly close connection to their daily meals. Pork, a kind of popular material, can be easily gotten from the market. It'll fully satisfy your taste buds no matter be braised with soya sauce, stewed, pan-fried, sauteed, simmered or roasted. With the improvement of people's living quality, more attention is paid to eating ways and the best cooking methods for every part of pork to maintain the nutrition at maximum.

## 1 BOSTON SHOULDER 颈背肌肉
Tender, with a slight crispy taste, well-proportioned muscle and fat.
肉质细嫩，微带脆，肌肉和脂肪分布比较均匀

**Cubed Steak** 嫩牛排
Cooking Methods
Braise / Pastry

**Pork Cubes** 猪肉粒
Cooking Methods
Braise / Cook in Liquid / Broil

**Blade Steak** 嫩肩部排
Cooking Methods
Braise / Pastry

**Smoked Shoulder Roll** 烟熏肉
Cooking Methods
Roast / Cook in Liquid

**Boneless Blade Boston Roast** 无骨肩胛嫩肉
Cooking Methods
Braise / Roast

**Blade Boston Roast** 肩胛嫩肉
Cooking Methods
Braise / Roast

## 2 CLEARPLATE 脂类
White solid fat in low room temperature, with fragrance.
于室温下呈中低密度凝固的白色固体油脂，具有醇厚的香味

**Fat Back** 肥膘肉
Cooking Methods
Pastry / Cook in Liquid

**Lard** 猪油
Cooking Methods
Pastry / Cookies / Quick Breads / Cakes / Frying

## 3 JOWL 猪下巴
Tender, with slightly crispy taste, lean in fat.
肉质细嫩，微带脆，瘦中夹肥

**Smoked Jowl** 烟熏下巴肉
Cooking Methods
Cook in Liquid / Broil / Barbecue / Pastry

## 8 PICNIC SHOULDER 前肩肉
Tiny fat between muscles, and either BBQ or grilling is perfect.
肌肉间的少许脂肪，不论是BBQ或者烤制均非常完美

**Fresh Arm Picnic** 鲜猪前腿
Cooking Methods
Roast

**Smoked Arm Picnic** 熏前腿
Cooking Methods
Roast / Cook in Liquid

**Arm Roast** 前腿烤肉
Cooking Methods
Braise

**Ground Pork** 猪肉馅
Cooking Methods
Roast / Panbroil / Pastry

**Neck Bones** 猪颈骨
Cooking Methods
Cook in Liquid

**Fresh Hock** 鲜猪蹄
Cooking Methods
Braise / Cook in Liquid

**Sausage/Roll** 香肠肉
Cooking Methods
Pastry / Braise / Bake

**Smoked Hock** 熏猪蹄
Cooking Methods
Braise / Cook in Liquid

**Link/Sausage** 香肠
Cooking Methods
Pastry / Braise / Bake

**Arm Steak** 前腿肉排
Cooking Methods
Braise / Pastry

## 7 BACON (SIDE PORK) 猪腹 (肋肉)
Striped, tender, with obvious muscle fiber, and suitable for sauting.
呈条状的瘦肉，肉质细嫩，有明显的肌肉纤维，适宜爆炒

**Spareribs** 小排/猪肋
Cooking Methods
Bake / Broil / Panbroil / Pastry / Cook in Liquid

**Slab Bacon** 大块腊肉
Cooking Methods
Bake / Broil / Panbroil / Pastry

**Salt Pork** 咸肉
Cooking Methods
Broil / Panbroil / Pastry / Cook in Liquid

**Sliced Bacon** 烟熏培根
Cooking Methods
Bake / Broil / Panbroil / Pastry

## 6 THIGH 后腿
Fit for mixing with sauce and marinating.
适宜蘸酱拌食，腌制做酱

It is soft and sweet, a few of slender fascia organization.
肉质软甜，脂肪少，有纤细筋膜组织

**Chuck Steak Boneless** 无骨后腿肉
Cooking Methods
Marinate / Grill / Broke

## 4 LOIN 猪腰肉
Very tender, fat-free, and fit for baking, roasting and sauting.
肉质柔嫩，没有油脂，适合用来烘焙、烤或炒

**Rib Roast** 肋排烤肉
Cooking Methods
Roast / Broil / Panbroil / Pastry

**Rib Chop** 肋排
Cooking Methods
Roast / Broil / Panbroil / Pastry

**Loin Chop** 腰肉排
Cooking Methods
Roast / Broil / Panbroil / Pastry

**Sirloin Chop** 里脊肉排
Cooking Methods
Braise / Broil / Panbroil / Pastry

**Cubed Steak** 嫩牛排
Cooking Methods
Braise / Broil / Panbroil / Pastry

**Butterfly Chop** 蝴蝶排
Cooking Methods
Braise / Broil / Panbroil / Pastry

**Top Loin Chop** 上腰肉排
Cooking Methods
Braise / Broil / Panbroil / Pastry

**Sirloin Cutlet** 里脊肉片
Cooking Methods
Braise / Broil / Panbroil / Pastry

**Country-Style Ribs** 乡村排骨
Cooking Methods
Roast / Braise / Cook in Liquid

**Back Ribs** 后排骨
Cooking Methods
Roast / Braise / Cook in Liquid

**Smoked Loin Chop** 烟熏腰排
Cooking Methods
Roast / Broil / Pastry

**Canadian-Style Bacon** 加拿大风味熏肉
Cooking Methods
Roast / Broil / Panbroil / Pastry

**Boneless Top Loin Roast** 无骨上腰肉
Cooking Methods
Roast / Broil / Pastry

**Boneless Top Loin Roast (Double)** 去骨上腰肉卷
Cooking Methods
Roast

**Tenderloin** 里脊
Cooking Methods
Roast / Braise / Pastry

**Blade Loin** 肩部腰肉
Cooking Methods
Roast

**Center Loin** 中段腰肉
Cooking Methods
Roast

**Sirloin** 里脊肉
Cooking Methods
Roast

## 5 LEG 腿

**Boneless Leg (Fresh Ham)** 无骨腿肉 (鲜腿)
Cooking Methods
Roast

**Sliced Cooked "Boiled" Ham** 切片熟火腿
Cooking Methods
Hot / Serve Cold

**Boneless Smoked Ham** 无骨烟熏火腿
Cooking Methods
Bone

**Center Ham** 中段烟熏火腿
Cooking Methods
Braise

**Boneless Smoked Ham Slices** 无骨烟熏火腿片
Cooking Methods
Broil / Panbroil / Pastry

**Center Smoked Ham Slice** 中段烟熏火腿片
Cooking Methods
Broil / Panbroil / Pastry

**Smoked Ham, Rump (Butt)Portion** 烟熏腿肉，臀部
Cooking Methods
Roast / Cook in Liquid

**Shank Portion** 腱子肉部分
Cooking Methods
Roast / Cook in Liquid

### TABOO OF PORK
• Don't eat excessive-cooking pork; Deep-fried bacon is unhealthy; Washing pork with hot water is unscientific. Taking in too much lean pork is also not good for health.
• Don't eat pork with cysticercosis; Don't eat measly pork.

### SECRET FOR CHOOSING PORK
Fresh pork skin is milky and glossy. Muscle takes on a dark color, nearly crimson, which is elastic and with fragrant aroma. If you press the meat, it'll rebound at once. Normally, frozen pork is solid. After being unfrozen, the color, smell and water content stay unchanged without abnormal taste.

# Bicycle Tram and Metro

Design: **Tatiana Trikoz**
Client: **City Projects by Varlamov and Katz**

Set of illustrations made to promote public transport in Moscow.

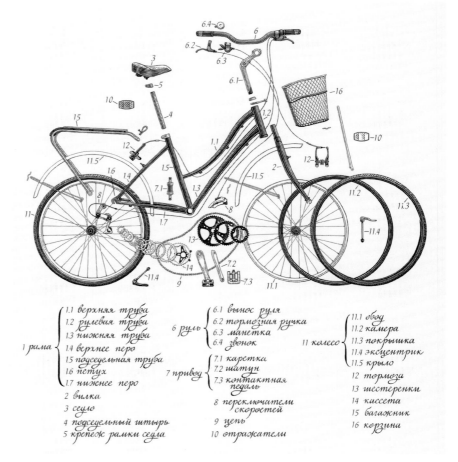

1 рама
1.1 верхняя труба
1.2 рулевая труба
1.3 нижняя труба
1.4 верхнее перо
1.5 подседельная труба
1.6 петух
1.7 нижнее перо
2 вилка
3 седло
4 подседельный штырь
5 крепеж рамки седла

6 руль
6.1 вынос руля
6.2 тормозная ручка
6.3 манетка
6.4 звонок
7 привод
7.1 каретка
7.2 шатун
7.3 контактная педаль
8 переключатели скоростей
9 цепь
10 отражатели

11 колесо
11.1 обод
11.2 камера
11.3 покрышка
11.4 эксцентрик
11.5 крыло
12 тормоза
13 шестеренки
14 кассета
15 багажник
16 корзина

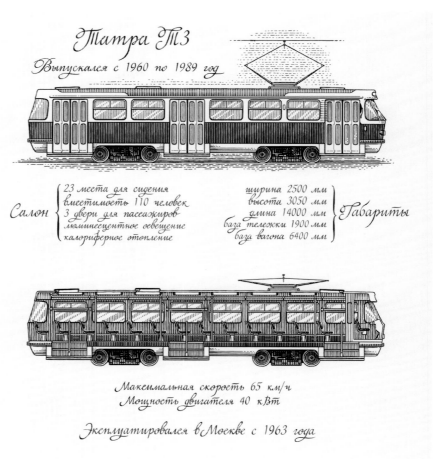

## Татра Т3

Выпускался с 1960 по 1989 год

Салон
23 места для сидения
вместимость 110 человек
3 двери для пассажиров
люминесцентное освещение
калориферное отопление

Габариты
ширина 2500 мм
высота 3050 мм
длина 14000 мм
база тележки 1900 мм
база вагона 6400 мм

Максимальная скорость 65 км/ч
Мощность двигателя 40 кВт

Эксплуатировался в Москве с 1963 года

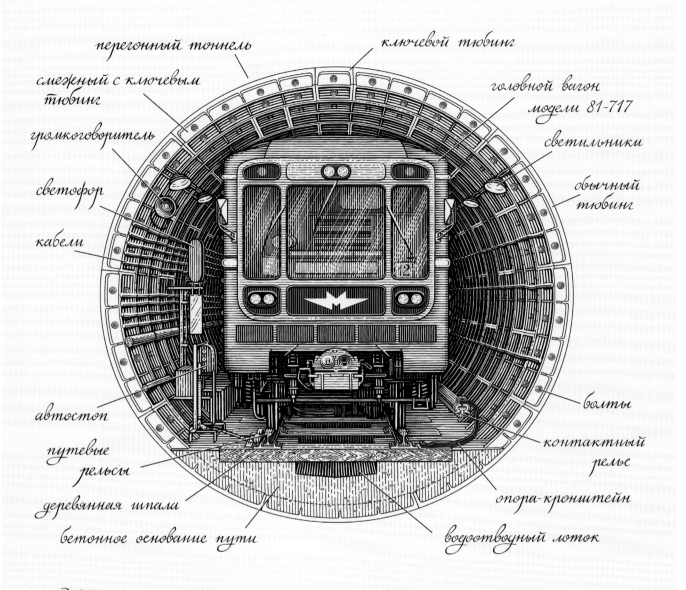

перегонный тоннель

ключевой тюбинг

смежный с ключевым тюбинг

головной вагон модели 81-717

громкоговоритель

светильники

светофор

обычный тюбинг

кабели

автостоп

болты

путевые рельсы

контактный рельс

деревянная шпала

опора-кронштейн

бетонное основание пути

водоотводный лоток

*Первый метрополитен в России открылся в Москве 15 мая 1935 года*

## KLM's Dreamliner

Agency: **Vizualism**
Design: **Chantal van Wessel**
Client: **Holland Herald, KLM**

A cutaway of KLM's new airplane with some interesting facts and data about the plane.

# KLM Takes Care

Facts & figures of the Boeing 787-9

# Deconstructing the Dreamliner

The new Boeing 787-9 is a perfect example of how aircraft manufacturers keep on innovating. Here are some facts & figures of this higher-power and lower-impact plane.

66 ele

The Dreamliner's ma
is 252,650kg. T
of some 66 ele

**11,500km**

The maximum range of the 787-9 is 11,500km. This approximately covers the distance between Amsterdam and Hawaii.

Average seat pitch World Business Class 42 inch/107cm (flatbed 190cm).

Kitchen

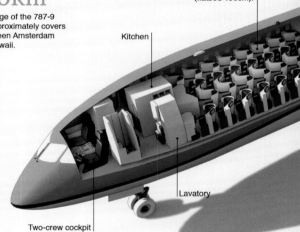

Lavatory

Two-crew cockpit

**294 passengers**

The Boeing 787-9 Dreamliner is configured to carry a total of 294 passengers, including crew.

-9(

The special pa
temperature
KLM co-develo
so that the airc
is applie

KLM, Holland Herald, dec 2016/jan 2017

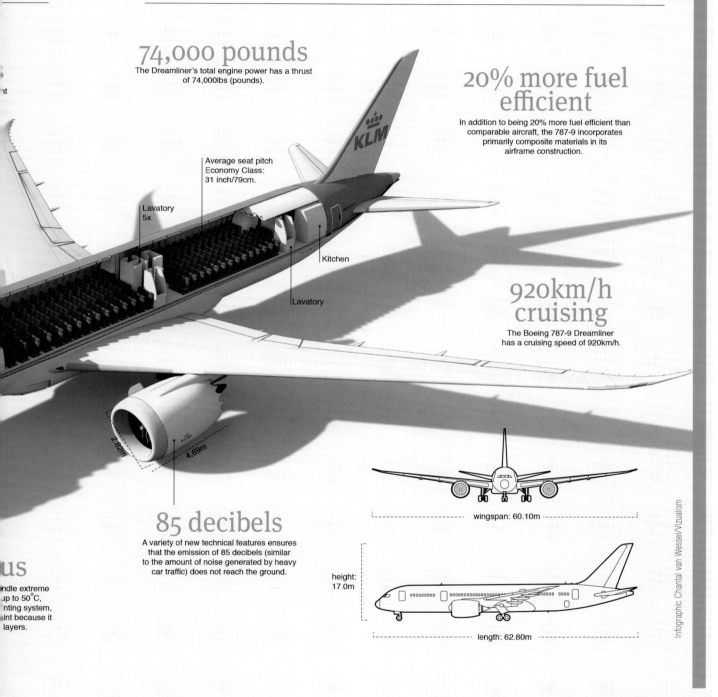

## 74,000 pounds

The Dreamliner's total engine power has a thrust of 74,000lbs (pounds).

## 20% more fuel efficient

In addition to being 20% more fuel efficient than comparable aircraft, the 787-9 incorporates primarily composite materials in its airframe construction.

Average seat pitch
Economy Class:
31 inch/79cm.

Lavatory
5x

Kitchen

Lavatory

## 920km/h cruising

The Boeing 787-9 Dreamliner has a cruising speed of 920km/h.

2.82m

4.69m

## 85 decibels

A variety of new technical features ensures that the emission of 85 decibels (similar to the amount of noise generated by heavy car traffic) does not reach the ground.

wingspan: 60.10m

height:
17.0m

length: 62.80m

us

ndle extreme
up to 50°C,
nting system,
int because it
layers.

Infographic Chantal van Wessel/Vizualism

KLM, Holland Herald, dec 2016/jan 2017

# Steam Locomotive Infographic Design

............................................................

**Design: Juyoon Park**

Juyoon Park visualized the history and mechanism of the steam locomotive in this infographic. Each element was designed with font and color according to the time.

## LOCOMOTIVE NO.491

| | |
|---|---|
| 국 가 | 미국 |
| 운행 지역 | 콜로라도 주 |
| 운행 기간 | 1928 – 1963 |
| 소 유 | 콜로라도 레일로드 뮤지엄 |

Denver & Rio Grande Western Railroad

## 1812

### Salamanca

Matthew Murray

살라만카는 상업적으로 성공한 첫번째 증기기관차다. 살라만카는 처음으로 두개의 실린더를 사용했다. 이 기관차는 살라만카 전투에 웰링턴 공작의 승리의 이름을 따서 명명되었다.

## 1813

### Puffing Billy

William Hedley

퍼핑빌리는 1813-14년 엔지니어 윌리엄 헤들리, 조나단 포스트와 대장장이 티모시 해크워스에 의해 만들어진 초기 증기기관차다.

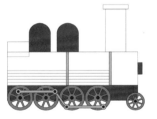

## 1825

### Locomotion No. 1

George & Robert Stephenson

로코모션 No.1호는 승객을 공공 철도선 스톡턴과 달링턴 철도여객을 운송하는 최초의 증기기관차다. 1824년에 조지 앤 로버트 스티븐슨 회사에 의해 만들어졌다.

# STEAM LOCOMOTIVE

Steam locomotives were first developed in Great Britain during the early 19th century and dominated railway transport until the middle of the 20th century. From the early 1900s they were gradually superseded by electric and diesel locomotives.

Smoke stack

Head light

Boiler

Steam dome

Main air reservoir

Trailer truck wheel

Cylinder

## HISTORY OF LOCOMOTIVE

### 1808
**Catch me who can**
Richard Trevithick

이 기관차는 최고속도 19km/h에 달했다. 그러나 상대적으로 부서지기 쉬운 주철 철로에너무 무거워고 인증이었던 트레비딕의 전시회는 명자 빨리쳐냐기 발생되고 허물러지않다.

### 1812
**Salamanca**
Matthew Murray

살라만카는 상업적으로 성공한 첫번째 증기기관차다. 살라만카는 처음으로 두개의 실린더를 사용했다. 이 기관차는 실린카가 주변에 열처된 공장의 승리의 이름을 따라 명명되었다.

### 1813
**Puffing Billy**
William Hedley

퍼핑빌리는 1813-14년 엔지니어 윌리엄 헤들리, 조나단 포스터와 대장장이 티모시 해크워스에 의해 만들어진 초기 증기기관차다.

### 1825
**Locomotion No. 1**
George & Robert Stephenson

로코모션 No.1호는 승객을 공공 철도선 스톡턴과 달링턴 철도여객을 운송하는 최초의 증기기관차다. 뉴캐슬에서 조지 로버트 스티븐슨 회사에 의해 만들어졌다.

### 1830
**Planet**
Robert Stephenson

플래닛호는 1830년 로버트 스티븐슨 엔 컴퍼니에서 리버풀과 맨체스터 철도를 위해 만들어진 초기 증기기관차다.

## LOCOMOTIVE NO.491

Denver & Rio Grande Western Railroad

국 가  미국
운행 지역  콜로라도 주
운행 기간  1928 - 1963
소 유  콜로라도 레일로드 유지엄

## STRUCTURE

**Boiler**
보일러
증기를 발생하기 위하여 불을 끓이는 장치

**Cylinder**
실린더
증기기관에서 피스톤이 왕복운동 하는 부분

**Wheel**
차륜
직접 차체를 지탱하고 차량의 구동

**Driver-cab**
운전실
증기기관을 조작하거나 운전하는 공간

## PRINCIPLE

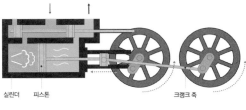

실린더   피스톤                          크랭크 축

→ ▨ 과열증기   → ▨ 배기증기   ⋯▸ 작동방향

# Between the Words

................................

Design: **Nicholas Rougeux**

"Between the Words" is an exploration of visual rhythm of the punctuation in well-known literary works. All letters, numbers, spaces, and line breaks were removed from the entire texts of classic stories like *Alice's Adventures in Wonderland*, *Moby Dick*, and *Pride and Prejudice*—leaving only the punctuation in one continuous line of symbols in the order that they appear in texts. The remaining punctuation was arranged in a spiral starting at the top center with markings for each chapter and classic illustrations at the center.

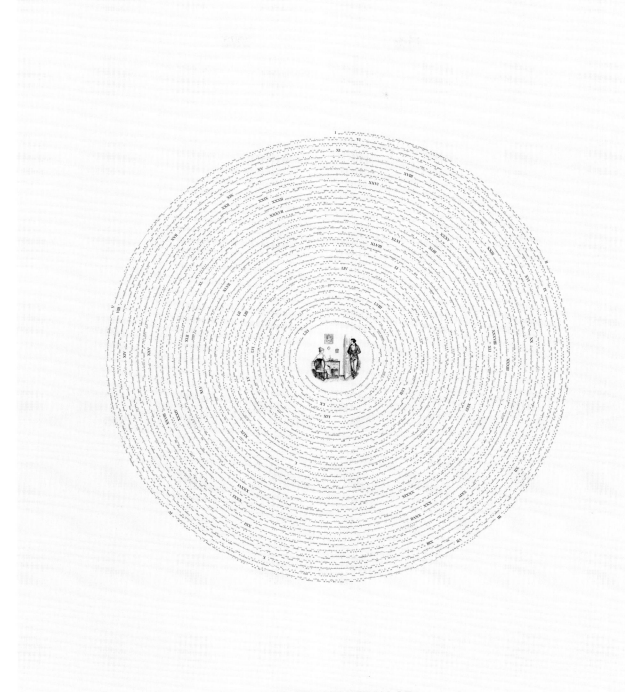

THE PUNCTUATION OF

## PRIDE AND PREJUDICE
*by Jane Austen*

By Nicholas Rougeux

THE PUNCTUATION OF
## MOBY-DICK; OR, THE WHALE
*by Herman Melville*

THE PUNCTUATION OF
## ALICE'S ADVENTURES IN WONDERLAND
*by Lewis Carroll*

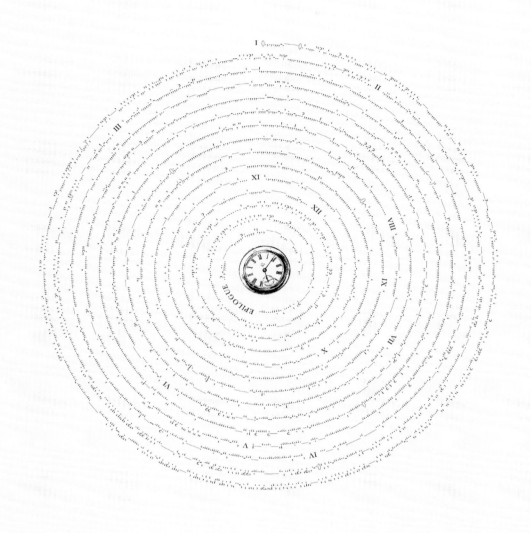

THE PUNCTUATION OF
# THE TIME MACHINE
*by H. G. Wells*

By Nicholas Rougeux

# Color Moon Days

Agency: **ohSeven Studio**
Design: **Yunje Park**

Yunje Park's expressed his feelings and colors of the clothes that he wore over the past 42 days by borrowing the concept of moon cycle.

He classified the phase of the moon—the dark moon, the waning moon, the crescent moon, the waxing moon, and the full moon—into 9 levels and marked his feelings from 1 to 9 using each phase. The waning moon shows that his feeling is negative. The waxing moon shows that his feeling is positive. The full moon shows that his feeling is the best.

The Moon is divided into 5 parts horizontally—each part represents respectively coat, top, pants, socks, and shoes from top to bottom. The color corresponds to the color of the clothes.

Yunje usually wears colorful clothes so he decided to analyze the color that he chose and to see if there is any connection between his feeling and the color of the clothes.

As a result, he discovered that the color of the clothes changed according to his feelings—he usually feels good on Saturday and Sunday so he wears the clothes in bright colors, like red; on the contrary, he feels bad on Tuesday so he wears in dark colors, like black or grey.

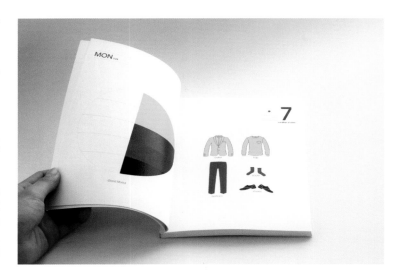

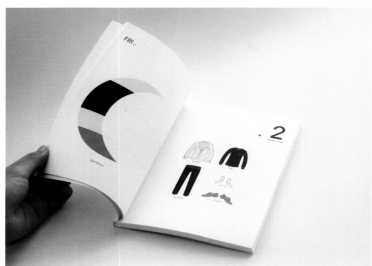

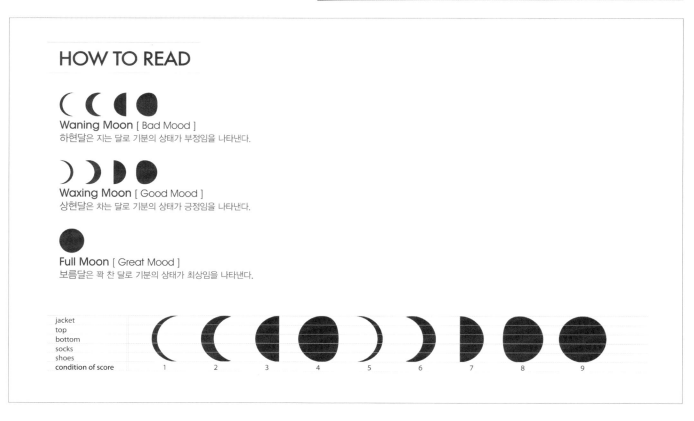

## HOW TO READ

**Waning Moon** [ Bad Mood ]
하현달은 지는 달로 기분의 상태가 부정임을 나타낸다.

**Waxing Moon** [ Good Mood ]
상현달은 차는 달로 기분의 상태가 긍정임을 나타낸다.

**Full Moon** [ Great Mood ]
보름달은 꽉 찬 달로 기분의 상태가 최상임을 나타낸다.

jacket
top
bottom
socks
shoes
condition of score  1  2  3  4  5  6  7  8  9

# COLORMOON DAYS

| | | | | | | | | | |
|---|---|---|---|---|---|---|---|---|---|
| outer | | | | | | | | | |
| top | | | | | | | | | |
| bottom | | | | | | | | | |
| socks | | | | | | | | | |
| shoes | | | | | | | | | |
| condition of score | 1 | 2 | 3 | 4 | 5 | 6 | 7 | 8 | 9 |

Waning Moon
Bad Mood

Waxing Moon
Good Mood

Full Moon
Great Mood

When I felt bad, I usually wore black and gray colors, on Tuesday.

When I felt good, I usually wore red colors, on Saturday and Sunday.

# Visualiser

..................

Agency: **Ilk Studio**

Visualiser is an ongoing music visualization project. The sound data of the track is animated alive using an array of graphic shapes and colors. The size, position, rotation, and color of each shape is controlled by the spectrum data from the sounds. When the track is paused, the resulting visual snapshot of the song is then produced as a hi-resolution image.

**TOUR DE FRANCE** / 01:58.6

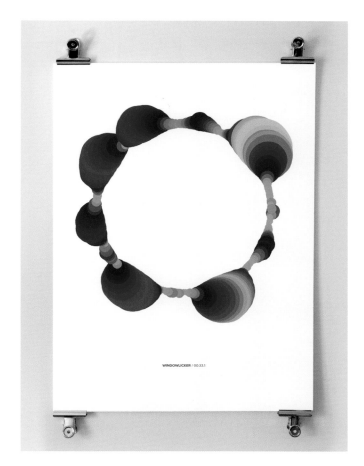

WINDOWLICKER / 00:33.1

WINDOWLICKER / 01:24.4

PHAT PLANET / 00:48.2

PHAT PLANET / 02:03.1

# Music Structures

Design: **Andrés Fernández Torcida**

The project addresses the discipline of music in a visual way.

It consists of two parts—a timeline that shows the composer's life period and important events of musical culture; a systematic study where three forms of graphic representation of the music are studied and a developed one with more possibilities is offered. Andrés first drew the sketches on paper and then brought the ideas into being by applying Adobe Illustrator.

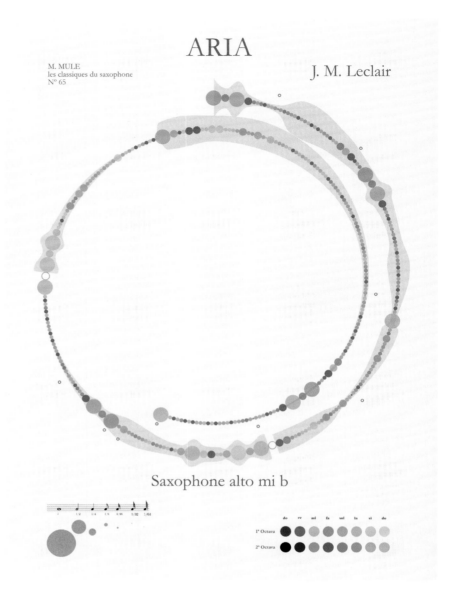

ARIA

M. MULE
les classiques du saxophone
N° 65

J. M. Leclair

Saxophone alto mi b

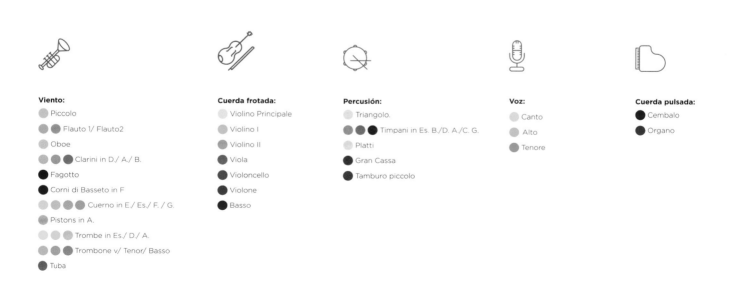

**Viento:**
- Piccolo
- Flauto 1/ Flauto2
- Oboe
- Clarini in D./ A./ B.
- Fagotto
- Corni di Basseto in F
- Cuerno in E./ Es./ F. / G.
- Pistons in A.
- Trombe in Es./ D./ A.
- Trombone v/ Tenor/ Basso
- Tuba

**Cuerda frotada:**
- Violino Principale
- Violino I
- Violino II
- Viola
- Violoncello
- Violone
- Basso

**Percusión:**
- Triangolo.
- Timpani in Es. B./D. A./C. G.
- Platti
- Gran Cassa
- Tamburo piccolo

**Voz:**
- Canto
- Alto
- Tenore

**Cuerda pulsada:**
- Cembalo
- Organo

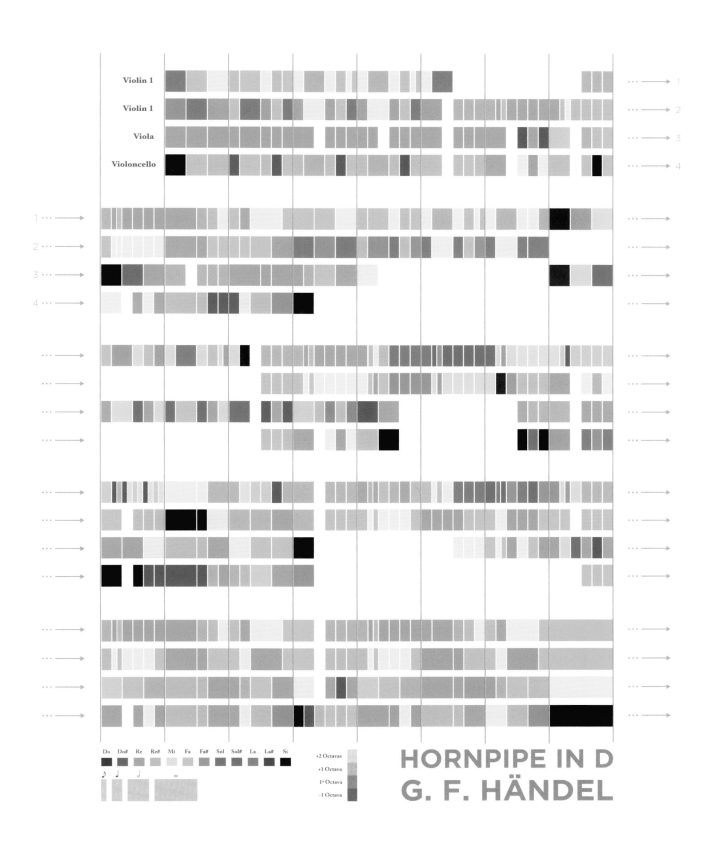

HORNPIPE IN D
G. F. HÄNDEL

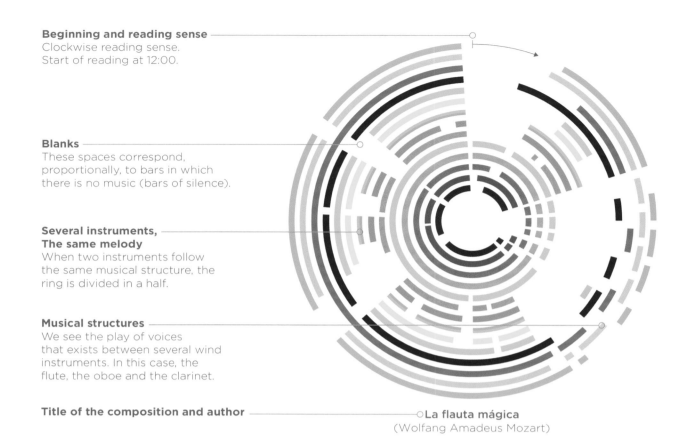

**Beginning and reading sense**
Clockwise reading sense.
Start of reading at 12:00.

**Blanks**
These spaces correspond,
proportionally, to bars in which
there is no music (bars of silence).

**Several instruments,**
**The same melody**
When two instruments follow
the same musical structure, the
ring is divided in a half.

**Musical structures**
We see the play of voices
that exists between several wind
instruments. In this case, the
flute, the oboe and the clarinet.

**Title of the composition and author**

La flauta mágica
(Wolfang Amadeus Mozart)

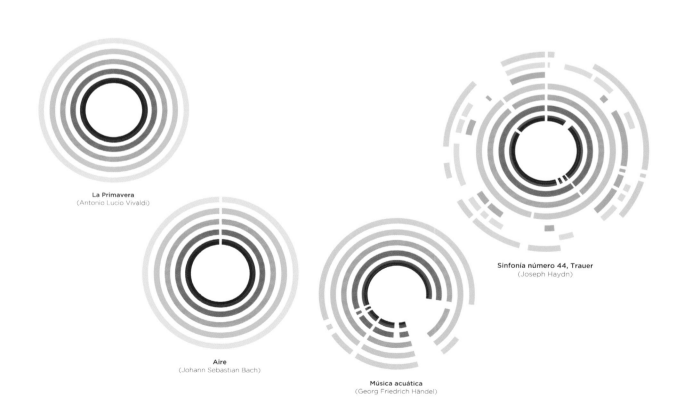

**La Primavera**
(Antonio Lucio Vivaldi)

**Sinfonía número 44, Trauer**
(Joseph Haydn)

**Aire**
(Johann Sebastian Bach)

**Música acuática**
(Georg Friedrich Händel)

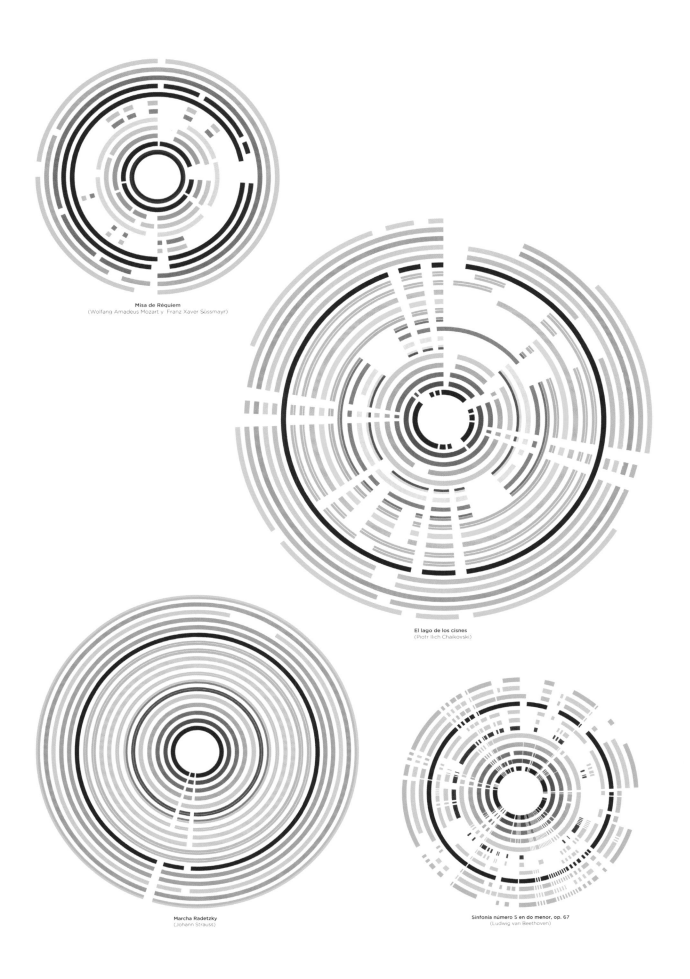

Misa de Réquiem
(Wolfang Amadeus Mozart y Franz Xaver Süssmayr)

El lago de los cisnes
(Piotr Ilich Chaikovski)

Marcha Radetzky
(Johann Strauss)

Sinfonía número 5 en do menor, op. 67
(Ludwig van Beethoven)

## Outer Space Series

Agency: **Archie's Press**
Design: **Archie Archambault**

Archie's Outer Space Series includes various illustrations of the planets in Solar System and the Milky Way. The Solar System is an incredible collection of planets, comets, asteroids, and moons. Here they are, neatly organized in perfect orbit around the Sun. The viewers can know more from each map of the planet.

The Milky Way is a spiral galaxy with so many stars that it is almost impossible to count all of them. This map marks the location of the Earth to give some perspective on humanity's place in the universe.

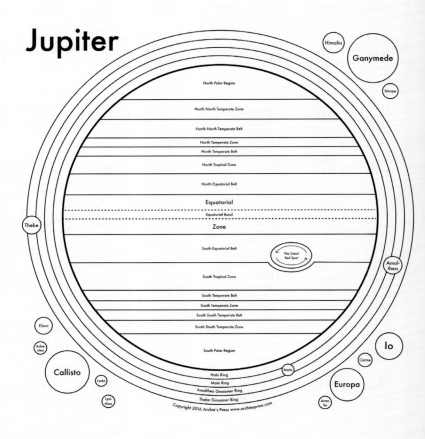

## The Sun

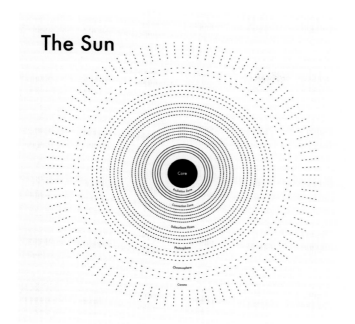

## Mars

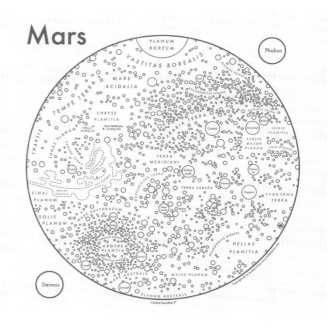

## Solar System

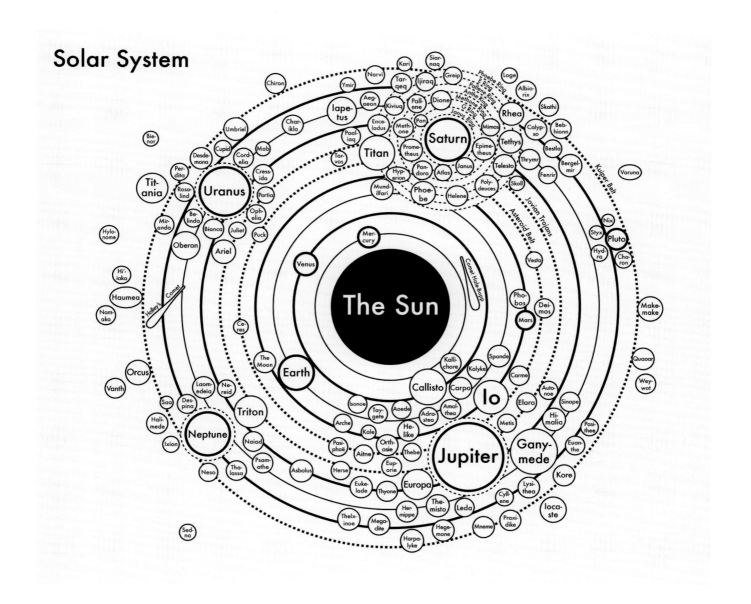

# Map of Fictional Places

Design: **Federica Fragapane**
Art Direction: **Federica Fragapane**
Client: *Corriere della Sera*

This is a piece of artwork for the column Visual Data on *La Lettura*, the cultural supplement of *Corriere Della Sera*. The visualization shows the geographical location of 48 places in 46 fictional works. The places were selected by justtheflight.co.uk. The actual sites are those that have provided inspiration in the creation of the place, or in which there was the shooting of the film or the television series. For each fictional destination are indicated: the author, the tile, the name of the place, and the name of the actual site. Every place is connected with a line to its geographical location on the map.

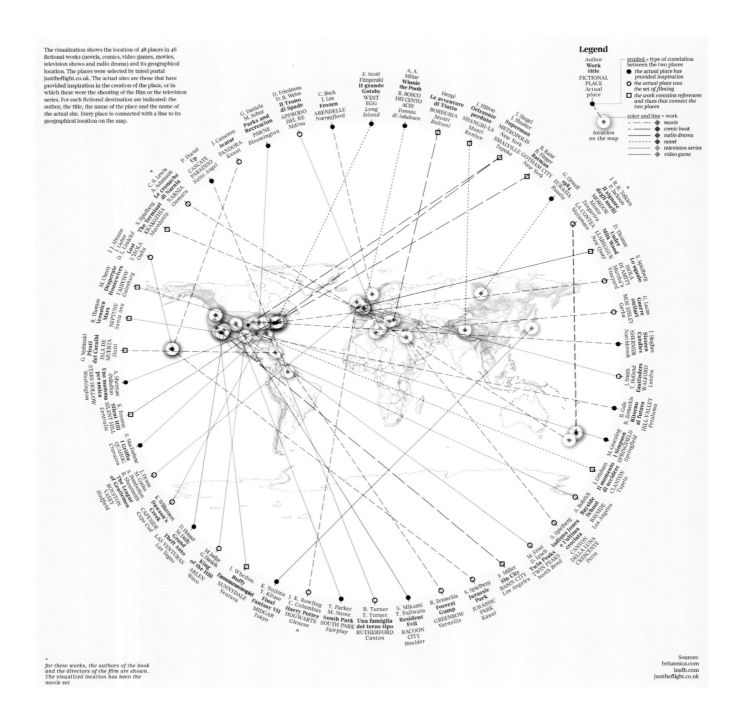

## 203 × Infographics Lab

*www.infographicslab203.com*

Design Studio 203 started its business in 2003 as a small design studio, specializing in graphic design and editorial design. As time goes by, its business ranges are extended. Nowadays it owns 203 × Design Studio, 203 × Infographics Lab, and 203 × SOSOBOOKS. Its main business sections are editorial design, infographics, magazine, and publications printed in a small volume.

*P.096, 097, 098, 099, 198, 199, 200, 201*

## Agris Bobrovs

*www.agrisbobrovs.lv*

Agris Bobrovs is a graphic designer and illustrator who enjoys shapes and colors in minimalist style.

*P.116-117*

## Alexandra Erkaeva

*www.behance.net/erkaeva*

Alexandra Erkaeva is a designer with over ten years of experience in graphic design and illustration. Her work is mainly focused on logo, identity design, print design, illustration, and mobile game design.

*P.104-105*

## Ana Cuna

*www.lawebdelacuna.com*

Ana Cuna is an illustrator and art director based in Madrid, Spain. She began her career by working for some graphic design studios and publicity agencies in Madrid. Now she is a freelance art director and illustrator based in Madrid. She collaborates with brands like *Monocle*, Inditex, Microsoft, *Boat International*, *Yorokobu*, *Pacha*, Fox, MINI, Vueling, etc.

*P.144-145, 146-147, 148-149, 154-155*

## Andrés Fernández Torcida

*www.andresft.com*

Andrés Fernández Torcida is a graphic designer specialized in infographics and data visualization. He is an enthusiast of data and infographics. After studying and finishing his studies in naval engineering, he entered the world of graphic design, infographics, and data visualization.

*P.226-229*

## Angel Sanz Correa

*www.behance.net/angelsanzcorrea*

Specialised in identity, editorial design, and infographics, Angel Sanz Correa always seeks meaningful visual and conceptual connections between seemingly distant concepts. He pays equal attention to tangible tools and digital ones.

*P.040-041*

## Anton Yermolov

*www.behance.net/yer-band*

Anton is an illustrator from Crimea who is also specialized in infographics and web design. He has worked with companies like Megafon, Microsoft, Kaplan, Yandex. Currently, he is working at Pixies studio in Moscow, Russia. His technical and design backgrounds influence his style of work.

*P.100*

## Archie Archambault

*www.archiespress.com*

Archie Archambault creates simple maps of complicated subjects to convey information quickly and efficiently. He has mapped over 100 cities, anatomical parts, celestial bodies, and governmental structures. His favorite shape is a circle because it is simple and perfect.

*P.230-231*

## Big Group

*www.biggroup.co.uk*

Big Group is a London-based marketing agency that has been helping various clients to connect with their markets and customers for over 25 years. Whether it is an immersive event or an award-winning integrated campaign, they always find the Big solution.

*P.202-203, 205*

## Biqi Zhang

*www.behance.net/631437669a632*

Biqi Zhang is now studying Graphic Design at Nanjing University of the Arts. Her favorite animal is cats.

*P.206-207*

## Bunkyo Gakuin University

*www.u-bunkyo.ac.jp*

Bunkyo Gakuin University, situated in central Tokyo and the suburban area of Saitama, is one of the private universities in Japan. It is comprised of four undergraduate faculties and four graduate schools in the fields of Business Administration, Foreign Studies, Human Studies, and Health Science with an enrollment of 4,700 students.

*P.092-093*

## CLEVER°FRANKE

*www.cleverfranke.com*

CLEVER°FRANKE combines strategy, design, and technology to create data-driven tools and experiences that enable change. They collaborate with forward-thinking clients, such as Google, Philips, Here, and *Wired* magazine, exploring the wealth of data at hand and designing cutting-edge ways to bring value to the surface. Along the way, they discover untapped value and hidden business opportunities that help their clients to innovate and grow.

*P.058-059*

## Creamcrackers

*creamcrackers.fr*

Creamcrackers, a.k.a. Sebastien Morales is a freelance graphic designer and illustrator. Specialized in data visualization and computer graphics, he works for large-scale French and international companies, institutions, and schools, including SNCF, Air France, Science Po, Arte, and many others. His style stands out with the purity of form. He dedicates himself to making a drawing readable at any scale.

*P.189*

## DAEKI & JUN Studio

*www.daekiandjun.com*

Daeki Shim and Hyojun Shim are graphic designers and founders of DAEKI & JUN design studio based in Seoul. Apart from running their studio, they give lectures at universities in South Korea. They have won and been selected by more than 80 international design awards, including Red Dot Award, Graphis Annual, STA 100, and TDC Tokyo.

*P.090-091, 208-209*

## Dan Revell

*www.behance.net/danrevell9afa1*

Dan Revell is a freelance designer and recent graduate of the University of Brighton. He is adept at stripped-back typography and hand-made imagery.

*P.196-197*

## Dongchern Cin

*followtheyellowbricks.com*

Dongchern Cin studied graphic and information design at Hongik University and graduate school. He worked for several years at AHN GRAPHICS. In addition, He designed and produced products at ARDIUM. He gave lectures on information design and editorial design at various universities including K'Arts and Hongik University. Currently, he runs a small design company. He is interested in designing and working on infographic, geographic, and data visualization.

*P.170-171*

## el abrelatas

*www.elabrelatas.com*

el abrelatas is an infographic and graphic designer based in Spain.

*P.150-151, 180-181, 182-183, 184-185*

## Ella Zheng Meisi

*www.behance.net/ellaisweird*

Ella Zheng is a Singaporean designer and illustrator who enjoys experimentation, craft, and the endless pursuit of self-improvement. Trained in both Fashion and Graphic Design, she hopes to be able to nurture Singaporean's mindset towards design.

*P.077*

## Estudio Pum

*www.estudiopum.com*

Pum is a graphic design studio based in Porto (PT) and São Paulo (BR). They have been focused on designing, illustrating, and creating things alike since 2013. Pum sees design as an experience and a learning process, which can be beautifully made and fills the everyday needs that a professional work requires.

*P.012-013*

## Federica Fragapane

*www.behance.net/FedericaFragapane*

Federica Fragapane is a freelance information designer. She studied in Milan and her M.Sc. thesis was selected and published on *ADI Design Index 2015*. One of her projects received the Honorable Mention at Kantar Information is Beautiful Awards 2014 and she won Silver Medal at European Design Awards 2017.

Federica Fragapane's work is characterized by a constant research for new aesthetics and forms created by a stream of dialogue between the contents and the visual elements.

*P.044-045, 046-047, 138-139, 232*

## Hong Sungwoo

*hongsungwoo.kr*

Hong Sungwoo is an independent illustrator and graphic designer. The majority of his work is focused on illustrations for infographics. He enjoys working with simple, geometric shapes, limited color, and vector graphics, while mixing some jokes in between.

*P.158-159*

## Ilk Studio

*ilkstudio.com*

Ilk Stuido is founded by Matt Booth, a UK based multi-disciplinary designer who produces a rich mix of work for screen, print, device, and product.

*P.224-225*

## Irina Oloeva

*www.be.net/shuga*

Irina Oloeva is from Saint-Petersburg, Russia. She works as a freelance graphic designer, specializing in visual identity, packaging design, lettering, infographics, and editorial design.

*P.160-161*

## Joey Ng

*www.behance.net/ngjoey*

Joey Ng is a Singaporean illustrator and designer currently based near Toronto, Canada. She has a degree in Animation and is on her way to obtain a degree in Illustration. Her greatest passions, apart from drawing, are sculpting and playing computer games. Her favorite medium of expression is to draw, but she is also very much fond of design, photography, motion, and sculpture.

*P.094-095*

## Jumping Space Studio

*www.jumpingspacestudio.com*

Based in Jakarta, Jumping Space Studio provides fresh and highly-innovative creative services. They have a distinct detail-focused approach towards the surroundings they create. They have extensive practical knowledge of commercial design, brand identity, ATL-BTL, and exhibition design.

*P.114-115*

## Justyna Sikora

*sikorajustyna.pl*

Justyna Sikora is a young graphic designer with an MA degree from the School of Fine Arts in Wroclaw. He is currently working as a trainee at büro uebele visuelle kommunikation in Stuttgart, Germany. He enjoys the minimalistic vector style.

*P.086-089*

## Juyoon Park

*www.behance.net/juyoon117*

Juyoon Park is a Korean designer specialized in digital media design at Hongik University. Currently, he is working on motion graphic design.

*P.216-217*

## Kamil Iwaszczyszyn

*www.behance.net/kaiwa*

Kamil Iwaszczyszyn, born in Poland in 1986, works now in Luxembourg and is best known for his modern designs in the fields of illustration and typography. His style is marked by functionalism and simplification.

Specialized in illustration and graphic design, Kamil joined the team of HUMAN MADE in 2014. The agency is strong in visual communication and information design, with an aim to educate and inspire the audience through powerful visual designs.

*P.174-177, 178-179*

## Kevin Teh

*tehdesigner.net*

He likes tea, cats, and typography. He aims to reinforce a positive experience through design by paying attention to details as much as he can.

*P.018-019*

## Krystyna Oniszczuk-Dylik

*www.behance.net/oniszczukdylik*

Krystyna Oniszczuk-Dylik is a graphic designer specialized in editorial, illustration, and motion design. She graduated from the Department of Graphic Arts at the Jan Matejko Academy of Fine Arts in Cracow. She works as a freelance senior graphic designer, occasionally as a lecturer in graphic design. In her works, she combines the fine art with utility.

*P.190-191*

## Kürşat Ünsal

*www.kursatunsal.com*

Kürşat Ünsal is a freelance graphic designer and illustrator based in Bodrum, Turkey. He has been designing for over 10 years. He is adept at vector illustration and icon design. Before becoming a freelancer, he has worked as an art director for some advertising agencies and international magazines.

*P.106-107*

## La Tigre

*www.latigre.net*

La Tigre is a multidisciplinary creative consultancy specialized in refined visual design solution and data visualization for small to large, local and global clients.

Backed with their strategic process based on research, they convert clients' ideas, visions, and inspirations into a system of visual expressions that elevate brands and create distinction. Their visual language is simple yet sophisticated, with a contemporary look and an attention to geometry.

*P.140-142*

## Laura Palumbo

*www.behance.net/Laurapal*

Laura Palumbo is a freelance graphic designer and illustrator. She is based in Italy between Florence and Gallipoli, her hometown. She likes traveling and TV series and she has always been obsessed with drawing and illustration since she was a kid.

*P.118-119*

## Leo Natsume

*www.behance.net/leonatsume*

Leo Natsume is an illustrator and multi-disciplinary digital designer who currently focuses on advertising and design agencies around the world. He has received some international design awards and his work has been featured on several websites like Bēhance and magazines.

*P.186-187*

## Lienke Raben

*www.behance.net/lienke*

Lienke Raben's work sees a graphic, doodle-ish, and hand-lettering style. Most of her illustrations have a bright yet limited color palettes. She now works in an Amsterdam-based design agency called in60seconds.

*P.120-121*

## Liow Heng Chun

*www.behance.net/hengchunliow*

Liow Heng Chun is a designer and art director based in Malaysia and Dubai. He works on a variety of projects from brand identity, publication, wayfinding, and environmental graphics.

*P.030-033*

## Lysanne de Water

*www.studioinform.nl*

Lysanne de Water has a passion for analyzing, structuring, and visualizing information. After she graduated from the Willem de Kooning Academy, she continued working on information design where she investigates new and effective ways of using visualizations. With her work, she likes to communicate with others and tell a clear and complete story.

*P.028-029*

## Malik Thomas-Smeda

*www.malikthomas.co.uk*

Malik Thomas-Smeda is an award-winning illustrator and graphic designer based in the northwest of England. He is passionate about detailed vector illustration, infographics, and digital design. He creates work that is inspired by popular culture, music, fashion, and architecture.

Malik's style is graphic, bold, and carefully considered with attention to detail. He works digitally using hand-drawn techniques that focus on line work, isometric shapes, and patterns to achieve a highly-rendered image.

*P.172-173*

## Massimiliano Mauro

*www.behance.net/massimilianomauro*

Massimiliano Mauro is an Italian designer focused on graphic design, art direction, and information architecture. His client includes iPad App, *Wired* magazine.

*P.060-063*

## Matthew Benkert

*www.mattbenkertdesign.com*

Matthew Benkert is a graphic designer based in Los Angeles. He graduated from the ArtCenter College of Design in Brand Identity Design. He enjoys designing across multiple mediums including print, UI, and motion. Inspired by Swiss and International design and streetwear/fashion branding, Matthew's style is mostly bold, simple, and typographic.

*P.070*

## Moritz Stefaner

*truth-and-beauty.net*

Moritz Stefaner works as a "truth and beauty operator" on the crossroads of data visualization, information aesthetics, and user interface design.

With a background in Cognitive Science (B.Sc.) at the University of Osnabrueck and in Interface Design (M.A.) at the University of Applied Sciences Potsdam, his work beautifully balances analytical and aesthetic aspects in mapping abstract and complex phenomena. In the past, he has helped clients like the OECD, the World Economic Forum, Skype, dpa, FIFA, and Max Planck Research Society to find insights and beauty in large data sets.

*P.054-057*

## Murat Kalkavan

*muratkalkavan.com*

Murat Kalkavan is an illustrator and designer located in Istanbul. He is a graduate of the Fine Arts Academy of Marmara University and enjoys creating character designs, concept art, and game visuals of all kinds.

He has worked with various advertising agencies in Turkey, such as Medina Turgul DDB, Tribal Worldwide, Alice BBDO, Leo Burnett, TBWA, Concept, 4129Grey, and Rafineri.

*P.124-125*

## Nadieh Bremer

*visualcinnamon.com*

Nadieh Bremer was a trained astronomer, who later turned into a data scientist and a self-taught data visualization designer. After working for a consultancy and fintech company where she discovered her passion for the visualization of data, she is now working as a freelancing data visualization designer under the name "Visual Cinnamon." She focuses on uniquely crafted (interactive) data visualizations that both engage and enlighten its audience. Secretly, she quite enjoys venturing into data and generative art as well.

*P.050-051, 052-053*

## Ngooi Su Hwa

*behance.net/SuHwa*

Ngooi Su Hwa is a graphic designer and illustrator based in Malaysia whose main sphere of interest lies in illustration, publication, and branding. She holds a bachelor of degree in Graphic Design from The One Academy of Communication Design in Malaysia. After graduation, she

had been freelancing for clients including Malaysia Airlines, Samsung, and Caltex.

Su Hwa's work shows illustration at its busiest but remains balanced with her use of shapes and composition. Throughout her portfolio, there are sprawling landscapes that encompass a great amount of detail, layer upon layer of vibrant colors, and a handful of simplified shapes.

*P.132-133, 134-135, 136-137*

## Nicholas Rougeux

*www.c82.net*

Nicholas Rougeux has been a digital artist and website designer for more than 17 years. He specializes in creating data visualization/art and building highly usable websites and tools focused on knowledge sharing. He is mostly self-taught and always enjoys learning more. He creates and sells artwork based on data on a variety of topics like transit, music, and literature. His work has been displayed in publications like *Wired*, *The Guardian*, *Fast Company*, *Huffington Post*, and *Mental Floss*.

He enjoys creating precise artwork based on data and let the data determine the final style. The work that he creates is less about informing and more about inspiring others to look at something in a new way.

*P.048-049, 218-221*

## Olga Günther

*olga-guenther.de*

Olga Günther is a graphic designer and illustrator based in Saarbrücken, Germany. She specializes in editorial and infographic work and has a true love for simple forms, geometric shapes, patterns of all kinds, well organized and nicely illustrated information, and all things related to screen

printed and hand-crafted. She is a member of the design collective Bureau Stabil. In her work, the world is flat; the shapes are bold; the colors are bright; and the details are important and significant.

*P.108-109, 110-111, 112-113*

## ONO Creates

*www.onocreates.com*

ONO Creates is an independent design studio based in Singapore that spans multiple disciplines. It is founded and run by two happy folks, Med and Jing, who are constantly seeking new challenges. The unlikely pair share a common goal: to do the good work and to live the good life.

*P.162-163, 164, 165*

## Pablo Cabrera

*www.badvstudio.com*

Pablo Cabrera is an art director based in Madrid, Spain. He is passionate about illustration and communication. He loves nature, Volkswagen California, and big cups of coffee in the morning. His illustrations center on geometric shapes, from flat design to isometric perspectives. He likes creating storytelling microworlds, using depths and spaces.

*P.080-085*

## Paul Button

*www.sectiondesign.co.uk*

Paul Button has been a data illustrator for nearly 10 years. Currently, he works as a senior information designer at Signal Noise. He loves working on pieces related to history or cult media (TV/movies). He tries to design in a very methodical and rational way.

*P.023*

## Paula Rusu

*www.paularusu.com*

Paula Rusu is a freelance illustrator and graphic designer based in Bucharest, Romania, whose work is defined by bold colors and clean shapes. Passionate about everything related to visual arts, she strives to become better and better at what she does and always takes on new challenges.

Paula's work is either really vibrant and colorful or completely black and white, no in-betweens. She approaches several different styles throughout her work, starting with clean vector mono-line illustrations and ending with noise shaded complex compositions.

*P.126-127*

## Peter Grundy

*grundini.com*

Peter Grundy, a.k.a. Grundini is a designer and illustrator who turns complex information into simple visual stories for clients who seek invention and imagination.

*P.192-195*

## Raquel Jove

*www.rebombo.com*

Born in Cadiz, Spain in 1984, Raquel Jove is a designer and illustrator. In 2009 she set up Refres-co, her own studio, along with another designer. Later she decided to expand her knowledge and studied a master's degree in graphic design at the Instituto de Artes Visuales. After three years, she decides to continue learning and advancing creatively by joining Raúl Gómez and forming a creative tandem with which she develops projects related to design, illustration, and art direction. At the same time, as a tireless creative, she develops personal projects that help her continue to grow in her day-to-day life. In 2017, she creates a new design studio with her partner Raúl Gómez, called Rebombo.

*P.204*

## Re-lab

*www.behance.net/Re-LAB*

Founded in 2011, Re-lab has believed in the power of information and extended its influence by designs. With bountiful energy and experimental spirit, Re-lab keeps pushing its limits to bring valuable and important data to the audience in creative and interesting presentations!

Re-lab has devoted much time doing projects related to a variety of topics and issues. Social movements, cultural diversity, environmental issues, and educational affairs have inspired Re-lab to bring about their creativity with infographics, motion graphics, and interactive websites.

*P.166-167, 168-169*

## relajaelcoco

*www.relajaelcoco.com*

Relajaelcoco is a graphic design studio founded by Pablo Galeano and Francesco Furno. It specializes in graphic design, editorial design, infographics, virtual reality, and illustration. Over the last year, the studio's main aim has been to research new ways to express and create contemporary visual systems. For relajaelcoco, good vibes and a pleasant experience are the foundation for achieving sparkling results.

*P.010-011, 102-103*

## Rodion Kitaev

*www.behance.net/gerondot*

Rodion Kitaev has been illustrating for more than 10 years. He works with both Russian and foreign publications and organizations. He works with magazines such as *Esquire*, *Forbes*, *Men's Health*, *GQ*, *Psychologies*, *Port*, *Hollywood Reporter*, etc. He usually combines different techniques, such as pencil, pastel, watercolor, gouache, markers, and Photoshop.

*P.026-027*

## Rutger Paulusse

*www.gwer.nl*

Rutger Paulusse is an illustrator based in Amsterdam, the Netherlands. Originally trained as a graphic designer, his interest moved to the field of illustration at some point. Rutger focuses on designs for both online and in print, playing around with graphic shapes, bold colors, dimensions, and space. These elements merge into his very own recognizable and vibrant style.

*P.076, 078-079, 156-157*

## Samu Coronado

*www.sin-con.com*

Samu Coronado, a.k.a. SINCON is an illustrator and graphic designer based in Madrid, with a passion for infographics. His style is quite fluid and it is constantly evolving.

*P.038-039, 042-043, 152-153*

## Sara Piccolomini

*www.behance.net/sarapic*

Born in 1990 in Milan, Sara Piccolomini is an information and visual communication designer specialized in data visualization, infographics, and map illustration. She usually works for newspapers and magazines that deal with the visual representation of information. She often gets inspired by old renaissance books of astronomy or geography. She also loves using geometrical shapes and pastel colors.

*P.068-069, 071, 072-074*

## Saskia Rasink

*www.saskiarasink.com*

Saskia Rasink is a freelance illustrator based in Amsterdam, the Netherlands. She studied illustration at AKV St. Joost in Den Bosch, the Netherlands, and graduated in 2013. Her work is best described as graphic, colorful, and full of details. Colors and patterns are important aspects of Saskia's work. She draws inspirations from Scandinavian design, interior, nature, architecture, cities, and traveling. Her work is often described as old, graphic illustrations from the 1950s and 1960s, but with a modern twist. Her client list includes Nordstrom, *Vanity Fair France*, iAmsterdam, KLM Airlines, American Express, *Jamie Magazine*, Knight Frank, and many others.

*P.122-123, 128-131*

## Studio Mistaker

*www.studiomistaker.com*

Studio Mistaker is a Rome-based creative studio born in 2016, established by Martina Tariciotti and Riccardo Casinelli. They make infographic projects, illustrations, brand, and editorial design. They are also information designers at *La Repubblica*, the most important Italian newspaper. They love basic shapes and simplicity because they trust in clearness as a strong element of design.

*P.014-015, 016, 017, 188*

## Surgery & Redcow

*www.surgeryredcow.com*

Surgery & Redcow is a London-based independent brand strategy and creative consultancy. They create simple, yet brilliantly crafted print, digital marketing, and communication tools that enable a brand to stand out from the crowd.

*P.020-021, 022, 024-025*

## Tatiana Trikoz

*www.behance.net/Tata_T*

Born in 1983 in Russia, Tatiana Trikoz is a freelance illustrator based in Tbilisi, Georgia.

*P.212-213*

## TukiToku

*www.behance.net/tukitoku*

Hailing from Bandung, West Java Indonesia, TukiToku, a.k.a. Tetuko Hanggoro is a creative designer based in Singapore. He is a branding designer by day, a full-time nocturnal artist at night.

Having worked with numerous clients including inSing, *Forbes* Indonesia, and UPS, TukiToku has not stopped himself from creating his own personal projects— a move derived from his inventive passion and provocative perspectives in the arts. He has participated in a myriad of exhibitions including Tiger Translate, Noise Singapore, and Ten Images for Ithaca.

*P.036-037*

## Valerio Pellegrini

*www.be.net/valeriopellegrini*

Valerio Pellegrini is a communication designer based in Milan. Specifically,

he deals with data visualization, graphic design, illustration, and editorial design. He collaborates with research laboratories and studios in Italy and works as a freelancer for the United States, Great Britain, Holland, Japan, and China.

*P.064-065, 066, 067*

## Vizualism

*www.vizualism.com*

Vizualism is a Dutch design studio specialized in infographics, data visualization, and animations. They are visual storytellers; fully committed to informing people through clarity and transparency, regardless of any style.

*P.034-035, 214-215*

## Yuanyuan Zhang

*www.behance.net/quanzi33*

Yuanyuan Zhang is a visual designer based in Beijing, China. She likes exploring the different aspects of life. She always tries to enrich her designs by seeking new styles.

*P.210-211*

## Yunje Park

*www.ohsevenstudio.com*

Yunje Park is a graphic designer working at ohSeven Studio in Seoul, specializing in packaging design, brand design, and development. She prefers a design with a strong impression that is colorful and memorable. She pursues a trendy design and believes that every design should have its own reasons.

*P.222-223*

# ACKNOWLEDGEMENTS ————————

We would like to thank all of the designers involved for granting us permission to publish their works, as well as all of the photographers who have generously allowed us to use their images. We are also very grateful to many other people whose names do not appear in the credits but who made specific contributions and provided support. Without these people, we would not have been able to share these beautiful works with readers around the world. Our editorial team includes editor Jessie Tan and book designer Wu Yanting, to whom we are truly grateful.